Public Policy and Land Exchange

This original contribution to the field is the first to bring economic sociology theory to the study of federal land exchanges. By blending public choice theory with engaging case studies that contextualize the tactics used by land developers, this book uses economic sociology to help challenge the undervaluation of federal lands in political decisions. The empirically based, scholarly analysis of federal–private land swaps exposes serious institutional dysfunctions, which sometimes amount to outright corruption. By evaluating investigative reports of each federal agency case study, *Public Policy and Land Exchange* illustrates the institutional nature of the actors in land swaps and, in particular, the history of U.S. agencies' promotion of private interests in land exchanges.

Using public choice theory to make sense of the privatization of public lands, the book looks in close detail at the federal policies of the Bureau of Land Management and the U.S. Forest Service land swaps in America. These pertinent case studies illustrate the trend to transfer federal lands notwithstanding their flawed value appraisals or interpretation of public interest, thus violating both the principles of equality in value and observance of specific public policy.

The book should be of interest to students and scholars of public land and natural resource management, as well as political science, public policy, and land law.

Giancarlo Panagia is Associate Professor at Westminster College, Salt Lake City, Utah, USA.

Routledge Studies in Environmental Policy

Public Policy and Land Exchange

Choice, law, and praxis

Giancarlo Panagia

Routledge
Taylor & Francis Group

LONDON AND NEW YORK

First published 2015
by Routledge
2 Park Square, Milton Park, Abingdon, Oxon OX14 4RN

and by Routledge
711 Third Avenue, New York, NY 10017

First issued in paperback 2017

*Routledge is an imprint of the Taylor & Francis Group,
an informa business*

British Library Cataloguing-in-Publication Data
A catalogue record for this book is available from the British Library

Library of Congress Cataloging-in-Publication Data
Panagia, Giancarlo, author.
  Public policy and land exchange : choice, law, and praxis /
Giancarlo Panagia.
    pages cm. — (Routledge studies in environmental policy)
    Includes bibliographical references and index.
  1. Public lands—United States.   2. Development rights transfer—
Law and legislation—United States.   3. Real property, Exchange of—
United States.   4. Government sale of real property—United
States. I. Title.
  KF5605.P36 2015
  343.73′025—dc23
  2014045166

ISBN 13: 978-1-138-50677-0 (pbk)
ISBN 13: 978-1-138-79750-5 (hbk)

Typeset in Sabon
by Apex CoVantage, LLC

To Janine and Susan Jane, true heroines in the protection of the public's lands, and to my godson Zack, who hopefully will be given a chance to enjoy them.

Contents

Foreword

"Sometimes, it takes an outsider to give us a fresh perspective on our own system." That is what a researcher for the Polish Academy of Sciences said to me in 1995 about my first book project (published in 1998) about the history of environmental and natural resources law in his country. And that is precisely what the Italian scholar Giancarlo Panagia has done so magnificently in this book.

The product of a decade of careful study, during the course of which the author completed not one but two doctorates at American universities, the book chronicles and analyzes the endemic corruption plaguing public–private land swaps in the western United States. That corruption has received virtually no attention in the public media, but it affects every American concerned not only with the state of our public lands but with effective, efficient, honest, and transparent governance. The cozy relationships between federal land management agencies and private landowners in the western United States have resulted in a massive financial rip-off of the American public and the denigration of the lands the public owns.

Dr. Panagia's analysis is at once comprehensive and concise, a scholarly tome written with a journalist's eye for capturing and holding the reader's attention. Each chapter starts with a different case study of a problematic public–private land swap, which helps to keep the analysis grounded. Viewing the problem from various angles, ranging from the historical to the economic, the sheer amount of research (in both primary and secondary sources) synthesized by the author is impressive. Perhaps because of those multiple angles of analysis, Dr. Panagia manages to avoid simplistic accounts and – what is more important – simplistic solutions that are commonly found in works by public lands scholars with ideological axes to grind. This book should be applauded by both environmentalists and public choice theorists, two groups that do not often overlap.

Finally, Dr. Panagia offers four proposals for reforming the system of public–private land swaps, which combine the great merits of sensibility, modesty, and real potential for ameliorating, if not completely resolving, the problem. This book should be required reading for government policy-makers and media opinion-makers. It also should be read by every American who cares about the proper management of our public lands and tax dollars.

Dan Cole
Indiana University, USA

Acknowledgments

My academic career has been influenced in the most part by two amazing mentors and scholars. I will never be able to repay either one for the selfless advice, friendship, and support I received from Daniel "Dan" Cole and John Hepburn. I would never have been able to achieve this major goal of publishing a manuscript without their unwavering effort to convince me that this research needed to be published. Why two scholars of their caliber would ever invest their brains, patience, and time and blindly support me in my endeavors probably is an issue for posterity. But I'm eternally grateful to both of them for believing in me. I also thank John Johnson, Randel "Randy" Hanson, Eric Dannenmeier, and Andrew Klein. Without their support and invaluably unique perspectives, I would have never completed any of my doctoral works. In addition, Frank Emmert has mentored me with such expertise and guidance that my career has fully developed thanks also to his suggestions. William "Bill" Rodgers deserves the real credit for teaching me the importance of researching and writing on federal land exchanges; his class at ASU law school opened my eyes to a subject I hardly knew at the time. But the passion to write in this field came from conversations with Janine Blaeloch and Susan Jane Brown, who showed me how hard work and perseverance in the protection of nature and its resources eventually pays off. I am indebted to Ray "RJ" Maratea, Jeffrey "Jeff" Nichols and Robert "Bob" Rains for showing me the way out of a dark tunnel during the drafting of this book. Not only did they provide editorial work, but they gave me invaluable advice in how to spice up the writing of each chapter in this book. Their contribution has allowed me to survive at a time in which this project was too overwhelming for me. RJ merits one more mention. Several times in the last few years, he was the one providing invaluable feedback every single time I felt I had reached an impasse on this project. He was the one who would spend time over the phone to give me ideas about new "hooks" in this project.

In terms of editorial work, Sean Desilets, Faith Long, Nan McEntire, Natasha Saje, and David Stanley played an important role in my drafts and edits of this manuscript. I am also grateful to Dean Lisa Gentile, staff (especially Ashley Kramer and Debby Scharffs), and students at Westminster

College. The School of Arts & Sciences offered me the opportunity to teach at such a great institution. Without a doubt, I have the good fortune to be surrounded by Justice Studies students who keep alive in my research and teaching a passion to address what is wrong with our system of laws and practices. They represent a future much brighter than our present times. Amy Fairchild has offered me guidance and deserves my eternal gratitude for putting up with my moody behavior for over five years. This project would have never got this far without her unwavering optimism and true belief in my capacity. Additionally, Fathom Croteau, my research assistant, has kept me sane long enough for me to complete this project.

My fortune in life has surrounded me with friends who have been constantly giving advice and encouraging progress in this and other endeavors: Kathryn "Kate" Pascarosa, Zachary "Zack" Pascarosa, Russell "Russ" Costa, Christine "Christy" Seifert, Scott Gust, Christine "Christy" Clay, Brent Olson, Hikmet Loe, David "Dave" Hoch, Bridget Newell, Gary Marquardt, Seong-In Choi, Bradley "Brad" Porfilio, Barbara "Barb" Smith, Sara Demko, John Contreras, Jennifer "Jen" Ritter, Carol Jeffers, Daniel "Dan" Shertzer, Shamby Polichronis, Michael "Mike" Zarkin, Marilee Coles-Ritchie, and Leonardo Figueroa-Helland. Their friendship has allowed them throughout the times to see only my good qualities rather than the overwhelming bad ones. Finally, I also want to express my eternal gratitude to Roxanne Derda and Susan Boland. At different stages of my manuscript draft, I shamelessly relied on their extremely exquisite library research skills; they are the reason why the research in this book is so compelling. I wholeheartedly thank each person in this two-page list for showing to me what true friends would do for me and my career.

The staff at Taylor and Francis has throughout each stage fully supported my scholarship and deserves my personal bow to their devoted professionalism. In particular, I would like to mention Helen Bell, Louisa Earls, Marie Roberts, and Annabelle Harris. Without their unrelenting support, this project would have never seen the light of day. Their encouragement and patience have allowed me to complete a project that over a year ago still seemed impossible to me. They gave a chance to a then assistant professor in a small liberal arts college in Utah; what happened afterwards reflects their committed effort to get my confidence boosted to a point where my level of comfort with their supervision did the unthinkable: a completed manuscript. I owe you so much, thank you from the bottom of my heart!

Finally, I could not complete these acknowledgments if I didn't give the ultimate credit to my mom, Vittoria D'Agostino. Her love of nature in all its forms opened my eyes to a world of books depicting its preservation. My mom used to take me to the local library in the city parks of Messina and Florence, Italy, and encouraged me to read books about forests and the beauty of their habitats. Thank you, mom – I owe it to you to appreciate nature as much as I do. The D'Agostino family has been relentlessly supportive of me and my endeavors and taught me the importance of life lessons that I will always treasure and inspired my journey in this world. In addition, my brother and dad from the Panagia side of the family, in their own ways, have blindly supported me notwithstanding that our political views are as antithetical as the present American political parties' rift. Least but not last, I wish to thank you, Peg Bortner, in forcing me to persevere in overcoming professional roadblocks.

1 Introducing the sour taste

In December 1980, the General Accountability Office (GAO), an independent agency providing investigative services to the U.S. Congress, issued a draft review of a proposed land exchange involving the Chattahoochee National Forest in Georgia. The proposal was for 1,330 acres of private land to be swapped for 667 acres of U.S. Forest Service (USFS) land. Originally, in November 1979, the federal lands were appraised by an independent contractor at $328,000. A year later, the same appraiser found the value to be unchanged. The GAO was concerned that the appraiser had failed to consider the added value of a state road being constructed through the federal land. Although the appraiser had indicated that the highest value of the forestlands was residential development, no indication of this value increase was reflected in either appraisal. Thus, the GAO contacted the U.S. Forest Service chief, recommending that he disapprove and terminate the exchange.

Four months later, in April 1981, the GAO submitted its complete review of the proposed exchange in the Chattahoochee National Forest (GAO 1981). In addition to the prior problems, the GAO now pointed out that Forest Service officials, by equalizing the difference in the values of the private and public lands, had rounded off a total of $1,189 in favor of the private owner. Also, the GAO discovered that the proponent of the land swap was not even the owner of an 80-acre tract included in the offered lands. The GAO questioned why the Forest Service would pay for the appraisal of lands not even owned by the proponent.

This GAO document is just an example of investigative documents that this book collects to study the history and public policy related to federal land swaps between private parties and the U.S. government. In such swaps, the federal government trades public lands to private parties in return for private lands.[1] In the present study, special attention is paid to federal policy

---

1 In these land exchanges, the federal government swaps with private parties public lands in return for private lands in the interest of consolidating federal ownership into larger contiguous areas.

and case law concerning swaps conducted by the Bureau of Land Management (BLM) and the USFS. In particular, this book covers and analyzes extensively two recurring issues in land swaps leading to litigation: the interpretation of the statutory terminology "public interest" as used in federal law and the valuation of public lands traded to private ownership.

This book presents a legal analysis of several representative land swaps in the form of case studies. It proffers a legal analysis of several cases interpreting federal statutory law before both judicial and administrative panels. Federal public policy has changed since the first statute that governed land exchanges at the end of the nineteenth century. However, problems with land swaps, particularly the under-valuation of federal lands, have continued ever since. Although the General Exchange Act (GEA) of 1922 changed the legal requirements for land swaps from the original terminology of equal acreage to the present requirement of equal value, courts, by granting wide discretion to the BLM and the USFS, allow suspect valuation practices to escape judicial review. Even the Interior Board of Land Appeals (IBLA), the administrative court for the Department of the Interior (DOI), is very receptive to conferring wide discretion to the BLM. The IBLA is especially consistent in its unwillingness to overturn the judgment of the BLM even in cases that favor private parties' claims against the government.

A valid solution to this impasse over the valuation of federal lands and the public interest determination of land swaps could be provided by the courts. Currently, though, both administrative judges and federal courts have declined to impose restraints on the agencies. The rule so far has been the dismissal of most challenges on procedural matters such as lack of standing, or, if the merits are reached, bowing to agency discretion. It could be that judicial oversight of land appraisal and public interest determination controversies are the final bulwark against the undervaluation of federal lands.

The past and now present problem

What makes these particular land transactions relevant to the public are the established trends, embedded in BLM and USFS policies, to transfer federal lands despite flawed land appraisals and faulty public interest determinations. These trends lead to a loss of economic value for the public and a consequent sour aftertaste for all of us.

This book examines why the BLM and the USFS consistently undervalue public lands and fail to respect the statutes which require the public interest to be served by all federal land swaps. The public interest, ostensibly the motivation for any land swap, requires a full consideration of the needs of the government and the people. In addition, how the constant undervaluation of federal lands affects the needs of diverse communities is still an unresolved issue.

This book investigates the undervaluation of the federal lands swapped by the BLM and the USFS and focuses on case studies in which the BLM and the USFS exchanged federal lands with private parties despite knowledge that the public lands were being undervalued. While land swaps have had success as a means to acquire private lands, the federal agencies have lost value in these exchanges by undervaluing federal lands. It is necessary to determine the causes of persistent undervaluation of public lands or disregard for the public interest in the transaction. Investigative reports of each federal agency allow an understanding of the institutional nature of the actors in land swaps where both the BLM and the USFS have historically failed to protect the interests of the public (Draffan and Blaeloch 2000).

At some point of socialization in their careers, some agencies' officials lose their multiple-use management ideals and reacquire, instead, what public choice theory refers to as self-interest. Firestone expresses this when he states: "Cultures are most effective in shaping behavior when their adherents cannot imagine any other way to behave. As soon as alternatives become available, deviance and cultural conflict can occur" (1990:108–109). This self-interested behavior contributes to the depreciation of the public interest, thus leading to the undervaluation of federal lands, a truly misunderstood chapter of U.S. land policy (Espey 2001).

From history to policy

By developing a historical time frame from the late 1890s to the present, this book intends to analyze the historical and legal changes pertaining to the interpretation of terms related to land swaps. Careful consideration of the chronology of events surrounding land swaps has led some authors to believe that the causes of undervaluation of lands or improper public interest determinations can be found in the general atmosphere of federal land and resource privatization which developed in the last decade of the twentieth century and has been common to both agencies.

Therefore, it is by conscious decision that this book focuses on the history, public policy literature, and investigative reports of land-swap issues covering a time span over one century. Thus, the disciplines most relevant to this project are history and law. Historical and legal evaluations help demonstrate the divide between public and private interests in land swaps. Under the rational choice model, in the words of Little, "the general idea is to explain specific social phenomena as the aggregate result of large numbers of rational persons making choices within a specific social and natural environment" (Little 1991:65). A description of human agency where commitments, beliefs, and cultures account for behavior helps explain self-motivated actions of public officials through public choice theory.

Why do we apply theory to make sense of faulty land exchanges? Land swaps are little known throughout American society. The total annual loss of value in land swaps conducted by the federal government, at both the administrative and legislative levels, is staggering. The use of public choice to understand public officials' behavior is the first step to improve agencies' practices before we can create policies which ascertain a more encompassing valuation and public interest determination of lands.

This project evaluates possible alternatives to the present land-swap process. In particular, it evaluates whether, in case the current problematic policies continue, "free market environmentalists" are correct in arguing that once those lands are in private hands the market will accurately determine their highest and best uses. They argue that privatization would be socially beneficial even if the federal government simply gave the lands away through exchange transactions, as it often did in the late nineteenth century.

Federal land swaps have been the subject of legal scholarship only since the publication of a 1964 article on sales and exchanges of federal lands. That article summarized federal exchange procedures and was essentially a guide to acquiring public land. At the time the problems in such exchanges, according to the author, "were the location and acquisition of acceptable private land to be offered" (Moran 1964:45).

The article addressed the needs of developers and businesses interested in acquiring public lands from the BLM. The author stressed that in land swaps "the procedures provide a wide area of discretionary power to such [a governmental] official; success in any instance depends upon the manner in which that discretion is exercised" (Moran 1964:49). The article instructed lawyers and their clients to complete land swaps by taking advantage of the complacency and discretionary practices of the Bureau's employees. The author concluded that all that was necessary for a swap to succeed was "closer contact between the administering officials and the representatives of private interests and an understanding by each of the problems of the other" (Moran 1964:50). According to the article, contrary to the policy of withdrawing public lands from potential private acquisition, the federal government should have disposed of these lands for economic development by private parties. Land exchanges, according to him, were created to facilitate private acquisition of public lands.

To prevent such skewed viewpoints and to give the BLM a clear mandate of forest and range management, Congress passed the Federal Land Policy and Management Act (FLPMA) in 1976. In confirming the withdrawal of the public domain (now renamed public lands) from private acquisition, Congress mandated the BLM to properly manage these land assets using several different approaches, such as range, grazing, recreation, and wilderness.

After a decade of land swaps conducted by the BLM and the USFS[2] under the new statute, in 1985 the Senate requested the GAO to review the exchange programs as actually implemented. In fact, due to budget cuts, the agencies had resorted to increased use of swaps to eliminate problems created by in-holdings – islands of private lands interspersed within larger

---

2 A particular provision of the FLPMA, section 206(a), made the exchange procedures applicable also to the USDA, thus, to the U.S. Forest Service. 43 U.S.C. § 1716(a) (1976).

federal and state land management areas. Therefore, the study commissioned by the Senate was to inquire about the land-swap process and make recommendations for improvement. The results of the study were somewhat perplexing. Although the "GAO found that the land exchange process [was] working well" (GAO 1987:2), several concerns were raised. The major area of concern was "cases when equal value was not obtained" (GAO 1987:3) in violation of FLPMA.

These alarming results prompted Congress to introduce a new bill, drafted by the natural resources development industry, to specify rules and procedures for appraisals to prevent failures to obtain equal value. In 1988, Congress finally passed the Federal Land Exchange Facilitation Act (FLEFA) to "facilitate and expedite land exchanges by providing more uniform rules pertaining to land appraisals and by establishing procedures for resolving appraisal disputes" (GAO 2000:7). FLEFA was supposed to guarantee that all swaps would garner equal value.

Congress mistakenly assumed that FLEFA would be a panacea for controversial land valuations. FLEFA created a new bargaining and negotiation process to handle the case of appraisals being challenged by either party to a swap. FLEFA also conferred on the agencies the power "to approve adjustments in the values of lands exchanged as a means of compensating a party for incurring [land swaps] costs" (Draffan and Blaeloch 2000:79). These changes did not track the recommendations of the GAO, which had chastised these very same practices. Representative Ron Marlenee had previously said that the practice of the BLM and USFS of transferring selected lands to pay for the exchange's administrative costs was tantamount to "giving away or selling off federal lands to a vested few, those [private parties] who are involved in the exchange" (U.S. House of Representatives 1986).

In sum, the GAO had found that both the BLM and the USFS had "adjusted" valuations in violation of the law. In direct response, Congress, rather than following the recommendation of the GAO, rubber-stamped the practice. Since then, authors have stopped critiquing this practice because it is now legal.

Environmental scholars question the practices of the agencies, especially when federal officials are being left at the mercy of private interests. Local communities and national politicians constantly pressure these officials into giving in to the requests of land developers. In addition, the agency's officials might become captive to private parties' interests (Brown 2000). Finally, in other instances, the same agency officials find themselves in a conflict of interest through a never-ending "revolving door" system (Draffan and Blaeloch 2000).

Espey (2001) has shown the true complexity of these issues surrounding land exchanges. She found that the political affiliation of the president is an explanatory variable of the preferential treatment that private businesses receive in land exchanges. Espey is disillusioned about the solutions proposed by other authors to solve the status quo. She notes that the same problems have been present for more than a century and will continue despite increased scrutiny or changes to the law.

In spite of this harsh criticism, the DOI and U.S. Department of Agriculture (USDA) still commission studies to determine the cause of losses of value, without asking for public accountability of their own officials. For example, The Appraisal Foundation (TAF), an organization authorized by Congress to promulgate business standards and appraiser qualifications, found that the organizational structure of the USFS allowed undue influence of realty personnel over the agency's appraisers (TAF 2000). In response, the agency reorganized the hierarchy of land appraisers, but problems have surfaced since then at the level of ranger districts. In this case, the data point more to the individual choice of the federal official to benefit the private party than to coercion from agency superiors.

Since the impartiality of the individual federal official is at stake, Stengel (2001) suggests that the solution to the undervaluation of federal lands is public accountability for the land officers and appraisers. She believes that a "mutual dependent relationship" between federal agencies and private businesses undermines the impartiality of individual officers and that criminal liability would restore a level playing field (Stengel 2001).

Another study by TAF (2002) confirmed that improper interference from the agency's offices in Washington, DC, has cost the nation millions of dollars in federal asset losses. On June 19, 2003, Secretary of the Interior Gale Norton announced the DOI's plans to consolidate all its agencies' appraisal functions into a single office. Under the new policy, appraisers would report up the chain of command to other appraisers rather than to realty specialists. This was to ensure appraiser independence and that appraisals would be in accordance with professional standards to provide unbiased appraisals consistent with the public interest. The DOI had decided that this change would put to rest any allegations of political manipulation of appraisals at the BLM, the Bureau of Reclamation, the Fish and Wildlife Service, and the National Park Service. Two years later, the DOI's Office of the Inspector General (OIG) issued a report on the BLM's use of the new policy. The OIG remained worried about the practices developing around the new policy. These concerns challenged the presumed independence of DOI review-appraisers (DOI 2005:1).

Throughout its chapters, this book highlights the fact that the current faulty appraisal determinations adopted by the agencies are intimately connected to conflicting tensions of federal policies based on conservation of public lands for future development rather than preservation (Gonzalez 2001). With this interpretative key it is easier to see how federal land exchanges have become an increasingly popular tool for land management agencies and private developers to transfer property. According to Espey, Republicans are "historically more inclined than Democrats to support the interests of business expansion by relinquishing federal lands" (Espey

2001:482), while the Democrats have used land exchanges as a means to purchase lands for conservation purposes (Gonzalez 2001) or for biodiversity, habitat protection, and ecosystem management (Ragsdale 1999).

To make sense of a system of policies that have changed throughout the last century and yet the outcome remains the same, this book starts with the coverage of public choice theory, which helps readers understand the behavior of agency officials facing the exigencies of narrow economic markets of exchange. Once readers are comfortable understanding the economic terms of exchange transactions, a historical coverage of public policy relative to land swaps will lead us to present federal statutes, regulations, and legal precedents that regulate the field. Afterwards, the book presents legal cases which will help the reader better understand the present status of law and how this status quo maintains intact two unresolved issues: questionable public interest determinations and undervaluation of federal lands. Afterwards, coverage of governmental studies will reflect how for more than two decades the United States has tried unsuccessfully to solve either one of these issues. Finally, a closer look at a 2003 reform initiated by the DOI demonstrates how even this measure has failed to create a positive solution to the problems faced by agencies in their completion of land swaps.

The book chapters are subdivided along the lines addressed above. Chapter 2 is a reading of federal land swaps through the lenses of economics and law. Here the use of public choice theory enhances the reader's understanding of problems involved in land swaps. Chapter 3 provides an historical overview of legislation passed by Congress related to the federal land-swap program from its inception at the end of the nineteenth century to the present day. Chapter 4 first includes a study of different statutes and regulatory requirements governing land swaps. This chapter describes, in particular, the procedures of land swaps. The next part of the same chapter reviews case law and administrative judge decisions concerning public interest and appraisal determinations leading to completion of federal land swaps. Chapter 5 presents the current controversy in the federal land exchange debate in the words of governmental investigative reports. Chapter 6 details the 2003 reform of the appraisal function within the DOI and subsequent governmental reports investigating the success of this reform.

Finally, the Conclusions provide suggestions for future policy-making. The book addresses the importance of tools such as judicial review and public accountability, which, if properly used, might make a positive impact on land-swap outcomes. Unfortunately, despite the fact that the GAO recommended a moratorium on land swaps, both the BLM and the USFS have continued their practices of undervaluing federal lands and approving faulty public interest determinations, as attested to by ongoing litigation nationwide.

References

Brown, S.J.M. (2000). David and Goliath: Reformulating the Definition of "the Public Interest" and the Future of Land Swaps After the Interstate 90 Land Exchange. *Journal of Environmental Law and Litigation, 15*, 235–293.

Draffan, G. & Blaeloch, J. (2000). *Commons or Commodity? The Dilemma of Federal Land Exchanges.* Seattle, WA: Western Land Exchange Project.

Espey, M. (2001). Federal Land Exchanges: 1960–1999. *Contemporary Economic Policy, 19*, 479–487.

Firestone, W. F. (1990). Accommodation: Toward a Paradigm-Praxis Dialect. In E. G. Guba (Ed.), *The Paradigm Dialog* (pp. 105–124). Newbury Park, CA: Sage Publications.

Gonzalez, G. A. (2001). *Corporate Power and the Environment: The Political Economy of U.S. Environmental Policy.* Oxford: Rowman & Littlefield.

Little, D. (1991). *Varieties of Social Explanation: An Introduction to the Philosophy of Social Science.* Boulder, CO: Westview Press.

Moran, R. L. (1964). Sales and Exchanges of Public Lands. *Rocky Mountain Mineral Law Institute, 15*, 25–50.

Ragsdale, J. W. (1999). National Forest Land Exchanges and the Growth of Vail and Other Gateway Communities. *Urban Lawyer, 31*, 1–45.

Stengel, A. (2001). Insider's Game or Valuable Land Management Tool? *Tulane Environmental Law Journal, 14*, 567–596.

The Appraisal Foundation. (2000). *Evaluation of the Appraisal Organization of the USDA Forest Service.* Washington, DC: Author.

The Appraisal Foundation. (2002). *Evaluation of the Appraisal Organizations of the Department of Interior Bureau of Land Management: Including a Special Evaluation of an Alternative Approach Used in St. George, Utah.* Washington, DC: Author.

U.S. Department of the Interior. (2005). *Managing Land Acquisitions Involving Non-federal Partnerships* (DOI Report No. W-IN-MOA-0085–2004). Washington, DC: U.S. Government Printing Office.

U.S. General Accounting Office. (1981). *Forest Service: Land Exchange Activities in the Chattahoochee and Oconee National Forests.* Washington, DC: U.S. Government Printing Office.

U.S. General Accounting Office. (1987). *Federal Land Acquisition: Land Exchange Process Working But Can Be Improved.* Washington DC: United States Government Printing Office.

U.S. General Accounting Office. (2000). *BLM and the Forest Service: Land Exchanges Need to Reflect Appropriate Value and Serve the Public Interest.* Washington, DC: U.S. Government Printing Office.

U.S. House of Representatives. (1986). 99th Cong., 2nd Sess., Cong. Record, Aug. 11, Washington, DC, 20607–20608.

2 Public choice and land exchange practices

In 1999, the BLM completed the DeMar Exchange, in which it acquired 239 acres of private lands surrounded by public land covered by the Desert Tortoise Habitat Conservation Plan. The desert tortoise is a threatened species,[1] and the Plan gives the BLM authority to exchange lands to fulfill its preservation goals. The private landholder's appraiser submitted a preliminary valuation of the offered lands of $7,000 per acre. However, the BLM's appraisal valued them at approximately $1,000 per acre. This was because the private owner's appraisal had assumed the possibility of land development, which is severely restricted by the Plan. According to the law, "the lands must first be appraised at their fair market value, taking into consideration any reduction in value that corresponds to development restrictions caused by endangered species" (Frischknecht 2005:999–1000). The landowners turned down the BLM appraisal.

BLM officials decided to bargain, explaining later that they disagreed with the agency's appraisal and felt the landowner would refuse other offers. They thought that the landowner's "refusal to accept governmental appraisal valuations was not a reasonable investment-backed expectation, but an attempt to game the system for greater compensations" (Frischknecht 2005:1018). However, in accordance with FLEFA, they began negotiations. According to FLEFA, federal land managers may bargain with landholders to resolve conflicting appraisals. The parties reached a valuation of $7,440 per acre, exceeding even the private appraiser's valuation. The BLM completed this exchange even though its own chief appraiser denounced the new valuation as not supported by credible evidence. The GAO later concurred (GAO 2000:17).

Introduction

The use of this example introduces the reader to flawed land exchanges that some federal agencies still complete each year. In this chapter, the use of

---

1 According to § 3(20) of the Endangered Species Act, a species is threatened whenever it "is likely to become an endangered species within the foreseeable future throughout all or a significant portion of its range."

theory attempts to explain why agency officials still complete these flawed land swaps. I propose that, in order to better understand why the BLM and the Forest Service complete land exchanges where the government loses value, we must examine public choice theory. Thus this chapter employs an economic analysis of federal land swaps. Public choice theory provides an analysis of individuals' behavior and their impact on the transactions. This choice of theory is adopted to explain agency officials' practices that demarcate a shift where allegiance to the organizational is replaced by individualism and self-interest (Nelson 1997:211). Basically, individuals within the organizational structure maximize their own utility, vis-à-vis their own interest. Thus it is necessary to study how public choice theory inspires this rebellion of the individual against the communitarian interests of the governmental agency. Accounting for individuals' behavior, this theory provides the foundation of the analysis concerning the practices of individual employees within federal agencies. This analysis explains how issues of organizational mismanagement (principal/agent problems) and capture, combined with improper, unethical, and in a few instances criminal, behavior by individual officials could be the cause of the loss of equal value in land swaps.

In general, economic theory helps us understand why actors choose specific strategies. Therefore, this chapter uses public choice theory to make sense of the unabated privatization of public lands at an economic loss. This economic analysis applies public choice theory to the behavior and practices of both the private owners or developers and the federal agencies' officials. In practice, the land-swap process reflects issues of self-interest; the capture of agencies or their personnel by interest groups; instances of duress; and decisions influenced by the revolving door through which federal officials join the ranks of land development firms. These are all examined to make sense of current land-swap practices which fail to protect the public interest.

Economics theory holds that the cooperation of the subjects involved in a transaction increases opportunities to augment joint returns and reach socially efficient outcomes, but reality may differ. According to economics theory, any contractual agreement should be presumed to be mutually beneficial in the absence of fraud, distress, or grossly unequal bargaining position (Cole and Grossman 2005:167). Even if bargaining positions are fairly equivalent, parties could still be expected to fight hard over surplus value. Thus in land swaps, private landowners may have a stronger incentive to gain the last dollar than do government regulators, who do not personally stand to gain or lose from the transaction (Cole 2009).

Ultimately, the land-swap market is not a normal market with many buyers and sellers. It is a very thin market[2] in which one of the parties – the

---

2   A market is thin or narrow when only a low number of buyers and sellers are in the position to exchange or swap.

government – suffers from principal/agent problems. Failure to properly supervise subordinates and the abuse of power over other officials both increase the opportunities for rent seeking[3] by private parties (Cole and Grossman 2005:60). Given that market failure[4] is common in the thin market of federal land exchanges, federal land realty managers should consider alternatives to this status up to and including the power of eminent domain.

Under FLPMA Section 1715(a), when BLM lands are landlocked[5] the Secretary of the Interior may exercise the power of eminent domain only if necessary to secure access to those lands and only if the acquired lands are confined to as narrow a corridor as possible. Prior to the enactment of FLPMA, the Secretary and the BLM had no power of eminent domain absent specific authorization from Congress (*U.S. v. 82.46 Acres of Land* 1982:475). No similar restriction limits the authority of the Secretary of Agriculture to acquire private lands within the National Forest System.

According to Cole (2007), the government possesses the power of eminent domain and, as a prescriptive measure, should use it as a bargaining chip to extract equal value in land transactions. In fact, as suggested pointedly by Merrill, "eminent domain's purpose is to overcome barriers to voluntary exchange created when a seller of resources is in position to extract economic rents from a buyer. . . . [otherwise] This 'thin market' setting . . . can lead to monopoly pricing by the seller" (1986:65). So the question becomes, why do agencies fail to use this tool? Public choice theory provides an answer – self-interest. Of course, since only one-fourth or one-fifth of land swaps are disadvantageous to the government, public choice theory does not provide a full explanation. In fact, additional theories of administrative agency behavior need to explain how some agency officials work very hard to benefit the public at large; others are captured; and finally, others are simply trying to get through the day while ruffling as few feathers as possible in accordance with the satisficing[6] model (Cole 2007).

Our theoretical analysis must explain first how policy is created before it is [mis]implemented. However, this analysis cannot be done without a historic overview. The management of public lands in the nineteenth century was a matter of the acquisition and disposition of the public domain (Culhane 1981). With the successive policies enacted over the last century to first dispose of and more recently to manage unclaimed lands in the public

---

3 "A rent in this context refers to an economic benefit acquired by an entity through its ability to escape the competitive pressure of markets" (Cross 1999:356).
4 According to economics theory, a market failure is experienced whenever the allocation of resources by a free market is not efficient.
5 Landlocked refers to any parcel of real property which has no access or egress to a public street and cannot be reached except by crossing another's property.
6 According to economics theory, the satisficing model describes how people make decisions among options open to them and within prevailing constraints aiming for a satisfactory result, rather than an optimal solution.

domain, conflicting paradigms of interests arose concerning those lands. Culhane (1981) ably describes the administration of these lands by the USFS and the ancestors of the BLM in terms of the conflict created by the differing policies of land management.

It was a debate of conformity-capture. From one perspective, the Forest Service (once called the Bureau of Forestry) was a highly regimented agency more immune to business pressure than the BLM and its ancestors (Culhane 1981:2). According to Herbert Kaufman (1960), this perspective saw a highly conformist agency created under the philosophy of progressive-conservation and following the principles of scientific management. At the other end of the spectrum, Phillip Foss (1960) examined the two agencies, the Grazing Service and the General Land Office (GLO), which eventually were combined to create the BLM. He saw them as powerless entities, influenced by their clientele to such an extent that he deemed them to be in a state of captivity. Foss highlighted interest groups as the leading policy of the BLM and its predecessors. It should be remembered that historically the GLO was not a management agency but a bureaucratic land disposal unit. It disposed of the public domain by transferring lands into private hands in a variety of ways, including land sales and grants.

In the nineteenth century, the natural resource management established in federal administrative policy was utilitarianism, where the greatest good for the greatest number could be achieved by technologically exploiting nature. The western frontier was considered limitless and its natural resources were to be commodified and exchanged in a capitalist economy protected by libertarian principles under the Constitution (Culhane 1981). Eventually, however, Americans began to realize that natural resources were indeed exhaustible and sought to protect them from waste. According to Culhane, the conservationist perspective arose as a response "to the destruction caused by the utilitarian plunder economy" (Culhane 1981:4). However, other authors challenge this interpretation as reductionist. While acknowledging that conservationism presented itself as protecting natural resources for later use, they argue that conservation was intended by business elites to protect resources from quick exploitation by small operators (Gonzalez 2001). These elites, the argument goes, expected that the government would transfer these lands to them at a time when competition was being dismantled and an oligopoly of large industries would reap the benefits of conservation (Gonzalez 2001).

This philosophy was quickly adopted by President Theodore Roosevelt's administration and put into practice by the USFS under the leadership of "Grand Master" Gifford Pinchot (Wilkinson 1992:126). According to one scholar, "progressive conservation was based on . . . principles central to the progressive era as a whole: opposition to the domination of economic affairs by narrow 'special interests' (that is, large business firms)" (Culhane 1981:4–5). This position has been critiqued by Gonzalez, who believes that at the time of the passage of the 1891 General Land Law Revision Act, also known as the Forest Reserve Act, which provided the president with the power to set aside forest reserves, the interests of timber companies were well represented in Congress. Thus large timber companies sponsored the conservation of forests for the supposed benefit of many (Gonzalez 2001). Gonzalez argues that conservation policies of the time, reflective of elite groups, were actually geared to conserve forests for future use while also driving weaker competitors out of the lumber market. He "contends that these policies were the outgrowth of an upper-class and corporate-based policy network" (Gonzalez 2001:23). This interpretive key helps highlight the fact that the current faulty appraisal practice adopted by federal agencies is intimately connected to the policy of conserving public lands for present development (Gonzalez 2001). Accordingly, land swaps have become an increasingly popular means for federal agencies to support the use of public lands by relinquishing them to private business (Espey 2001:482).

In what follows, I argue that Culhane's interpretation of the principles of conservation in forestry, as exemplified by Gifford Pinchot's practices, deserves close attention. Culhane suggests that opposition to wasteful natural resource exploitation was a need of the Progressive Era, but conservation advocates were unable to preserve the forests from the timber barons, whose constituency, according to Gonzalez, was actually represented by Pinchot. However, conservation policy quickly withdrew timber from small operators, who did not own private forests and, therefore, were driven out of business, allowing timber barons to profit from government-subsidized purchases of public forest wood during the construction boom of the 1950s and 1960s. Gonzalez states, "The basic principle of conservation was 'wise use,' with the emphasis on wise, for the progressive conservationists were reacting to rapacious, short-term, profit-maximizing, utilitarian exploitation . . . of the forests" (2001:5).

Pinchot's conservationism stood for the wise use of resources. Both Theodore Roosevelt and Gifford Pinchot emphasized how the wise use of natural resources should provide for the future the greatest good for the greatest number (Dana and Fairfax 1980:1). This agenda ultimately favored business constituencies. When this progressive conservation is placed on the continuum of land-use theories, its commodification of natural resources is very similar to utilitarianism. Both are use-oriented and stand in opposition to the beliefs of the Wilderness Society (created in 1935) and the 1960s preservationist environmental organizations, which believed in the intrinsic value of nature found in its beauty and wildness.

Preservation's criticism comes from those authors who, adopting the precepts of laissez-faire capitalism, embrace a utilitarianism that chastises any inefficient use of natural resources. According to this utilitarian view, public lands should be privatized. In fact, property rights advocates argue that environmental resources should be reallocated by the free market. One critic, though, points out that "this 'one-size-fits-all' view, however, is frequently driven by ideology . . . rather than the result of a thorough examination of the evidence" (Jaeger 2005:130). Feldman joins the argument by challenging the very idea of public lands ownership and proposes their sale in pursuit of a balanced federal budget (1997:2–4). Summarizing these points, Sinden explains why such perspectives have some support: "Based on . . . a litany of anecdotes describing the incompetence and corruption of federal land managers, the free marketeers argue that all federal lands . . . should be sold off to private parties" (2007:599).

In this climate, some propose transferring control of federal forests to local representative boards, because after all, governmental agencies are the largest destroyers of natural resources (Nelson 1997). Calabresi and Bobbitt (1978) discuss the decentralization of decision-making as a negative element. According to their analysis, "The more decentralized the process becomes, the less sure we are that the acceptable national rules are in fact being applied; the suspicion of bias, advantage, or corruption is heightened" (Calabresi and Bobbitt 1978:54).[7] In fact, according to two economists, federal–private contractual transactions are "riddled" with "patron-client ties between government officials and businessmen" (King and Szelenyi 2005:218). One way to explain this rapport is that "patron–client relationships . . . [become] commodified – because private entrepreneurs . . . need to have resourceful patrons in the bureaucracy to get deals done" (King and Szelenyi 2005:221). The dangers of such relationships cannot be overstated because in the field of land swaps, increased decentralization has actually led to local offices becoming captured by private interest groups or, worse yet, their personnel being harassed. In fact, historically, local government decisions are heavily influenced by economic interests, which end up setting policy (Draffan and Blaeloch 2000).

In recognition of the dangers of agency capture, another policy scholar acknowledges that the agencies are excessively influenced by their clientele (Culhane 1981:17). Foss brilliantly illustrated this argument in his study of BLM land management policies prior to the 1970s. The history of the BLM has been one of capture,[8] where local business interests were successful in implementing their own policies at the local level. More important to my argument, another public lands scholar analyzes data showing that federal employees' jobs and salaries may depend on the successful

7 In communist countries, it was not only a matter of individual corruption but also systemic impediments to resource conservation. The centralized government owned economic enterprises and, therefore, directly depended on their financial success by overexploiting natural resources.
8 According to political scientists, a governmental agency is captured when it is largely influenced by the economic interest groups, which are directly affected by its decisions and policies. Regulatory capture becomes possible when private companies offer better remuneration to a selected few agency workers. Striving to make the private company happy while hoping to later gain successful employment with that company the individual agent's behavior ties them to a policy model supported through agent's capture.

completion of swaps, resulting in the "capture" of the agency process and its employees (Vaskov 2001:91). On the same note, Brown suggests both BLM and USFS are "captive" to private interests because the government has failed to provide them with sufficient funds to conduct environmental studies or appraisals during swap negotiations. This "capture" creates conflicts of interest when the agencies' officers deal with businesses which actually pay for those studies and appraisals (Brown 2000). In these cases, the preferences of the dominant economic elite overshadow management by imposing their values in the implementation of policies (Gonzalez 2001).

From a mainstream perspective, Lowi (1979) counters that the delegation of power to federal agencies is predicated on the belief that special interests have not captured policymaking at the agency level. Regarding land exchanges, it could be argued that delegation "is a political-economy response to the great specificity[9] of landed assets. This specificity makes compensation decisions informationally complicated, subject to strenuous political lobbying and potentially socially very costly" (Frieden 2000:144). Thus, wide discretion is afforded to agencies to set policies, because legislators assume that policy decisions will be worked out with special interest groups.

As explained above, one of the most direct means that the corporate community has to affect policymaking is the governmental appointment process. According to Miliband (1969), the appointment process in advanced capitalist societies leads to the designation of individuals who are disposed to the capitalist status quo and to businesses' policy preferences. Current data show an increase in political appointees coming from law school, which is mainly based on the teaching of relatively conservative values. This takes place in a system like the United States, in which Republican administrations show stronger tendencies toward the protection of business interests (Espey 2001). These new progressive conservationist appointees believe that "production decisions should remain in the private sector" (Dowie 1996:108) and that the removal of market barriers and the addition of corporate welfare (e.g. through tax exemptions) would eliminate obstacles to their exploitation of resources in public lands.

In support of Miliband's claim, other authors posit that members of the economic elite (e.g. Gifford Pinchot) have historically relied on appointments to government agencies in order to have superior access to the policy formulation process. In this regard, Domhoff argues "that the highest levels of the executive branch . . . are interlocked constantly with the corporate community through the movement of executives and lawyers in and out of government" (1978:253). Thus, through this intimate and constant relationship among the corporate community and the executive branch, their policy

---

9 The specificity is due to the presence of very thin markets.

proposals are injected into the process. As a member of the economic elite,[10] Gifford Pinchot was appointed to a director position within the USFS at the time of this agency's inception (Gonzalez 2001). As a result of Pinchot's appointment, his ideas were incorporated into the policies of the USFS.

Under current USFS policies, former public domain lands disposed to private ownership are being reacquired. The tool adopted for this reacquisition is a land swap, which fulfills the consolidation of fragmented holdings and the promotion of more effective land management (Glicksman 1997:652). However, are these land swaps benefitting the management of public lands?

Law and economics: the market and its failure

As the goal of this chapter is to find solutions which could help the BLM or the Forest Service achieve economically efficient allocations while meeting the public interest[11] and equal value requirements, my economics analysis introduces an interpretive theoretical key. This section will explore public choice theory, which helps better explain the status quo of the economics of land exchanges.

At its core, economics attempts to determine a better allocation of scarce resources (Keohane and Olmstead 2007:2). In the land-swap market, the importance of a transaction stands at the intersection of supply and demand: the market sets, through supply and demand, the valuation and price of an item or lands. Assuming economists are correct, economics reveals how a reasonably expected increase in the value of land should be reflected in an up-to-date market price (Cole and Grossman 2005:50).

However, economies may suffer from market failure. Economists believe that markets fail when they are unable to achieve an efficient allocation of resources (Jaeger 2005:72). Guido Calabresi and Philip Bobbitt (1978) looked at the U.S. economic market and pointed out an important element: the presence of scarce essential resources in the supply market. Their analysis may be extended to different items that are presently scarce (Calabresi and Bobbitt 1978:151). We may consider their starting point of analysis as an element of comparison in the land-swap market. The demand is high, but the supply (a limited number of landowners offering lands back to the federal government) is low. In other words, it is a thin market.

---

10 President Theodore Roosevelt was another member of the economic elite, as were many other conservationists and preservationists in the country. Clearly, not all the economic elites were on the side of protecting corporations' interests. According to historian Donald Worster (2011), no other U.S. president ever went so far in the preservation of the natural environment as did Teddy Roosevelt.

11 Public interest has been interpreted to include commercial uses such as livestock grazing, mineral extraction, and logging; recreational uses such as fishing, hunting, birding, boating, hiking, and off-roading, and conservation of biological, archeological, historical, and cultural resources.

As suggested by Cole (2009), land-swap markets are not normal markets with lots of buyers and sellers. They are very thin markets in which one of the parties – the government – is in a situation that increases the chances for rent seeking by the other parties. "Compensation demands . . . can be part of rent-seeking efforts as parties engage in extortion, holding up agreement unless they are offered more" (Libecap 2002:145). In these cases, when voluntary negotiations break off, use of the eminent domain power should be considered an appropriate alternative to extortionate measures (Pogrund Stark 2007:637). Indeed, this thin market represents the status quo in federal land exchanges with private parties; a thin market for offered lands decreases the chances that governmental agencies can shop around for better customers. As proposed by Merrill, regardless of a thin market's cause, the potential for rent seeking makes the choice by an agency to use eminent domain economically efficient for the public interest (1986:76). According to Hellegers (2001), agencies should turn to eminent domain whenever a particular parcel of land is needed for public purposes and the agencies would otherwise be forced to purchase on the open market at an inflated cost. This is the typical scenario of a thin market, and the purpose of eminent domain is to overcome any thin market obstacles (Hellegers 2001:934).

To better understand the political economy of land swaps, we have situated the decisions of agency officials in the context of the market. Swaps take place in the form of contractual transactions in thin markets. Therefore, my analysis begins with a broad overview of the economics of land transactions, their markets, inefficiencies, and failures. Thus, we understand how contract and market theory predict that land swaps should be efficient for both parties. On the other hand, land exchanges differ from normal markets in important respects, including the incentives of federal land managers and the thinness of the market, which result in deviations (i.e. market failures) from the predictions of contract and market theory. Each following subsection discusses these issues in more detail; we start our brief analysis in the following order: 1) a description of the land-swap market as it exists, with some estimations of total federal losses from bad swaps; 2) an account of contract theory, which presumes that swaps should be good for both parties; 3) an explanation of whether land-swap market failures occur because of (a) principal–agent problems and (b) public choice problems; and 4) a suggestion of how more frequent recourse to eminent domain might improve the situation.

The land exchange market

This first subsection provides a description of the land-swap market according to governmental reports published in the last two decades. In 1987, the GAO issued its first report on the specific practices of the BLM and Forest Service regarding FLPMA land-swap provisions. Among the land exchanges examined by the GAO, in 29 swaps equal value was not attained. The GAO only used a random sample of 61 BLM and 90 Forest Service land swaps. The GAO found that in three land swaps, the BLM office had waived the required cash equalization payments, while in 26 other swaps either the BLM or the Forest Service had actually adjusted or rounded appraisal values, therefore failing to achieve equal value from the nonfederal parties (GAO 1987:3).

These alarming data, showing agencies' failures to attain equal value in land swaps, prompted Congress to introduce a new bill, drafted by the very industry that the statute would regulate, to specify rules and procedures for appraisals to prevent these failures. In 1988, Congress finally passed FLEFA to "facilitate and expedite land exchanges by providing more uniform rules pertaining to land appraisals and by establishing procedures for resolving appraisal disputes" (GAO 2000:7). FLEFA was supposed to guarantee that all swaps would garner equal value.

In 1991, the DOI Office of Inspector General (OIG) more effectively reviewed the appraisals of lands exchanged by the BLM. In this case, the OIG hired an external reviewer to conduct the analysis. The reviewer confirmed that inadequate appraisal reviews were being accepted by the agency and that its officers were making land value adjustments at the expense of the public interest. A few years later, in 1996, the same OIG conducted an audit of BLM land swaps in Nevada. The new audit confirmed that the local state office had failed to obtain equal value in three of its four exchanges.

In 1998, the OIG for the USDA issued a report on a Nevada local district ranger office's land exchange practices, and this time the OIG uncovered the undue influences of private parties over the local USFS employees. In this investigation, the OIG uncovered data that showed malfeasance by a USFS lands and realty manager and two other staff managers. The same OIG later completed an evaluation report on another land swap conducted by the USFS in Nevada. In this instance, the USFS lands staff corrupted the validity of the appraisal process.

In March 2000, The Appraisal Foundation (TAF)[12] issued its first report evaluating the appraisal organization of the USFS. The data collected by TAF showed that undue influence was a normal practice of land-swap proponents and that land management line officers were compromising the independence of appraisers.

In 2000, the GAO also issued a new report confirming that both the BLM and the USFS had overvalued private lands and undervalued federal lands. Data showed that the agencies engaged in a practice of disapproving appraisals considered unsatisfactory by the private parties. Thus new appraisals

---

12 TAF is an independent organization headquartered in Washington, DC, that establishes the qualification criteria for state licensing, certification, and recertification of appraisers. The Foundation benefits the appraisal profession by increasing the quality of appraisals and by addressing issues critical to the advancement of professional valuations.

were prepared to accommodate the private proponents. The major finding was that both the BLM and the USFS "ha[d] given more than fair market value for nonfederal land they acquired and accepted less than fair market value for federal land they conveyed because the appraisals used to estimate the lands' values did not always meet federal standards" (GAO 2000:4).

The report proceeded to closely examine particular swaps. For example, the BLM had just completed the DeMar Exchange in 1999. There had been a wide gap in the two parties' valuations. According to a BLM source, "agency officials decided to bargain . . . because . . . the landowner would not otherwise reach agreement about the land's value" (GAO 2000:17). The DeMar Exchange shows how in a thin market a private party's extortion behavior may be compensated by disproportionate land valuations.

Finally, in 2002 TAF reported that the BLM appraisal organization was unduly influenced by private parties over the independence and objectivity of staff appraisers. This pressure, according to the report, was political in nature and had compromised the performance of the appraisers. Specifically, instances of undue political influence were shown to be present whenever a BLM state director was a political appointee.

Federal land exchanges: contracts

This section provides a description of contract theory, which holds that land swaps would ordinarily be economically beneficial for both parties. In federal land exchanges, "transacting parties are locked-in to a bilateral trading relationship, in the sense that the potential aggregate value of continuing the bilateral relationship is higher than terminating it and turning to alternative buyers or sellers" (Joskow 2005:321). In economics, a contractual transaction, such as a land swap, is a bilateral agreement in which the parties make reciprocal commitments (Brousseau and Glachant 2002:3). However, by envisioning land exchanges as a refined form of bartering in which roughly equally valued exchangeable goods are present, the picture of federal land swaps becomes clearer. In fact, according to Coase, "A person wishing to buy something in a barter system has to find someone who has this product for sale but who also wants some of the goods possessed by the potential buyer" (2005:35).

As the title of this section proposes, land swaps are contractual transactions concerning real property. In properly competitive markets, "Bargaining power should be equal and without a chance for any party to act opportunistically" (Cole and Grossman 2005:162). However, market competition, as a critical prerequisite for efficiency (a goal in land swaps), is lacking whenever a federal agency is trying to obtain environmentally sensitive lands. In these cases, the number of private owners willing to sell is severely limited, thus creating a thin market (Salamon 2001:1665).

In recognition of this reality, the New Institutional Economics model starts with the assumption that market competition is imperfect. According to Furubotn, "the 'neoinstitutional' environment . . . is a quite special one characterized by widespread uncertainty, asymmetrical information, opportunistic behavior, and many other 'frictional' features not found in the orthodox neoclassical system" (Furubotn 2002:75). In this framework, land-swap markets are not normal markets with many buyers and sellers. They are very thin markets compounded by the likelihood of rent seeking by any counterparts. As defined by Merrill, a "thin market" reflects "any situation where a seller can extract economic rents from a buyer" (1986:76). Accordingly, demands for over-compensation crop up as private landowners engage in extortion, holding up the signing of contracts until they receive more value from an agency (Libecap 2002:145). This represents the status quo in federal land exchanges with private parties; a thin market of offered lands decreases the chances that agencies can shop around for better customers. In these conditions, according to Coase, "if the costs of making an exchange are greater than the gains which that exchange would bring, that exchange would not take place" (2005:37). However, the BLM and Forest Service do conduct and complete swaps which they should not accept.

As pointed out by economists, the relevant level of analysis is the management of the transaction itself. Thus, in land swaps, the contractual transaction is the adopted unit of analysis (Brousseau and Glachant 2002:19). However, these transactions invite opportunism. According to Menard, "opportunism can generate contractual hazards" (2005:284); in these cases, the law must define and the agencies implement safeguard measures. The problem with this opportunism is that the perfect scenario for bargaining over the appropriate *ex post* quasi-rents is set by FLEFA's policies (Joskow 2005:322).[13]

Although the most important function of contract law is the protection of parties from such exploitive opportunism, the element of asset specificity renders the transaction a risky one. As suggested by Rubin, "The general form of opportunism is appropriating the 'quasi-rents' associated with some transaction . . . Such quasi-rents are often created by 'asset specificity,'[14] creations of valuable assets that are specialized to one transaction or trading partner" (Rubin 2005:213). Frieden goes even further in this form of analysis, proposing: "The specificity of an asset to a particular use creates two interrelated problems: valuation and opportunism" (2000:140). It is the high specificity of an asset which creates the potential for a possible hold-up situation, in which the detrimental *ex post* appropriation of the quasi-rent may take place in an improper item valuation (Menard 2005:285). The previous disbursements (e.g. appraisal or National Environmental Policy Act [NEPA] compliance costs) in furtherance of the land transaction create a bilateral dependency of the two parties. In such a scenario, "the parties to the

---

13 Quasi-rent is a term in economics that describes types of excess returns of temporary nature.
14 Asset specificity refers to the degree to which an asset is specialized; the more specialized the feature, the more difficult it is to transfer the asset to a different use.

transaction may then have an incentive to haggle over the distribution of the *ex post* quasi-rents created by the specific investments" (Joskow 2005:327).

To complicate matters even more, in the field of land swaps a new generation of somewhat shady characters has entered the game. Due to the peculiar circumstances of land-exchange markets, "In some cases, relevant information can be obtained through surveys of buyers, sellers, brokers, or facilitators who are directly involved in the exchange" (Benham and Benham 2002:370). A major problem in land exchanges is the fact that a complete knowledge of the market has never been a strength of the agencies. Thus, the world of federal land swaps has seen the proliferation of a peculiar form of entrepreneurship, also known as third-party facilitators. This third party is "an entrepreneur [that] connects two groups of people who otherwise would be socially disconnected . . . The entrepreneur, in his or her capacity as a middleman, straddles according to this argument a so-called 'structural hole'" (Nee and Swedberg 2005:793). Some environmentalists believe that a system of "built-in incentives" leaves the federal agency's local management at the mercy of unscrupulous "third-party facilitators" and businesses (Draffan and Blaeloch 2000).

Although facilitators add an additional cost element to the land transaction, they "can facilitate access to parties that provide information or resources" (Smith-Doerr and Powell 2005:379). Thus, the cumulative effect of using networks produces considerable economic benefits. As argued by some economists, "Networks represent informal relationships in the workplace and labor market that shape work-related outcomes. Social ties and economic exchange can be deeply interwoven, such that purposive activity becomes 'entangled' with friendship, reputation, and trust" (Smith-Doerr and Powell 2005:379). In addition, as the same authors continue in their analysis, "Networks are formal exchanges, either in the form of asset pooling or resource provision, . . . that entail ongoing interaction in order to derive value from the exchange" (Smith-Doerr and Powell 2005:379). Once these network relationships become formalized in repeated exchanges, the interdependence and interaction lead to a reduction in the need for formal supervision by governmental agents. The final result of this intermingling is that the network relations affect the information which is exchanged, the norms to which the parties adhere, and the people to whom they feel obligated (England and Folbre 2005:628).

Principal–agent (agency–official) problems[15]

Principal–agent problems are a reason that land swaps often fail to serve the public interest. In capitalism, opportunism or self-interest of agency officials

15 The principal is the federal agency or better yet the nation, while agency officials are the agents.

is a major obstacle to market efficiency. "The concept of 'principal-agent' is typically used to analyze this problem of self-interest. The prototypical principle[sic]-agent problem involves the difficulty that one actor (the principal) will have in getting another actor (the agent) to work on the first party's behalf" (Shapiro 2003:394). The main issue in this instance is the agent's self-referentiality, which relates to the frame of mind and perspectives with which such an actor approaches the work relationship with his or her employer (Salamon 2001:1631). According to Salamon, this framework leads to the conclusion that "the less the coincidence of interests and perspectives between principals and agents, the greater the risk of goal displacement and principal-agent difficulties" (Salamon 2001:1661). Thus, it becomes much more problematic for principals to ensure that their sets of values are implemented by their agents.

It is convenient to borrow terms from agency law. If we agree that BLM and Forest Service officials are agents for the principal, the nation itself, there are many circumstances in which the nation delegates its authority (Miller 2005:349). Basically, federal officials make resource-use decisions without being owners but only authorized agents (Libecap 2005:548). But as recognized by public choice theory and more generally by law and economics, because agents are utility maximizers[16] they will not necessarily act in the best interest of their principals (Jensen and Meckling 2003:164). The risk is that "anytime a principal assigns an agent with responsibilities, there are likely to be differences in motivation, incentives, and performance that lead to inefficiencies . . . The same thing holds for a society where public servants are charged with implementing the public's will" (Jaeger 2005:209). As explained by Posner, whenever a principal cannot directly supervise the agent's practices an agency problem arises. Each time agents engage in their delegated activities with low effort, moral hazard is created (Posner 2000:230). This behavior takes place especially when opposition norms, reflective of the interests and identity of individuals in agency positions, are more prevalent than the constraint of formal norms. As opportunism and malfeasance become routine (see the BLM's "alternative approach"), the opposition norms enable agents to seek out self-interested utility maximization (Nee and Swedberg 2005:805).

This dissonance (in supposedly shared perspectives) has economic relevance in the market in terms of what is known as agency costs. Agency costs are the direct result of the conflict between the agent's and principal's interests. Since the monitoring of delegated powers becomes necessary to curtail

---

16 Under this microeconomics concept as applied to our scenario of land swaps when making an economic decision, an agency official attempts to get the greatest value possible from expenditure of the least amount of bureaucratic red tape. His or her objective is to maximize the total value derived from the present occupation, eventually to obtain a better paying job in the private sector.

the agents' pursuit of their own interests at the expense of the principal's interest, the consequent monitoring costs are called agency costs (Gorga and Halberstam 2007:1134). The same economists point out: "The agency cost framework suggests that the greater the 'gap' between the agent and the principal, the greater the agency costs" (Gorga and Halberstam 2007:1134). Greater autonomy for agency officials results in an increase in the government's agency costs. "Agency costs are the sum of the costs of designing, implementing, and maintaining appropriate incentive and control systems and the residual loss resulting from the difficulty of solving these problems completely" (Jensen and Meckling 1992:262). Thus in this framework it is troubling that economic efficiency demands the devolvement of decision rights to agents at the local level (Jensen and Meckling 1992:264).

The current problem, according to Jensen and Meckling, is that there is no appropriate way to reward individual performance in a government agency. Failure to properly account for and reward actions on behalf of the principal's interests motivates agents to pursue their own self-interest, magnifying any dissonance in interests (Jensen and Meckling 1992:259–260). It is a major assumption in economics modeling that agency officials may have particular self-interests that do not necessarily align with the congressionally mandated public interest. "This is the root of the principle [sic]–agent problem" (Shapiro 2003:399). This problem is commonly known as bureaucratic drift, which is the decision of an agent to stray from congressionally mandated goals (Shapiro 2003:399). As argued by Jensen and Meckling, since individuals working for an organization may not share their principal's interests, a control system which ties the interests of the agent with those of the principal is necessary (1992:267). Basically, "self-interest on the part of individual decision-makers means that a control system is required to motivate individuals to use their specific knowledge and decision rights properly" (Jensen and Meckling 1992:270). Control in this case would be accomplished by compensating the agent more, such as with bonuses, and offering opportunities for job security and status or career advancement, thus allowing self-interest to be better aligned with the public interest.

If we apply this analysis to the present problems with land swaps, we realize that agency policy might indeed be impeded by the self-interests of the private party and the governmental agent. If indeed both parties tend to seek to maximize their utilities,[17] agency action might become inconsistent with the public interest mandated by the GEA or FLPMA (Shapiro 2002:52). In addition, land valuation uncertainty may allow actions by officials that are construed by watchdog organizations as exploitive of the situation and influenced by the agent's self-interest. By exploiting their positions as

---

17 Agency officials may maximize their utility by receiving gratuities or better paid job opportunities in the private sector, e.g. by being employed by the land developer with whom the land exchange was successfully completed.

decision-makers, the agents fail to act in the national interest, thus increasing agency costs (Shapiro 2002:53). Ultimately, the chance for opportunistic behavior by governmental officials is mainly dictated by the ethics of the individual and by whether his or her private interests may align with the public interest at large (Shapiro 2002:53).

Compounding the problem and the costs of the agency official's self-interest is the reality of government employment. According to Rosen, governmental occupations create risks of their own, "opportunities for misconduct increase as the successful agent's control over resources increases over the life cycle" (1992:190). Specific deterrence and loss of reputation are not foolproof inoculations against malfeasance. In fact, as Rosen suggests, analysts who have studied whether "social opprobrium, disapproval from one's peers, and loss of self-esteem have substantial deterrence value to many people . . . remain skeptical about their overall role in enforcing agency relations . . . [in fact] reputation is likely to be more efficacious earlier rather than later in the life cycle" (1992:190).

Asymmetric information is another reason that principal–agent problems occur. When agents have information not available to their principals, a conflict of interest between the parties may arise leading to economic waste, inefficiency, and corruption (Jaeger 2005:210). In fact, such behavior may escalate to a higher level of information asymmetry as members of a close-knit network within an agency collectively withhold information that could eventually lead to the discovery of opportunism and malfeasance (Nee and Swedberg 2005:805). In this environment, self-interested agents[18] who are decision-makers regulate private constituencies by keeping an eye on possible future employment with their regulatees (Kornhauser 1989:33). More specifically, if we adopt this form of analysis, we have to realize that "career government bureaucrats have their own careers to think about and furthering their own career may motivate them in ways that diverge from the will of the people" (Jaeger 2005:209). As Eyre points out, specifically referring to a contested land swap, "it is the involvement of BLM officials in Washington D.C. in the appraisal process, and the pressures that these officials put on the officials negotiating the exchange that was perhaps the biggest problem faced in the . . . exchange" (2003:293). This issue of self-interest with respect to a governmental agent's career is a major feature of the framework of principal–agent problems regarding land swaps. In order to appease their superior's requests, some agency officials would not contradict headquarters' orders fearing otherwise possible reprisal against their career.

As we have seen, agents who happen to be bureaucrats in economic life are normal utility maximizers. Therefore, "there is no reason to assume that [they] . . . suddenly become different and more benign when they enter the arena of government" (O'Neill 2006:161). As proof of this argument,

---

18 According to Shapiro, agency officials' self-interests vary from money, security, and status to policy (2003:399).

historically, "BLM's appraisers generally are evaluated by non-appraisers and their work performance is supervised by managers who are responsible for completing land transactions and exchanges" (TAF 2002:11). If O'Neill is correct, these bureaucrats, in their supervising position, might indeed add to the problem because their job is to complete land exchanges and maintain a good rapport with the private party involved in the land swap without creating problems in the process. When the district office's mantra is to avoid principal–agency problems at all costs, supervisors tend not to challenge questionable appraisals; therefore, supervision is lax.

Finally, we have reached a point at which we can highlight the crux of the matter in terms of control (or lack thereof) over an agent's practices. In fact, another problem may clarify why the agents are less susceptible to control by their principal. As pointed out by Shapiro, "an agency is not subject to the rulemaking requirements of the APA [Administrative Procedure Act] if it engages in contracting. Section 553(a)(2) of the APA provides an unqualified exclusion from every requirement of notice and rulemaking for rules relating to 'public property . . . or contracts'" (2002:57). This exclusion from the rules means no prior notice of negotiations for a land swap is published, which prevents any control of the agent by the principal because it is not possible to examine the contract proposed for the land swap. The data, which should be susceptible to challenge, are unavailable to the principal, rendering any successful challenge even more difficult.

Public choice problems

Public choice is commonly understood as an application of theoretical economics to the field of political science. "Just as economics reasoning holds that people are predominantly self-interested creatures, so public choice holds that political processes are likewise dominated by self-interest" (Gwartney and Wagner 2004:4). Under public choice, individuals are autonomous and self-interestedly pursue their preferences (Kirchner 2007:21). Private parties, motivated by their own financial interests, seek to extract economic rents from government agencies (Cross 1999:356). However, as public choice theorists teach us, bureaucrats are similar to their counterparts in the private sector. They pursue power, prestige, and wealth in the marketplace of future employment and have the same motivations as their counterparts (Gwartney and Wagner 2004:5). In addition, new institutional economics adds a twist to this theory. In accordance with its model, it is important "to make predictions of how actors change their behavior under different or changing institutional arrangements . . . It is necessary to make assumptions of how individual actors (methodological individualism)[19]

---

19 Methodological individualism as applied to economics reflects how social phenomena may be explained from the rational choice of individual agents as they react to changes in prices and incomes.

react to institutional changes" (Kirchner 2007:23–24). This is in fact the important lesson to learn; public choice theory since its inception focused its attention on individual decision-makers, but recently it has also extended its critical analysis to study the institutional structure in which they act (Cross 1999:381). Institutional changes may influence how individual agency officials rationalize the purchasing capacity of their stagnant incomes.

In fact, "in defining individual preferences differently in different contexts, public choice theory implicitly assumes, quite correctly, that different institutional settings foster different conceptions of self interest" (O'Neill 2006:167). More to the point, when economists refer to institutions they "mean any humanly devised mechanism or tool that influences individuals' incentives and choices by either constraining, guiding, or encouraging certain kinds of actions" (Jaeger 2005:126). In such cases the very same structure of institutions and the principal–agent problem combine to make the achievement of the public interest even more difficult and the pursuit of self-interest more possible. As stated by Miller, the agent's interests differ from the principal's; thus, when management lies under the agent's control, there is the danger that the agent might act in a self-serving fashion (facilitating a land transaction to secure future employment in the private sector in the pursuit of money, job security, and status) to the principal's detriment (Miller 2000:66). This argument thus summarizes both forms of analysis, institutional and individual, on which this entire chapter is premised.

Public choice theory explains other self-interested behavior. It proposes the idea of manipulation of legislative or regulatory policy through "rent seeking," which is "the diversion of resources from productive economic activities to efforts to obtain unearned benefits in the political arena" (Cole and Grossman 2005:60). The transfer of existing property rights through land swaps always carries the potential for rent seeking in the regulatory process because the private party seeks out unearned financial benefits in a thin market of land transactions (Gwartney and Wagner 2004:7). In any economic market including one relative to land exchanges, rent seeking takes two forms. First, "there are attempts by individuals or groups to gain rents within the rules of the game ('economic' rent-seeking)" (Span 2003:53). Second, "there are attempts to gain 'rents' outside the rules of the game ('criminal' rent-seeking)" (Span 2003:53).

To render matters more complicated for the interests of the principal, public choice theorists believe that public lands, as a natural resource, should be privatized to maximize their economic value. "There is a *prima facie* assumption in capitalist economic theory . . . that profit maximization by private enterprises maximizes welfare for society as a whole" (Feintuck 2004:14). However, that reasoning quickly opens the door for a slippery slope analysis. As Leys points out, evidence "suggest[s] that market-driven politics can lead to a remarkably rapid erosion of democratically determined collective values and institutions" (2001:4); thus, if this rapid erosion of collective values takes place, free-market policies could write the eulogy for equal value exchange in the public interest in particular. This is a direct consequence of the fact that public choice theorists offer their own concept of law and economics to argue in defense of some basic political and legal institutions in which individual self-interest will likely be more able to succeed (Kornhauser 1989:50). An additional critique of this theory that advocates the privatization of public lands comes from a recent application of Aristotle's *Politics* to the field of law and economics. Applying Aristotle's theory, we can recognize "his influential criticism of the market in terms of its encouragement of the desire for the unlimited acquisition of goods and thus the vice of *pleonexia*, the desire to have more than is proper" (O'Neill 2006:166). What makes the concept of *pleonexia* applicable to the market of land swaps is the potential for rent-seeking behavior of private landholders and agency officials who may both seek out self-interested, unearned economic benefits at the expense of the public interest of the land transaction.

Ultimately, public choice theory rests on the foundation of selfish, individualist behavior by all parties involved in the formulation and implementation of policy. More specifically, according to Farber and Frickey, the political process is subject to potential corruption by special interests; if this happens, the economic outcome may represents only the rent-seeking interest of a specific constituency rather than that of the public (1991:38). Historically, a few federal agencies have become captured or at least have been deemed susceptible to political pressures mounted by well-organized interest groups (Sunstein 1997:285).[20] Thus, as Croley points out, "Because regulation infrequently takes the form of highly specified legislation, interest groups seeking to advance their regulatory policy goals require . . . a willing bureaucrat or agency" (2008:16). Thus, the attainment of the public interest could be highly compromised because it has been garbled or perverted and now might reflect instead individual or group interests. Scholars have repeatedly called for increased judicial review of agency decision-making to combat agency capture (Cross 1999:359). Sunstein believes that if courts were to employ a "hard look"[21] standard of judicial review, the problem of impermissible rent seeking could be flushed out (1985:61).

Taking a "hard look" requires an approach which will be able to seek the true meaning of policies establishing the preservation of public lands. The Supreme Court affirmed in *Light v. United States* that "all the public lands of the nation are held in trust for the people of the whole country" (1911:537).

---

20 In addition to the BLM, other agencies have been rumored as captured by the industry. Among others, the Minerals Management Service, the Commodity Futures Trading Commission, the Federal Aviation Administration, the Federal Communications Commission, and the Food and Drug Administration, just to name a few.

21 In administrative law, the hard look doctrine is a legal principle that requires a court to carefully review an administrative-agency decision to ensure that the agency genuinely engaged in reasoned decision making.

However, this holding runs contrary to the values of the dominant economic and political group in U.S. society (Feintuck 2004:38). Accordingly, public choice theory explains how the true meaning of the public interest can be twisted to favor one group's agenda. Some authors reach the conclusion that "public choice theories can, [sic] quite properly be alternatively categorized as a sub-species of 'private interest theories' of regulation, within which regulatory systems are seen to be dominated by powerful private interests which subvert 'public' regulatory systems to their 'private' ends" (Feintuck 2004:8). In fact, as studies conducted by Cross confirm, data support the ideology that administrative action is influenced by self-interest (1999:370). Public choice theory "is premised entirely upon the outcomes of the pursuit of private interests, which, it is claimed, will ultimately reflect the best interests of general welfare" (Feintuck 2004:9). The Depression contradicted this assumption, as predicted by Keynes. As he pointed out, it is not a necessary consequence of the application of principles of law and economics that actions motivated by self-interest will always operate in furtherance of the public interest (Keynes 1926).

To begin with, the term public interest is a notion whose definition, according to some skeptical interpreters, is "either incoherent or a tyrannical imposition upon dissenters" (Farber and Frickey 1991:14). The range of the definition as it relates to economics is quite wide. On one side of the spectrum, some authors see the public interest as "the necessary exercise of collective power through government in order to cure 'market failures,' to protect the public from such evils as monopoly behavior, 'destructive' competition, the abuse of private economic power, or the effects of externalities" (Levine and Forrence 1990:168). On the other side, as Feintuck pointedly stated, "It seems that while an absence of definition for a concept potentially as central as 'the public interest' might appear to be helpful to an agency, in maximizing the scope of discretion available to it, the same absence may contribute to . . . leaving its agenda vulnerable to interest-group capture" (2004:140–141). Economists define regulatory capture as a situation in which government agents who regulate private industry become so closely linked and aligned with that industry's interests that they actually advocate for industry interests rather than the public interest (Jaeger 2005:209–210). According to public choice theorists, self-interested bureaucrats worry about their future employment. In a revolving-door system,[22]

22 In political science, the revolving-door system describes the movement of governmental personnel from employment as regulators to employment in the industries affected by their regulation. Political scientists believe that this movement creates an unhealthy relationship (regulatory capture) between the private industry and government, based on the granting of unearned economic benefits to the detriment of the public interest. Notable examples of the revolving door include Vice President Dick Cheney and Linda Fisher, deputy administrator of the Environmental Protection Agency, who took lobbyist jobs in military contracting and the pesticide and biotech industry, respectively.

few governmental officials are rewarded with more lucrative employment in the private sector if they favored the latter during their tenure as regulators. As a direct consequence, regulatory capture in the form of individual interests may very well influence agency practices (Cross 1999:357).

Following this critique, Croley surmises that in a captured agency "control runs in the direction *from* interest group *to* agency, opposite from what might be hoped for or supposed by a public-interest model of regulation" (2008:18). Agency officials' practices reflect the revolving-door system, "according to which administrators rotate in and out of government service and employment with regulated interests" (Croley 2008:95). This self-serving behavior has the potential of leading to corruption due to the vulnerability to market pressures of those officials who seek out money, job security, and status. When discretionary judgment enters this paradigm, concealed corruption may occur (Calabresi and Bobbitt 1978:123). Thus "if a society wants market pressures to win out but wishes to pretend otherwise, corruption can become an accepted way of life for such allocations" (Calabresi and Bobbitt 1978:123–124).

Per public choice theory, individuals seek out better opportunities; thus agency officials "cater to special interests . . . to advance their own interests, such as favorable future employment prospects" (Croley 2008:49). The theory pinpoints "two sets of considerations, one motivational and one structural" (Croley 2008:49). The motivational aspect represents the self-interest of agency officials. The structural aspect represents institutional bias in favor of an interest group. However, Croley disagrees with these so-called biases of agencies and their employees and critiques these assumptions. He argues that "illicit bargains between regulatees seeking regulatory favors and regulators seeking desirable future employment prospects seem unlikely" (2008:96). Per Croley, the illegality of the practice is sufficient disincentive to prevent it.

It would be naïve to support this argument that the existence of legal restrictions is a sufficient disincentive to human behavior, but Croley persists in this assumption and he goes even further in his analysis. He believes that actual agency employees are beyond doubt free of self-interest in their actions. He also assumes that by maintaining a code of professionalism "civil servants are the most difficult agency personnel for rent seekers to co-opt" (Croley 2008:274). Without proffering any factual evidence other than his "common sense," he states that "it seems especially unlikely that many regulators would make decisions hoping to improve their future employment prospects, notwithstanding the familiar 'revolving door' image" (Croley 2008:95).

In conclusion, public choice theory explains the present status quo of agencies' interaction with private parties, but these economic losses that the nation suffers in land swaps with land developers would not be prevalent without the support of other governmental institutions. More specifically, public choice theory calls for the courts to defer to agency decisions.

In other words, courts should not closely analyze the substance of agency decision-making if doing so would "severely impede the supply of regulatory goods to favored groups. In short, insofar as agencies aim to supply regulatory goods to rent-seeking interest groups, external oversight should not interfere" (Croley 2008:24). In fact, it has been the consistent jurisprudence of the Interior Board of Land Appeals (IBLA) and federal district courts to leave unchallenged, under the mantra of agency discretion, the decisions of agency officials. Therefore, this economic theory explains why the status quo remains unchallenged, since the administrative and judicial systems take a leave of absence each time they are asked to step in.

Eminent domain

When thin markets lead, in economics terms, to inefficient exchanges, should the power of eminent domain be the arm of last resort for federal exchanges? The concept of private property and its uses has always been open to different and contrasting views. However, in a capitalist society, as Jaeger points out, private ownership finds more economic utility in the development of lands rather than in their preservation for wilderness protection (2005:12–13). In the United States, given the history of westward expansion under successive land disposal policies, only some of the lands in need of preservation management are held as public lands, while the others are still in the hands of private landowners. If the Constitution and Congress confer power to the government to create management areas of public lands for conservation and preservation purposes, should the federal agencies use the power of eminent domain when private landholders become recalcitrant during the negotiation of land exchanges?

Describing this power in Lockean terms, Cole affirms that "representative governments possess the tacit consent of the governed, including property owners, to . . . regulate private property in the public interest" (2007:146). Conferring on the federal government the power to condemn private property is of the utmost importance. Eminent domain is the power to take private property by paying just compensation or market value, when it is needed for a public use (Cole and Grossman 2005:121). In a land-swap negotiation, if a federal agency is in the position to acquire a particular piece of property, e.g. for preservation purposes, "the owner of that parcel would have monopoly power with respect to the government. The owner would be able to extract from the government a price in excess of the opportunity cost for the property, thereby converting public surplus to private surplus" (Schill 1989:836).

Under case law, "the government's power of eminent domain is subject to two conditions enshrined in the 5th Amendment to the U.S. Constitution: (1) it must take the land for 'public use,' and (2) it must provide 'just compensation'" (Cole and Grossman 2005:144–145). The public use condition ensures that agencies make use of the eminent domain power only to further the public interest (Cole and Grossman 2005:145). However, the interpretation of public interest has been always a sort of chimera. So far, courts have acknowledged that "in a 'traditional taking'[23] where the government will own the land taken . . . [which] will be open to the public as a matter of right . . . it will be presumed that the taking satisfies the public use requirement" (Pogrund Stark 2007:612). Courts require the agency to show that the taking is necessary and that no reasonable alternative is available (Pogrund Stark 2007:641).

Just compensation is interpreted as the fair market value of the land, "Under the law, this compensation is valued by the price that a willing buyer would pay to a willing seller for the strip of land, with neither compulsion to buy or sell" (Crump 2001:135). As explained by Calabresi and Melamed (1972), when a scarce resource is sold it is unlikely that the market will supply a correct valuation.[24] In addition, any governmental attempt to establish the "correct" valuation will encourage private parties to spend their resources "to influence" agency officials rather than to agree on the correct appraisal (Baden 1997:136). As a consequence, rather than cozying up with private landowners, appraisers must instead keep their professionalism and "examine 'comparable sales' . . . to investigate the 'shadow [hypothetical] market' of somewhat similar properties . . . or to examine historical costs . . . i.e. to investigate how much the landowner paid . . . for the property" (Crump 2001:135–136).

Currently even the strictest interpretation of the takings clause[25] allows agencies to make use of eminent domain. In fact, in his dissenting opinion in *Kelo*, Justice Thomas argues that the "most natural reading of the Clause is that it allows the government to take property only if the government owns, or the public has a legal right to use, the property, as opposed to taking it for any public purpose or necessity whatsoever" (*Kelo* 2005:508). Furthermore, according to Justice Thomas, the condemnation power "is thus most naturally read to concern whether the property is used by the public or the government" (*Kelo* 2005:511). In other words, Justice Thomas, in examining the wording of the Clause, would limit its power only to those instances

23 In a traditional taking, property is condemned when a governmental entity compels the owner to transfer ownership of, or property rights in, real or personal property to the government.

24 A correct market value is "the estimated amount for which a property should exchange on the date of valuation between a willing buyer and a willing seller in an arm's-length transaction after proper marketing wherein the parties had each acted knowledgeably, prudently, and without compulsion." In the case of real estate property the correct valuation is recognized according to the land utility rather than its physical status (International Valuation Standards Committee 2007).

25 The Takings Clause is found in the last clause of the Fifth Amendment to the U.S. Constitution. This Clause limits the power of eminent domain by requiring the government to pay just compensation on taking private property for public use.

in which the general public acquires access to the condemned lands" (Mansfield 2005:262). Per Justice Thomas, eminent domain should be used by the agency when the government needs to acquire a specific parcel of land for its own mandated uses (Mansfield 2005:262). For him, the Clause would "require actual use by the public of the lands condemned" (Mansfield 2005:246). If we accept Justice Thomas's interpretation, in which public use means literally a property used by the public, a taking must include the acquisition, providing just compensation, of a facility that is physically accessible to the public (Merrill 1986:67). Even adopting this narrow interpretation of public use, land management agencies could use eminent domain in those cases in which thin markets cannot solve land exchanges due to diverging land valuations. The USFS has the authority to use eminent domain and yet as reported by the OIG, a local district ranger in Nevada preferred to acquiesce to the undue pressures of the private party unhappy with the USFS's appraiser's valuation (USDA 1998).

The problem facing federal agencies, however, is their refusal to use the eminent domain power and their willingness to pay a premium for private offered lands. If an agency acquires land on a willing-seller basis, without even considering the power of eminent domain, clearly the government is relinquishing the full control over the process to the private party. The problem lies in the agency, which declines to use eminent domain even when it considers the acquisition of a particular parcel of land necessary for the better management of its lands and the private party refuses to accept the agency's land valuation (Fink 1991). In the example offered by Fink, the agency "conducts its acquisition program in the Lake Tahoe Basin without condemnation proceedings, although the Tahoe Conservancy enabling legislation grants the agency a circumscribed authority to do so" (1991:540). Since both the OIG's and the GAO's studies confirmed that the Lake Tahoe basin is one of the two areas (the other one being Greater Las Vegas) in which land exchanges cause monetary losses to the federal agencies, it is interesting that, to date, neither the BLM nor the USFS has invoked such authority in this basin.

One major factor could explain this failure. According to Fink, any land swap should avoid increasing tensions in an already highly charged locale in which the local community, due to the economic need for expansion, abhors the eminent domain power. Due to the litigiousness surrounding land preservation in the Lake Tahoe region, the exercise of eminent domain could be interpreted by local residents as an abuse of power (Fink 1991:540). Ultimately, reliance on purchases from willing sellers, rather than eminent domain, avoids exacerbating resentment of federal intervention in the basin (Fink 1991:545). As suggested by Cole, in his analysis of the *Kelo* decision, "It is entirely possible, even probable, that governments, particularly in non-democratic countries, might protect some property rights (or the rights of some owners) more than others" (Cole 2007:154). This argument suggests that some landowners' rights (are land developers in this category?)

are overly protected in the United States over, for example, the rights of homeowners in blighted areas (but also that we might not live in a true democracy).

The threat of eminent domain remains merely a threat because interest groups prevent the BLM and the Forest Service from using it. Thus when governmental agencies and their regulatees spar over land transactions, the former tend to cave in to interest groups' guidance. This concept can be more properly described in these terms: a federal bureau headquarters may always reduce the bargaining power of an agency's local district or its intransigent officials by reducing the tenure of its senior bureaucrats or their appropriations (Rowley 1989:149). In this vein, any "markets are seen to respond to rent-seeking and rent-protection outlays mounted by the more effective interests groups" (Rowley 1989:149). Unlike Rowley, Becker sees this favorably, suggesting that the influence of interest groups may actually promote market efficiency. Interest groups may gain control of bureaucrats and politicians, thus achieving the control of political markets (Becker 1983). Market efficiency is then achieved by reallocating lands and their resources to those enterprises, which value it most in terms of its exploitation. Rowley criticizes this outcome and suggests that such "analysis unifies the view that governments correct market failures with the view that they favor the politically powerful" (1989:155).

Because of these perennial risks, eminent domain remains the best answer when a holdout owner refuses to sell at fair value. As Jaeger points out, "the stark reality that we must make trade-offs . . . seems often to be missed by individuals whose own interests are narrowly focused, especially when the opportunity costs are at the community or societal level" (2005:5). Calabresi and Melamed recognize that eminent domain would solve the problem of recalcitrant landowners: "If society can remove from the market the valuation of each tract of land, decide the value collectively, and impose it, then the holdout problem is gone" (1972:1107).

Discussing solutions

Any possible solutions to controversies over land exchanges should be centered on achieving the receipt of equal value by federal agents in each land swap. But what constitutes equal value or just compensation? Courts have been wrestling with this issue for over a century. Short of an entire deconstruction of the law and economics perspective,[26] the solution has to be found within the paradigm of a political–economic institution: law. As argued by Ulen, the law serves the function to promote the efficient use of

---

26 "To deconstruct means to demonstrate that a given set of legal principles really is a political tool used by powerful member of society to protect their positions against disadvantaged [others]" (Crump 2001:332).

resources (1989:223). In fact, law can devise ways to perfect market swaps in terms of joint returns and social efficiency reflective of preconceived principles.

Specifically, policy enactment should be geared first to guarantee the agents' compliance with their mandates. If courts require the trustworthiness of the agents in their implementation of federal policy, any solution has to account for the element of distrust toward the same agents. According to Levi, institutionalized distrust of agency's officials is paramount to building a set of procedures to monitor and protect against agents' malfeasance (2000:154). As Levi suggests, organizational and institutional defenses are necessary. By increasing the monitoring of agents' activities (as transaction costs), the ultimate result should be beneficial to the public interest. "This is the Smithian, even the Hobbesian, insight, elaborated in the work of recent transaction cost theorists . . . the investment in transaction costs, similarly to the investment in production costs, can make possible exchanges otherwise not possible and increase the overall number of exchanges" (Levi 2000:154).

The side effect of policy enactment, as Sunstein reminds us, is that over-regulation may actually lead to underregulation (the overregulation–underregulation paradox). In fact "by adopting a draconian standard, legislators can claim to support the total elimination of [fraudulent swaps]; but legislators and regulated [parties] know that administrators will shrink from enforcing the law . . . Hence . . . legislative incentives . . . will not in practice harm politically powerful groups" (Sunstein 1997:287–288). Judicial deference to agency decision-making then leaves in place the officials' unwillingness to enforce the law. Thus although many politicians oppose as a solution any statute that delegates to the courts the power to oversee the interpretation of public interest, there is no other institutional body able to effectively do so (Feintuck 2004:161).

It is naïve to think that by just giving meaning to the term public interest we would solve any controversy surrounding land swaps. How do we start to generate information about a concept which is still unclear? We should come to terms with the fact that "simply encouraging the judiciary to be more active in pursuit of public interest values does not help, if there is no clear conception of what those values are" (Feintuck 2004:174). More importantly, the political will necessary to ensure that newly enacted regulatory programs become established is very unlikely to last long enough to also prevent their capture by special interests (Croley 2008:61). Immediately following the GAO studies proving serious problems in the appraisal practices of the Forest Service and BLM, only window-dressing initiatives were adopted (the creation of the Office of Appraisal Services Directorate) and no longitudinal follow-up studies were conducted.

We now have to add to our analysis individual rational behavior in the context of federal land swaps. I posit that a possible solution has to come from a law that deters unethical behavior. What makes the present status quo in the field of land swaps even worse is "that the rate of crime is significantly related to the perception that the expected benefits of criminal conduct exceed the expected costs (for the criminal), including the risk of detection, arrest, and conviction, plus opportunity costs" (Cole and Grossman 2005:276). Indeed, as studies conducted by Rowley demonstrate a "criminal [i]s a rational utility maximizer" (1989:164). Given that studies of human behavior suggest people decide to act criminally based on their perception of the likelihood of their arrest, conviction, and punishment, it becomes clear why defrauding U.S. agencies with questionable swaps may continue unabated. As Rowley explains it, "criminals, benefiting from 'special interests,' will lobby more effectively than non-criminals to abate the severity of the detection/punishment control mechanism" (1989:164).

Moreover, as statistical analysis confirms organizational crime tends to be naturally efficient. As pointed out by Crump, "we can develop an economic equation that compares the criminal actor [public official, private appraiser, and/or private landowner defrauding the government]'s utility to the mathematically expected deterrent of the sanction, including factors for defects in detection, apprehension, adjudication and application" (2001:34). Just as multiple regression analysis has been used to study the deterrent effect of the death penalty, an equation for the criminal public official, private appraiser, and/or private landowner's expected utility could be created. In organizational crimes, such elements would include the prospective criminals' expected utility, the probability of conviction, the conditional probability of a prison sentence given a conviction, their utility if acquitted of criminal charges, their utility if convicted but subject to suspended sentence, and their utility if they actually have to go to prison. We gather that if criminal prosecution and conviction of appraisers in land exchanges were to become part of the future landscape of federal law enforcement, calls for immediate detection rather than imprisonment of malefactors would be supported by lobbyists for land development interest groups.

This chapter has tried to trace a theory that better explains why agencies' officials may favor some private developers in land swaps. Public choice theory gives a thorough analysis of the economics linked to an official's decision-making. Ultimately, however, people make choices in accordance with their societal role and the social norms they learned (Sunstein 1997:7). A combination of social norms, a distinctive societal role, and a personal upbringing (into selfishness?) might lead some to believe that defrauding federal agencies in land swaps is socially acceptable. This would go hand-in-hand with the revolving-door model, where officials shift sides and join private development firms. What is important to point out, though, is the framework of individualism and even selfishness that permeates land swaps. In this arena, markets are centered on the general acceptance of cultural norms, which may lead to uncooperative behavior among the parties and ultimately to socially inefficient outcomes (Sunstein 1997:385). That is why Glicksman is right when he states: "Expecting disgruntled [private landholding] westerners to make voluntary sacrifices of their perceived private interests to the public good may seem utopian and foolish, and cramming civic virtue and responsibility down their throats may seem pointless" (1997:669).

Thus we are left with the hope that agencies will decide to exercise the eminent domain power when private owners are recalcitrant about completing land swaps which are not fully advantageous for them. The Land and Water Conservation Act of 1964 earmarks a specific fund for the acquisition of lands for outdoor recreation and wildlife purposes. However, Republican administrations have regularly left it underfunded. Espey points out the presence of "a statistically significant negative relationship between expenditures from the Land and Water Conservation (LWC) Fund and the number of land exchanges, indicating that when there is more money for the federal agencies to buy land, they are less inclined to exchange lands with private parties" (2001:98).[27]

Since appropriations for the Fund have steadily decreased under Republican administrations, it would be interesting to see whether by using the threat of eminent domain a different appraising of lands would follow. Federal agencies have the eminent domain power, and because economic agents are subject to their decision making, they could certainly use that power (Brousseau and Fares 2000:415). Instead, holdouts manipulate the system and the final result is that wheeler-dealers profit from the game of extortion. Private landholders simply threaten to log their private parcel of land surrounded by wilderness and then complete a spectacular land swap worth millions of dollars when they finally resell the lands previously held in public ownership (Blevins 2010:A1).[28] Thus, it is true "that people with inholdings could force land exchanges to take place by creating a credible threat" (Paul 2006:124).

Conclusion

Public choice theory explains why one-fourth of federal land exchanges (GAO 2000) end in substantial governmental losses. In order to fully comprehend the seriousness of the problem, we must not disregard the importance

27 In 1997, President Clinton signed a bill earmarking $250 million from the LWC Fund to buy 7,500 acres in the Headwaters Forest, a grove of ancient redwoods in Northern California. Two years later, the government finally purchased the forestlands at the final price of $480 million.

28 In 1989, a land speculator, Tom Chapman, bought a 240-acre inholding in the Gunnison National Forest in western Colorado for $1,000 per acre. He threatened to build a million-dollar log cabin unless the Forest Service bought his inholding for $5,500 per acre. Eventually, Chapman brokered a land swap with the Forest Service, acquiring 105 acres of public lands near the ski town of Telluride. Once Chapman took title to the selected public lands, which the Forest Service appraised at $640,000, he immediately sold them for over $4 million.

of public choice theory and how it emphasizes two sets of considerations: motivational and structural. As described earlier, the motivational aspect concerns self-interested behavior on both sides of the exchanges. According to economic sociologists Portes and Sensenbrenner, "social life consists of a vast series of primary transactions where favors, information . . . are given and received. Social capital arising from such reciprocity transactions consists of an accumulation of 'chits' earned through previous good deeds to others, backed by the norm of reciprocity" (2001:129). As we have seen, the revolving-door system has permitted administrators to rotate in and out of government service and regulated interests, making them receptive to appeals from the private sector.

In addition, agency capture has for decades rendered governmental officials easy targets for manipulation. As historian Richard White suggests, once a governmental agency is captured, it is largely influenced by the interest groups, which directly affect its decisions and policies (1991:409). When private companies offer better remuneration than federal agencies, a selected few officials, striving to make the private outfit happy and hoping to gain successful employment with that company, may tie themselves to a policy model which economically benefits the private employer to the detriment of the agency and the public interest. It is through this institutional capture that these self-interested officials may benefit private interests at the expense of public ones.

However, institutional capture and self-interested agents are only part of the problem to be solved. Most importantly, as pointedly argued by Frieden, it is "the great specificity of land to its current use [which] leads to the great difficulties of arriving at a commonly accepted valuation and provides powerful incentives for owners to exert political pressure for favorable treatment" (2000:146). Because of this, the courts should exercise their authority to require procedurally and substantively sound appraisals. Thus, "due to the 'specificity' of land values, it is politically efficient for policymakers to delegate the problem of compensation to a body such as the judiciary that is better insulated from lobbying" (Span 2003:28).

On the other hand, as Calabresi and Bobbitt (1978) point out, the cost of good legal representation and appraisal expertise gives an advantage to the rich, which might distort the principles of the federal land exchange system. They conclude that "since people are not equal in their ability to state their cases, we [are] again faced with the necessity . . . of accepting *sub silentio* the notion that the ability to state a case is an acceptable criterion for allocating the good" (Calabresi and Bobbitt 1978:59).

However, not involving the courts merely perpetuates the status quo. Calabresi and Bobbitt argue that negotiations enhance the efficiency of the market. Yet, the pervasiveness of human selfishness has demonstrated that policies should be passed and implemented to counteract those tendencies to take advantage of the desperate demand for items in a market of scarce but essential natural resources. If the solution is the enactment of new federal policies, such as increased use of eminent domain, it remains true that "if a new program is to be successful, the officials responsible for implementing it must have sufficient focus and persistence to develop new procedures and to apply them in the face of possible resistance" (Fink 1991:552).

In order to provide answers, we should ask whether it is time to create a new independent federal agency whose only purpose would be the negotiation of land swaps (Eyre 2003:293). Eyre proposes: "Although it is hard to imagine any governmental agency being completely free from political pressures, the creation of a new government agency composed of federal appraisers may be the best way to avoid many of the problems faced by the federal land exchange process" (2003:293). This argument is based on the faulty premise that "because the new agency would be given the sole responsibility of negotiating federal land exchanges it would be free from many of the constraints and pressures that the BLM suffers from [sic]" (Eyre 2003:293). However, this assumption is based on the optimistic belief that top governmental bureaucrats, politicians, and lobbyists will not be able to extend their influence into the new agency.

As a solution, I propose to use public choice theory with a new perspective. In its "constitutional perspective," this theory advocates institutional reform only when improvements are adopted within constitutional rules. "This perspective requires that we shift attention away from the analysis of policy choice by existing agents within existing rules, and towards the examination of alternative sets of rules" (Brennan and Buchanan 2004:420). The solution, a new set of rules regulating the transfer of property rights between private owners and federal agencies and vice versa, is also embraced by Brousseau and Glachant. They believe this "reallocation of property rights can overcome economic agents' propensity to be opportunistic" (Brousseau and Glachant 2002:7).

Accordingly, given the Kaldor-Hicks efficiency criteria,[29] the power of eminent domain is a viable alternative. In fact, as long as the contractual

---

29 According to the two economists, Nicholas Kaldor and John Hicks, the efficiency criteria used to assess market allocations explain how "net social welfare can be enhanced by changes in entitlements, even if some individuals suffer losses as a result" (Cole and Grossman 2005:12). In accordance with the Kaldor criterion, as long as one party is better off (winner) after the reallocation of resources and this person can afford to compensate whoever is left worse off after the completion of the market transaction, market efficiency is enhanced. Per the Hicks criterion, the amount of resources that those who are left worse off after a market reallocation may offer to the winner(s) to forego the previous reallocation would cause the former an even greater loss in net social welfare. According to these criteria, reallocations in entitlements are neither necessarily based on voluntary market transactions nor require equal compensation for the change to the previous allocation. Thus, in our scenario of land swaps, governmental agencies' use of eminent domain would perfectly dovetail out of the efficiency reallocation enhanced by the Kaldor-Hicks criteria and could lead to a better reallocation of entitlements.

transaction is still efficient within Kaldor-Hicks, the market would be satisfied in terms of mutual and social efficiency. The use of eminent domain would reestablish parity of bargaining power, which is a fundamental goal for any market-efficient land swap. Otherwise, since the agencies are presently acting under capture by interest groups, mutual and social efficiency will continue to be severely compromised.

For a further solution, Congress might legislate to reopen those land exchange transactions in which the BLM or the USFS sustained losses. After, all as Schwartz postulated, "long-term contracts contain a variety of . . . reopener provisions that respond to the difficulties that imperfect indices cause" (1992:89). In fact, as North (2001) points out, some decisions need to be made which involve the altering of existing contracts. In certain instances, recontracting cannot be accomplished within the existing structure of legal rules in the property rights arena; therefore, those instances require an alteration in the rules to allow recontracting (North 2001:250).

The combined use of eminent domain and the option of recontracting previous land deals would empower the government to fulfill its mandate to exchange its public lands in the public interest. Governmental agencies could then overcome the current advantages of private landowners and achieve the requirement of equal value which underpins the scope of land swaps.

Table of Cases

Kelo v. City of New London, 545 U.S. 469 (2005)
Light v. U.S., 220 U.S. 523 (1911)
U.S. v. 82.46 Acres of Land, 691 F.2d 474 (10th Cir. 1982)

References

Baden, J. A. (1997). The True-Mann's West: Endangered and Forsaken? In J. Baden and D. Snow (Eds.), *The Next West: Public Lands, Community, and Economy in the American West* (pp. 107–129). Washington, DC: Island Press.

Becker, G. S. (1983). A Theory of Competition Among Pressure Groups for Political Influence. *Quarterly Journal of Economics*, 98(3), 371–400.

Benham, A. & Benham, L. (2002). Measuring the Costs of Exchange. In C. Menard (Ed.), *Institutions, Contracts, and Organizations: Perspectives From New Institutional Economics* (pp. 367–375). Northampton, MA: Edward Elgar.

Blevins, J. (2010, May 11). Controversial Real-Estate Speculator Tom Chapman Is Back on the Map. *Denver Post*, p. A-1.

Brennan, G. & Buchanan, J. M. (2004). Is Public Choice Immoral? The Case for "Noble" Lie. In J. C. Heckelman (Ed.), *Readings in Public Choice Economics* (pp. 413–418). Ann Arbor: University of Michigan Press.

Brousseau, E. & Fares, M. (2000). Incomplete Contracts and Governance Structures: Are Incomplete Contract Theory and New Institutional Economics Substitutes or Complements? In C. Menard (Ed.), *Institutions, Contracts, and Organizations: Perspectives From New Institutional Economics* (pp. 399–421). Northampton, MA: Edward Elgar.

Brousseau, E. & Glachant, J. M. (2002). The Economics of Contracts and the Renewal of Contracts. In E. Brousseau & J. M. Glachant (Eds.), *The Economics of Contracts: Theories and Applications* (pp. 3–30). Cambridge: Cambridge University Press.

Brown, S.J.M. (2000). David and Goliath: Reformulating the Definition of "the Public Interest" and the Future of Land Swaps After the Interstate 90 Land Exchange. *Journal of Environmental Law and Litigation, 15*, 235–293.

Calabresi, G. & Bobbitt, P. (1978). *Tragic Choices.* New York, NY: W. W. Norton.

Calabresi, G. & Melamed, A. D. (1972). Property Rules, Liability Rules, and Inalienability: One View of the Cathedral. *Harvard Law Review, 5*, 1089–1128.

Coase, R. H. (2005). The Institutional Structure of Production. In C. Menard & M. M. Shirley (Eds.), *Handbook of New Institutional Economics* (pp. 31–40). Dordrecht, Netherlands: Springer.

Cole, D. H. (2007). Political Institutions, Judicial Review, and Private Property: A Comparative Analysis. *Supreme Court Economic Review, 15*, 141–182.

Cole, D. H. (2009). Climate Change and Collective Action. *Current Legal Problems, 61*, 229–264.

Cole, D. H. & Grossman, P. Z. (2005). *Principles of Law and Economics.* Upper Saddle River, NJ: Pearson Prentice Hall.

Croley, S. P. (2008). *Regulation and Public Interests: The Possibility of Good Regulatory Government.* Princeton, NJ: Princeton University Press.

Cross, F. B. (1999). The Judiciary and Public Choice. *Hastings Law Journal, 50*, 355–382.

Crump, D. (2001). *How to Reason About the Law: An Interdisciplinary Approach to the Foundations of Public Policy.* Newark, NJ: LexisNexis.

Culhane, P. J. (1981). *Public Lands Politics: Interest Group Influence on the Forest Service and the Bureau of Land Management.* Baltimore, MD: Johns Hopkins University Press.

Dana, S. T. & Fairfax, S. K. (1980). *Forest and Range Policy: Its Development in the United States.* New York, NY: McGraw-Hill.

Domhoff, G. W. (1978). *Powers That Be: Processes of Ruling Class Domination in America.* New York, NY: Vintage.

Dowie, M. (1996). *Losing Ground: American Environmentalism at the Close of the Twentieth Century.* Cambridge, MA: MIT Press.

Draffan, G. & Blaeloch, J. (2000). *Commons or Commodity?: The Dilemma of Federal Land Exchanges.* Seattle, WA: Western Land Exchange Project.

England, P. & Folbre, N. (2005). Gender and Economic Sociology. In N. J. Smelser & R. Swedberg (Eds.), *The Handbook of Economic Sociology* (pp. 627–649). Princeton, NJ: Princeton University Press.

Espey, M. (2001). Federal Land Exchanges: 1960–1999. *Contemporary Economic Policy, 19*, 479–487.

Eyre, J. (2003). The San Rafael Swell and the Difficulties in State-Federal Land Exchanges. *Virginia Journal of Land, Resources, & Environmental Law, 23*, 269–294.

Farber, D. A. & Frickey, P. P. (1991). *Law and Public Choice: A Critical Introduction.* Chicago, IL: University of Chicago Press.

Feintuck, M. (2004). *"The Public Interest" in Regulation.* Oxford: Oxford University Press.

Feldman, M. D. (1997). The New Public Land Exchanges: Trading Development Rights in One Area for Public Resources in Another. *Rocky Mountain Mineral Law Institute, 43*, 2-1-45.

Fink, R. (1991). Public Land Acquisition for Environmental Protection: Structuring a Program for the Lake Tahoe Basin. *Ecology Law Quarterly, 18*(3), 485.

Foss, P. O. (1960). *Politics and Grass: The Administration of Grazing on the Public Domain.* Seattle: University of Washington Press.

Frieden, J. A. (2000). Evolving Voices in Land Use Law: A Festschrift in Honor of Daniel R. Mandelker: Part II: Discussions on the National Level: Chapter 3: Takings Issues: Toward a Political Economy of Takings. *Washington University Journal of Law & Policy, 3*, 137–147.

Frischknecht, P. P. (2005). Safety Nets and Side Effects: Regulatory Takings and Alternative Compensation Structures Created in Response to the Desert Tortoise Listing in Southern Utah. *Detroit Utah Law Review, 2005*, 997–1019.

Furubotn, E. G. (2002). Entrepreneurship, Transaction-Costs Economics, and the Design of Contracts. In E. Brousseau & J. M. Glachant (Eds.), *The Economics of Contracts: Theories and Applications* (pp. 72–98). Cambridge: Cambridge University Press.

Glicksman, R. L. (1997). Fear and Loathing on the Federal Lands. *Kansas Law Review, 45*, 647–670.

Gonzalez, G. A. (2001). *Corporate Power and the Environment: The Political Economy of U.S. Environmental Policy.* Oxford: Rowman & Littlefield.

Gorga, E. & Halberstam, M. (2007). Knowledge Inputs, Legal Institutions and Firm Structure: Towards a Knowledge-Based Theory of the Firm. *Northwestern University Law Review, 101*, 1123–1206.

Gwartney, J. D. & Wagner, R. E. (2004). The Public Choice Revolution. In J. C. Heckelman, *Readings in Public Choice Economics* (pp. 3–18). Ann Arbor: University of Michigan Press.

Hellegers, A. P. (2001). Eminent Domain as an Economic Development Tool: A Proposal to Reform HUD Displacement Policy. *Detroit College of Law at Michigan State University Law Review, 2001*, 901–963.

International Valuation Standards Committee. (2007). *International Valuation Standards* (8th ed.). London: IVSC.

Jaeger, W. K. (2005). *Environmental Economics for Tree-Huggers and Other Skeptics.* Washington, DC: Island Press.

Jensen, M. C. & Meckling, W. H. (1992). Specific and General Knowledge, and Organizational Structure. In L. Werin & H. Wijkander, H. (Eds.), *Contract Economics* (pp. 251–274). Cambridge, MA: Blackwell.

Jensen, M. C. & Meckling, W. H. (2003). Theory of the Firm: Managerial Behavior, Agency Costs, and Ownership Structure. In D. A. Wittman (Ed.), *Economic Analysis of the Law* (pp. 162–176). Malden, MA: Wiley-Blackwell.

Joskow, P. L. (2005). Vertical Integration. In C. Menard & M. M. Shirley (Eds.), *Handbook of New Institutional Economics* (pp. 319–348). Dordrecht, Netherlands: Springer.

Kaufman, H. (1960). *The Forest Ranger: A Study in Administrative Behavior.* Baltimore, MD: Johns Hopkins Press.

Keohane, N. O. & Olmstead, S. M. (2007). *Markets and the Environment.* Washington, DC: Island Press.

Keynes, J. M. (1926). *The End of Laissez-Faire: The Economic Consequences of the Peace.* London: Hogarth Press.

King, L. P. & Szelenyi, I. (2005). Post-Communist Economic Systems. In N. J. Smelser & R. Swedberg (Eds.), *The Handbook of Economic Sociology* (pp. 205–232). Princeton, NJ: Princeton University Press.

Kirchner, C. (2007). Public Choice and New Institutional Economics: A Comparative Analysis in Search of Co-operation Potentials. In P. Baake & R. Borck (Eds.), *Public Economics and Pubic Choice* (pp. 19–38). Berlin: Springer.

Kornhauser, L. A. (1989). The New Economic Analysis of Law: Legal Rules as Incentives. In N. Mercuro (Ed.), *Law and Economics* (pp. 27–55). Boston, MA: Kluwer Academic.

Levi, M. (2000). When Good Defenses Make Good Neighbours: A Transaction Cost Approach to Trust, the Absence of Trust Distrust. In C. Menard (Ed.), *Institutions, Contracts, and Organizations: Perspectives from New Institutional Economics* (pp. 137–157). Northampton, MA: Edward Elgar.

Levine, M. E. & Forrence, J. L. (1990). Regulatory Capture, Public Interest, and the Public Agenda: Toward a Synthesis. *Journal of Law Economics & Organization,* 6, 167–198.

Leys, C. (2001). *Market-Driven Politics: Neoliberal Democracy and the Public Interest.* London: Verso Books.

Libecap, G. D. (2002). A Transactions-Cost Approach to the Analysis of Property Rights. In E. Brousseau & J. M. Glachant (Eds.), *The Economics of Contracts: Theories and Applications* (pp. 140–158). Cambridge: Cambridge University Press.

Libecap, G. D. (2005). State Regulation of Open-Access, Common-Pool Resources Problems in Firms. In C. Menard & M. M. Shirley (Eds.), *Handbook of New Institutional Economics* (pp. 545–572). Dordrecht, Netherlands: Springer.

Lowi, T. J. (1979). *The End of Liberalism: The Second Republic of the United States.* New York, NY: W. W. Norton.

Mansfield, M. E. (2005). Takings and Threes: The Supreme Court's 2004–2005 Term. *Tulsa Law Review,* 41, 243–290.

Menard, C. (2005). A New Institutional Approach to Organization. In C. Menard & M. M. Shirley (Eds.), *Handbook of New Institutional Economics* (pp. 281–318). Dordrecht, Netherlands: Springer.

Merrill, T. W. (1986). The Economics of Public Use. *Cornell Law Review,* 72, 61–115.

Miliband, R. (1969). *The State in Capitalist Society.* New York, NY: Basic Books.

Miller, G. J. (2005). Solutions to Principal-Agent Problems in Firms. In C. Menard & M. M. Shirley (Eds.), *Handbook of New Institutional Economics* (pp. 349–370). Dordrecht, Netherlands: Springer.

Miller, G. P. (2000). Das Kapital: Solvency Regulation of the American Business Enterprise. In R. A. Posner, *Chicago Lectures in Law and Economics* (pp. 65–81). New York, NY: Foundation Press.

Nee, V. & Swedberg, R. (2005). Economic Sociology and New Institutional Economics. In C. Menard & M. M. Shirley (Eds.), *Handbook of New Institutional Economics* (pp. 789–818). Dordrecht, Netherlands: Springer.

Nelson, R. H. (1997). Is "Libertarian Environmentalist" an Oxymoron? The Crisis of Progressive Faith and the Environmental and Libertarian Search for a New Guiding Vision. In J. Baden and D. Snow (Eds.), *The Next West: Public Lands, Community, and Economy in the American West* (pp. 205–232). Washington, DC: Island Press.

North, D. C. (2001). Economic Performance Through Time. In M. C. Brinton & V. Nee, *Economic Performance Through Time* (pp. 247–257). New York, NY: Russell Sage Foundation.

O'Neill, J. (2006). Public Choice, Institutional Economics, Public Goods. In P.H.G. Stephens, J. Barry, and A. Dobson (Eds.), *Contemporary Environmental Politics: From Margins to Mainstream* (pp. 160–178). London: Routledge.

Paul, B. (2006). Statutory Land Exchanges That Reflect "Appropriate" Value and "Well Serve" the Public Interest. *Public Land & Resources Law Review, 27,* 107–129.

Pogrund Stark, D. (2007). How Do You Solve a Problem Like in Kelo? *John Marshall Law Review, 40,* 609–650.

Portes, A. & Sensenbrenner, J. (2001). Embeddedness and Immigration: Notes on the Social Determinants of Economic Action. In M. C. Brinton & V. Nee, *The New Institutionalism in Sociology* (pp. 127–150). New York, NY: Russell Sage Foundation.

Posner, R. A. (2000). Agency Models in Law and Economics. In R. A. Posner, *Chicago Lectures in Law and Economics* (pp. 225–244). New York, NY: Foundation Press.

Rosen, S. (1992). Contracts and the Market for Executives. In L. Werin & H. Wijkander (Eds.), *Contract Economics* (pp. 181–211). Cambridge, MA: Blackwell.

Rowley, C. K. (1989). Public Choice and the Economic Analysis of Law. In N. Mercuro (Ed.), *Law and Economics* (pp. 123–173). Boston, MA: Kluwer Academic.

Rubin, P. H. (2005). Legal Systems as Frameworks for Market Exchanges. In C. Menard & M. M. Shirley (Eds.), *Handbook of New Institutional Economics* (pp. 205–228). Dordrecht, Netherlands: Springer.

Salamon, L. M. (2001). The New Governance and the Tools of Public Action: An Introduction. *Fordham Urban Law Journal, 28,* 1611–1674.

Schill, M. H. (1989). Intergovernmental Takings and Just Compensation: A Question of Federalism. *University of Pennsylvania Law Review, 137,* 829–901.

Schwartz, A. (1992). Legal Contract Theories and Incomplete Contracts. In L. Werin & H. Wijkander (Eds.), *Contract Economics* (pp. 76–108). Cambridge, MA: Blackwell.

Shapiro, S. A. (2002). Matching Public Ends and Private Means: Insights from the New Institutional Economics. *Journal of Small and Emerging Business Law, 6,* 43–64.

Shapiro, S. A. (2003). Outsourcing Government Regulation. *Duke Law Journal, 53,* 389–434.

Sinden, A. (2007). The Tragedy of the Commons and the Myth of a Private Property Solution. *University of Colorado Law Review, 78,* 533–612.

Smith-Doerr, L. & Powell, W. W. (2005). Networks and Economic Life. In N. J. Smelser & R. Swedberg (Eds.), *The Handbook of Economic Sociology* (pp. 379–402). Princeton, NJ: Princeton University Press.

Span, H. A. (2003). Public Choice Theory and the Political Utility of the Takings Clause. *Idaho Law Review, 40,* 11–110.

Sunstein, C. R. (1985). Interest Groups in American Public Law. *Stanford Law Review, 38,* 29–87.

Sunstein, C. R. (1997). *Free Markets and Social Justice.* New York, NY: Oxford University Press.

The Appraisal Foundation. (2002). *Evaluation of the Appraisal Organizations of the Department of Interior Bureau of Land Management: Including a Special Evaluation of an Alternative Approach Used in St. George, Utah.* Washington, DC: Author.

Ulen, T. S. (1989). Law and Economics: Settled Issues and Open Questions. In N. Mercuro (Ed.), *Law and Economics* (pp. 201–231). Boston, MA: Kluwer Academic.

U.S. Department of Agriculture. (1998). *Title to Physical Improvements on the Zephyr Cove Land Exchange* (USDA Report No. 08003–4-SF). South Lake Tahoe, CA: Lake Tahoe Basin Management Unit.

U.S. General Accounting Office. (1987). *Federal Land Acquisition: Land Exchange Process Working But Can Be Improved.* Washington, DC: U.S. Government Printing Office.

U.S. General Accounting Office. (2000). *BLM and the Forest Service: Land Exchanges Need to Reflect Appropriate Value and Serve the Public Interest.* Washington, DC: U.S. Government Printing Office.

Vaskov, N. G. (2001). Continued Cartographic Chaos, or a New Paradigm in Public Land Reconfiguration? The Effect of New Law Authorizing Limited Sales of Public Land. *UCLA Journal of Environmental Law & Policy, 20,* 79–107.

White, R. (1991). *A New History of the American West, "It's Your Misfortune and None of My Own."* Norman: University of Oklahoma Press.

Wilkinson, C. F. (1992). *Crossing the Next Meridian: Land, Water, and the Future of the West.* Washington, DC: Island Press.

Worster, D. (2011). *A Passion for Nature: The Life of John Muir.* New York, NY: Oxford University Press.

3 History of federal land exchanges

On February 28, 2007, a U.S. district court in Arizona decided a challenge brought by the Greer Coalition against the USFS's decision to approve the Black River Land Exchange. The challengers claimed that the USFS had acted in violation of FLPMA. The USFS had approved the swap of 337.74 acres of two tracts of federal lands just north of Greer, Arizona, for 400 acres of private lands. According to the challengers, the USFS had violated FLPMA by its approving of flawed appraisals of the swapped selected lands.

The court was persuaded by the plaintiffs' argument "that the valuation of the federal land is flawed and likely too low based upon the appraiser's failure to consider . . . a land exchange in the Greer area occurring in 1994" (*Greer Coalition* 2007:1658). Since land appraisals are based on previous land swaps completed in the same area, the court disapproved of the appraiser's "handling and evaluation of the information regarding a 1994 land exchange involving federal property in the Greer area" (*ibid.*). As the plaintiffs claimed, "although the information regarding the 1994 exchange was disclosed to the Forest Service and appraiser there is nothing to suggest that it was even considered in valuing the federal land" (*ibid.*). By examining the evidence before the court, the judge found "the appraiser's omission of any reference of the 1994 land exchange to be puzzling" (*ibid.*). The court found in the administrative record that the USFS "requested that appraiser 'acknowledge and document [its] [sic] consideration of the additional market based data in [its] [sic] appraisal'" (*ibid.*). Yet, there was no record that the appraiser gave any consideration to the 1994 land swap.

Therefore, the judge concluded, "while the Court must afford discretion to the expertise of the appraiser, the Court's discretion only extends to the extent that there is a reasonable and rationale [sic] explanation addressing legitimate questions and issues associated with the appraisal" (*Greer Coalition* 2007:1658). The court found that the USFS had supplied no such rational answer. Faced with this failure, the court reasoned that the 1994 land swap's "omission from the appraisal of the current land exchange, is 'arbitrary and capricious'" (*ibid.*).

Introduction

This chapter provides historical evidence that supports the findings of the district court in the Black River Land Exchange and helps challenge those federal agencies' practices that keep on causing the same effect: individual enrichment at the expense of the national coffers. Land swaps are an integral part of federal natural resources policy. Much attention has been given to them in government reports and legal analysis; however, little has been done to situate them historically. The first "purpose" of this chapter is to illustrate a broad historical overview of land-swap policy. Here we will look through two lenses: one inquiring into American expansionism and another into constitutional and statutory law. Land-swap policy is the product of historical dynamics. A historical review beginning at the end of the nineteenth century will clarify the struggles over legislation purported to improve land swaps.

The second purpose of this chapter is to review the malfeasance that has surrounded land swaps from the start. This malfeasance has not gone without official remark. In fact, the GAO has shown in two recent instances (GAO 1987; GAO 2000) that at least two federal agencies have problematic appraisal processes that fail to obtain appropriate value in a proposed swap.

Unfortunately, this malfeasance has been going on for more than a hundred years, a reality that often is underappreciated in government review and critical historical analysis. This chapter seeks to document the blundering history of land swaps and chronicle the malfeasance that accompanied it. It highlights the BLM and USFS practices valuing nonfederal land at more than fair market value while appraising federal land at less than fair market value in violation of FLPMA (GAO 2000:4). Finally, it addresses a specific question: why it is that, although "ostensibly created to serve the public and protect public lands, lands exchanges have become a corporate welfare program, doling out prime lands and resources to powerful interests and yielding dubious benefits to the public?" (Draffan and Blaeloch 2000:6).

In answering this question, this chapter explores the growth of conservationist thought during the Theodore Roosevelt administration and examines the critiques of its detractors. It interprets conservationism as both a practical tool for preserving natural resources for future use and an instrument for driving competitors out of business. This chapter adopts the explanation provided by Gonzalez (2001:23), who suggests progressive conservation schemes advocate wiser use of natural resources and then offer public lands to private interests at low cost.

Historical policy foundations

In the nineteenth century, U.S. public land policy was simply a matter of "acquisition and disposition" of the public domain (Culhane 1981:2). In 1891, the Division of Forestry, a decade later renamed as the Bureau of

Forestry, was given a new mandate to conserve forest reserves, which were later renamed, under Gifford Pinchot's request, national forests (Wilkinson 1992:130). In 1905, the Bureau of Forestry became the Forest Service when the forest reserves, originally established by executive order under the DOI, were transferred to the Department of Agriculture (USDA). Over the course of the twentieth century, conflicts arose regarding disposal and, more recently, management of the lands of the public domain. Culhane (1981) describes the administration of these lands by the Forest Service and the ancestors of the BLM in terms of the dichotomy created by diverse land management policies.

This dichotomy was expressed in the debate of conformity-capture. From the perspective of political scientist Herbert Kaufman (1960), the USFS was a disciplined agency immune to pressure by special interests. His interpretation sees a highly conformist agency created under the philosophy of progressive-conservation and following the principles of scientific management. The opposing perspective was articulated by Phillip Foss (1960) in his study of the Grazing Service and the General Land Office (GLO), which were eventually combined into the BLM. They were described as weak entities thoroughly influenced by their "clientele" – western stockmen – to such an extent to be considered in a state of captivity (Culhane 1981:2). Foss highlighted how narrow interest groups co-opted policy-making for the newly created federal agency and its predecessors. This form of policy-making had become the near-exclusive province of organized lobbies since their agendas were deemed to be the ultimate form of good government. Both the Grazing Service and the GLO functioned as simple bureaucratic land disposal entities. They disposed of the public domain by transferring lands into private hands.

In the nineteenth century, the prevailing philosophy was one of techno-utilitarianism; according to this philosophy, "natural resources were inexhaustible" (Culhane 1981:3). The western frontier was considered limitless, and its natural resources were to be commodified and exchanged in a laissez-faire market (Culhane 1981:3). These principles served the rapidly industrializing United States as it operated with a near-religious belief in its mission. Indeed, "a combination of self-aggrandizing Calvinist theology, unswerving faith in science and technology, and the consumer appetites of a rapidly growing Euro-American population combined to utterly transform most of America's natural environment" (Burton 2002:58). Toward the end of the nineteenth century, however, Americans began to realize that natural resources were indeed exhaustible and sought to protect them from the wasteful abuse of a "utilitarian plunder economy" (Culhane 1981:4). Theodore Roosevelt's administration quickly appropriated a new philosophy and put it into practice. "With the establishment of the National Forest Service . . . and President Roosevelt's protection of millions of acres of federal land from unregulated resource exploitation, in the early days of the twentieth century the American conservation movement began to come of age" (Burton 2002:62).

According to Culhane (1981), this progressive conservation philosophy reflected an opposition to special interests' destruction of natural resources. On the other hand, Gonzalez (2001) believes that at the time of the passage of the 1891 General Land Law Revision Act, also known as the Forest Reserve Act, which provided the president with the power to set aside forest reserves, timber companies appropriated some of the conservationist rhetoric (White 1991:409). Timber executives supported the new progressive philosophy under the guise of watershed protection and forest conservation, in reality serving their own long-term future interests (Gonzalez 2001:1).

Through a synthesis of Culhane and Gonzalez, this chapter provides a plausible explanation for these opposing political approaches. The concept of forestry adopted by Theodore Roosevelt's conservationist administration was a response to the laissez-faire abuse of the public domain. Culhane suggests that opposition to natural resource exploitation was a need of that particular era, but conservation advocates were unable to preserve the forests from the timber barons, a constituency that, according to Gonzalez, was actually represented by Pinchot (Gonzalez 2001:25). Under progressive conservation theory, forests were simply managed for a future sustainable yield (Gonzalez 2001:25). Each time timber shortages occurred in the free market, private forest reserves were depleted. Conservation policy, by withdrawing timber, affected mostly small operators, who did not own private forests (White 1991:409). However, the same policy favored later on those companies, which took advantage of government-subsidized purchases of federal timber during the construction boom of the 1960s (Wilkinson 1992:136). Therefore, Gonzalez correctly states that "the basic principle of conservation was 'wise use,' with the emphasis on wise, for the progressive conservationists were reacting to rapacious, short-term, profit-maximizing, utilitarian exploitation . . . of the forests" (2001:25).

Land swaps in history: the beginning

The era of forest conservation on federal lands began in the mid-1870s, initially focusing on the goals of preventing floods and reducing dependency on foreign lumber. In the 1880s, the USDA created the Division of Forestry.[1] Its goal was to bring the management of the U.S. forest reserves, which were created in 1891, in line with European professional standards. The Forest Reserve Act of March 3, 1891, authorized the president "to set apart and reserve, in any State or Territory having public land bearing forests . . . whether of commercial value or not, as public

---

1 Although the charge to manage the forest reserves first went to the DOI in 1905, those responsibilities were transferred to the USDA and the Forest Service when this agency was created out of the already existing Bureau of Forestry.

reservations" (§ 24). President Harrison alone reserved over 13 million acres of forestlands between 1891 and 1894. A few years later, in early 1896, the National Academy of Sciences created the National Forest Commission to plan the withdrawal of future forest reserves. By 1897, presidential proclamations of forestland withdrawals covered an estimated 21,279,840 acres of public lands. The Sundry Civil Appropriations Act of June 4, 1897, created the Forest Management Act and the "in lieu" section that allowed land exchanges for the reacquisition of in-holdings (Dana and Fairfax 1980:1).

Congress passed the Forest Management Act, also called the Organic Act, in an attempt to restrain presidential proclamations of forest reserves. According to historian Paul Gates, the Act dealt a temporary blow to conservationist plans to withdraw public lands from general public disposition and entry, but the Act actually had a more traumatic effect upon lands still in the public domain (1968:568). As Gates notes, "most unfortunate was the inclusion in this act of the famous Forest Lieu Section" (1968:570). Originally, this provision, as drafted in the Senate bill, was to recognize only a settler's right to exchange lands within forest reserves once a claim had been initiated or finally acquired for other quarter sections situated outside of the reservations. But the House–Senate conference committee, under the direction of Rep. John Lacey of Iowa, replaced that provision with one extending the right of exchange to other commercial interests, including railroad and timber companies (Gates 1968:570).

Thus this section recognized the right of "settlers or owners of unperfected or patented lands within the reserves to relinquish their tracts and to select in lieu vacant land open to settlement in amount equal to that relinquished" (Gates 1968:570). According to Sen. Richard Pettigrew (1970),[2] who proposed the first draft of this section, the pro-railroad members of Congress were extremely effective in manipulating the bill to protect the economic interests of the railroads. Sen. Pettigrew's bill recognized only the right of settlers to swap forest reserve lands, while the House version included both the rights of settlers and of owners vis-à-vis railroad landholdings received through presidential grants (Gates 1968:570). Sen. Pettigrew argued forcefully that a powerful constituency had stripped the U.S. government of precious timber (Pettigrew 1970:17). He believed that, under the presidential plan of creating forest reserves, there was already intent to favor business interests. Thus, these reservations intentionally included desert lands "so that the railroads could exchange their odd sections of

2   Richard F. Pettigrew served as a U.S. senator for the newly created state of South Dakota from 1889 until 1901. He attacked his former Republican colleagues in his 1922 autobiography, claiming the Republican party was in the hands of trusts and corporations, running a political platform authored by gamblers and shylocks.

worthless desert land for lands of great value outside of the reservation" (Pettigrew 1970:18).

Pettigrew blamed for these manipulations Congressman Joseph Cannon,[3] chairman of the committee on appropriations and a major proponent of the "in lieu" device. Thus, Pettigrew defined "Cannonism [a]s the profession of selling the country to the rich so that they may be enabled to grow still richer by the exploitation of the poor" (1970:280). Under this scheme, a tool designed to protect the claims of pioneering homesteaders had become a loophole by which unscrupulous businessmen could pillage the resources of the western states (Pettigrew 1970:17).

According to Gates, "by permitting owners of near worthless land within the forest reserves to exchange them for equal acreages of the very choicest timberlands outside, Congress was setting up a system that invited whole-sale abuse and deprived the government of valuable resources" (1968:586). Stephen Puter (1908), a self-confessed looter of the public domain, referred in his autobiography to other frauds perpetrated in these lands. In describing the abuses of a particular railroad company in these land swaps, he claimed that "the whole thing is a low-down means of granting the Northern Pacific extraordinary powers in the selection of lands in lieu of its worthless hold-ings in two reserves" (Puter 1908:372). Ultimately, Pettigrew's sardonic comment clearly summarizes a constant element in the history of federal land policy: "These men became rich because, through their positions of public trust, they were able to betray the Government and the people into the hands of the exploiters" (1970:278).

In 1899, the GLO issued a report on the abuses surrounding the imple-mentation of the "in lieu" section, identifying specifically the practice of fraudulent claims filed by fictitious homesteaders to acquire title to lands located in the forest reserves. In spite of this report, virtually nothing was done to correct the problem. In fact, that same year Secretary of the Interior Ethan Hitchcock issued a ruling that made matters worse. He ruled that even unsurveyed lands could be swapped under the "in lieu" section.[4] Sec-retary Hitchcock even issued a decision whereby "owners of land within the reserves might even strip it of timber and then relinquish it and select other land elsewhere" (Ise 1920:178). In 1900, the Senate voted unanimously to ask the Secretary of the Interior to introduce a bill that would stop the abuses of the land-swap law.

Pressure for change mounted. Sen. Pettigrew made a strong argument in Congress that the DOI was exchanging timber-rich lands for "worth-less lands" held by railroad companies in order to "enlarge" the value of

---

3 As a Speaker of the House, Joseph Cannon blocked the governmental regulation of rail-roads and other industries. See Cheney and Cheney (1983).

4 Secretary Hitchcock overruled the decision made a year earlier by his predecessor Secretary Bliss, who had ruled against the selection of unsurveyed parcels in land exchanges.

their grants (U.S. Senate 1900:6288). He spoke in terms of congressmen acting "against the public welfare" (Pettigrew 1970:21). In his view, the public interest should have been interpreted as the interests of U.S. citizens rather than those of "the railroads['] . . . predatory interests who are the real government of the United States" (Pettigrew 1970:210). Binger Hermann, then-commissioner of the GLO, also "was troubled about the forest lieu provision of the Act of 1897 which allowed any owner or bona fide claimant to land within the reserves to relinquish the tract" (Gates 1968:573). The commissioner believed that land swaps should favor land settlers rather than be subject to fraud by timber interests. On June 6, 1900, Congress adopted his support of relinquishment of agricultural lands for "in lieu" land swaps. However, railroad interests were still protected under this legislation (Gates 1968:573).

Notwithstanding Sen. Pettigrew's adamant support of the requirement that land swaps be carried out only on the basis of appraisals, and thus be based on equal value rather than acreage, his counterpart in the House, Joseph Cannon, was successful in blocking the effort. He convinced his House colleagues to adopt language that indirectly protected the interests of big business. Cannon "inserted a provision that thereafter railroads could only exchange for surveyed lands" (Pettigrew 1970:279). But the law did not take effect until October 1, 1900. "Since it did not take effect for nearly four months, there was still time for most of the selections to be made on unsurveyed lands as before" (Ise 1920:181). According to a contemporary scholar, the pillaging continued under the letter of the law (Ise 1920:181). The window of opportunity left open for railroad companies allowed them to stake claims on unsurveyed lands, which would be traded later for reserved forestlands.

In reality, the provision limited exchanging the lieu scrip in a reserve with surveyed lands still in the public domain. But the land fraud continued. The nature of the fraud was such that it could be conducted under the veneer of legality. The fraudulent device was similar in each instance. "When three settlers in a township petitioned for the survey of the township the Government was bound to make the survey . . . [; thus] . . . railroad thieves would send three men into a township, would have them file three homestead entries . . . and then the railroads would locate their scrip upon these lands" (Pettigrew 1970:279–280). Sen. Pettigrew came to realize that they were "the tools in the hands of big business that were used to plunder the American people" (Pettigrew 1970:24). Ultimately the land exchange provision was there to help plunder "in the interest of capital" (Pettigrew 1970:25).

In 1902, newly installed Secretary of the Interior Hitchcock, upon learning about the land frauds throughout the West, began his term by firing the GLO commissioner, Binger Hermann. However, the corruption had extended to several people, including "land officers, attorneys, surveyors, inspectors, and men higher up" (Ise 1920:186). By 1904, many involved in the business of stealing governmental lands were being prosecuted (DOI 1904:21). Over 30 people were convicted and sentenced to prison for conspiracy to defraud the government, including Sen. John Mitchell and Congressman John Williamson.

Following reports from the Secretary of the Interior denouncing the effects of the "in lieu" section, President Roosevelt appointed the Public Lands Commission in 1903 to deal with management of the forest reserves. The Commission recommended the complete repeal of the "in lieu" section, or at least a rule requiring both equal value and equal acreage.[5] However, the onslaught of "in lieu" swaps continued (Draffan and Blaeloch 2000). John Ise, a forestry policy author, repeating the words of the 1903 annual report by the Secretary of the Interior, commented that "the Forest Lieu Act . . . was manifestly unfair to the government. It permitted an exchange in which it was certain that the government would lose" (Ise 1920:176). These practices went on until March 3, 1905, when Congress finally repealed the "in lieu" section.

Puter, who was convicted for his involvement in several schemes, commented that repeal occurred only because "all big corporations in the country could afford to kill the law, because it had outlived its usefulness, and the next move was to make a grandstand play before the country and pretend to bow to the people's will, and incidentally shut the stable door after the horse was gone" (1908:374). Indeed, the 1905 act validated all land exchange contracts entered into by the federal government just prior to the passage of the statute. A forest policy analyst of the time made clear the general consensus that "the exchanges made in connection with [this clause] were nothing that the government should proud of . . . but it was hardly to be expected that the government should bargain with private parties and not get cheated more or less" (Ise 1920:183). The San Francisco Mountains Forest Reserve in Arizona and its checkerboard style of land subdivision was an exemplar of the fraudulent swaps, thus timber cutting continued unabated in the forest reserve due to its preexisting contacts on allegedly surveyed lands (Ise 1920:183).[6]

The voice of Gifford Pinchot, America's first professionally trained forester, was absent during the time of the fraudulent appropriation. In 1898, he was appointed chief of the USDA Division of Forestry due to his advanced training in forestry and the need to protect the American forests. However, his ability

---

5 According to Pinchot, in a recommendation on March 7, 1904, the Commission transmitted to Congress the proposal to block the exchange of forest reserve lands under the "in lieu" section. The second recommendation followed on February 13, 1905. According to Roth and Williams (2003), Pinchot supposedly realized the in lieu land provision was dangerous, but he never had any idea of the gravity of the consequences of passaging this section.

6 The checkerboard land pattern is a constant reminder of the nineteenth century land grants, especially the railroad land grants, used by the federal government to develop its public domain lands in the western territories. This pattern has created in-holdings, parcels of lands owned by the government (state and federal) surrounded by private ownership or vice versa, following the decision of the federal government to retain some of its lands. The whole problem of intermingled private and public land holdings, checkerboard lands, predates the first act of Congress establishing a policy of federal land retention, the 1891 Forest Reserve Act.

to block "in lieu" land exchanges was limited. In his memoirs he rejoiced when "the pernicious lieu-land exchange was laid away for good and all. That was progress of the first water" (Pinchot 1947:258). He also commented that the framers of the "in lieu" section meant "that any lumber company, mining company, railroad company, cattle outfit, or any other large owners could get rid of their cut-over land, their worked-out claims, the valueless portions of their land grants, or any other land they had no use for, and take in exchange an equal area" (Pinchot 1947:118). Pinchot admitted that that was the purpose, yet he never acted against it. Because of this, he became the object of political attacks by members of Congress. "Representative Humphrey . . . criticized Pinchot for not having protested against the operation of the Forest Lieu Act, and several western men accused him of being in large measure responsible for the frauds arising under that act" (Ise 1920:293).

Throughout this period (1897–1905), the DOI was totally ineffective at impeding the process of land grabbing.[7] By the time the "in lieu" section was repealed on March 3, 1905, "unscrupulous land speculators successfully urged the creation of reserves simply because they contained worthless lands claimed by the speculators, which were there then traded for clear title to valuable properties on the unreserved public domain" (Dana and Fairfax 1980:64). The USDA, newly responsible for the forest reserves, was successful in lobbying against the exchange provision. By this time, however, railroad and timber companies had already significantly expanded their territorial assets. As Ise pointedly observed, "the Forest Lieu Act . . . had served as the means whereby individuals and corporations exchanged about 3,000,000 acres of land, much of it waste and cut-over land within the forest reserves, for valuable government land outside" (Ise 1920:182).

The manipulation of the "in lieu" system, together with the legislative requirement of equal acreage, showed the importance of a new player in the story – the cruiser – who is more familiar today as the appraiser of lands (Puter 1908:389). Puter reported that the honesty of a cruiser was significant because a cruiser held power over "either the contemplated purchaser of the tract or the one who sells an irreparable injury by any dishonest methods" (1908:389). Puter described the consequences for the public domain when federal agencies employed dishonest cruisers. He claimed that "a crooked cruiser is capable of swindling his employer out of thousands of dollars without becoming involved in criminal liability, because, if cornered he can set up as a defense that subsequent estimates exposing his dishonest efforts are the result of a difference of opinion between experts" (Puter 1908:389).

Unlike previous policy designed to foster agricultural settling of the western lands (e.g. the Homestead Act of 1862),[8] the Forest Lieu Section sparked

---

7 The Transfer Act of February 5, 1905, transferred management responsibility for the forest reserves to the USDA.

8 Homestead Act, Pub. L. No. 37–64, 12 Stat. 392 (May 20, 1862).

bitter controversy over the use of those lands, since, among other things, it inhibited homesteading (Weaver 2003:321). As President Roosevelt summarized in a letter to the Public Lands Convention, held in Denver in June of 1907, the country had "incurred the violent hostility of the individuals and corporations seeking by fraud . . . to acquire and monopolize great tracts of the public domain to the exclusion of the settlers" (Puter 1908:461). At the same time, the net results of the passage of the "in lieu" section of the 1897 Act ran contrary to the purpose of homesteading. An editorial in the *Portland Oregonian* of June 21, 1907, testified to this dishonorable period of mismanagement of the public domain. The editor criticized the anticonservationist agenda of the time and condemned "the abuses which were permitted . . . which enabled large corporations to exchange their worthless lands for good and still retain their good lands within a reserve" (Puter 1908:464).

Forestlands exchanges in the 1920s

Between 1911 and 1925, Congress passed several laws that helped consolidate federal forests throughout the country in support of the conservationist agenda. Dana and Fairfax describe the 1911 Weeks Act as "the most significant forestry legislation ever written. . . . This critical law authorized purchase of national forests in the East" (1980:101). The importance of the Weeks Act is the authority it gave to the Secretary of Agriculture "to recommend the acquisition of lands which were, in his judgment, necessary for regulating the flow of navigable streams and to purchase such lands" (Dana and Fairfax 1980:113; Weeks Act of 1911).

The Secretary of Agriculture had since 1905 enjoyed control of the forest reserves through the Forest Service. Now, the Weeks Act authorized the secretary "to organize acquired lands to be administered as national forests" (Dana and Fairfax 1980:113; Weeks Act of 1911). The Act essentially implemented the conservationist design to extend forest reservations to other parts of the country, especially the Northeast and the South. The statute conferred to the National Forest Reservation Commission, which was made up of three members of the government and four members of Congress, the power to purchase forestlands. The secretary received a mandate to select the forestlands to be purchased, and over the following two years the government purchased over 1.5 million acres.

Power to swap those lands was not conferred on the executive branch until 1925. The Weeks Exchange Act "authorized the exchange of land . . . for land within the exterior boundaries of national forests acquired under the Weeks Act of 1911 or the Clarke-McNary Act of 1924, on an equal-value basis" (Dana and Fairfax 1980:383). The Clarke-McNary Act had extended the powers of the Forest Service to purchase lands both for stream flow protection and for timber production. The Weeks Exchange Act granted to the agency authority to complete administrative land swaps for those in-holdings created by purchases under the Weeks Act.

Previously, in 1922, Congress had finally, with the General Exchange Act (GEA), legislated the power of the USDA to swap lands for in-holdings of equal value. The "General Exchange Act authorized the Secretary of Agriculture . . . to exchange surveyed, nonmineral land . . . in national forests established from the public domain for privately owned . . . land of equal value within national forests in the same state" (Dana and Fairfax 1980:381). The GEA was modeled after the "in lieu" land section, but this time the requirement of equal acreage was replaced with a requirement of equal value. The idea was still to expand forestry, but forest consolidation was now the driving force of congressional initiative.

The Act to Consolidate National Forest Lands, also known as the GEA of March 20, 1922, had become truly necessary to solve the problem of private in-holdings within national forests created by the checkerboard system. This pattern consists of square-mile blocks of land. During the Western expansion, railroad companies would receive alternate blocks in exchange for their promise to construct railways in the West. While some lands were transferred to private individuals for agricultural use, others were sold to timber companies for logging. The final result was an alternating design of private square-mile sections of land intermingled with property the federal government had originally retained. The first attempt at solving the problem of intermingled property had failed utterly in the period between 1897 and 1905. However, even the repeal of the "in lieu" land section still did not solve the in-holding problem. Consequently, from 1905 to 1922, Congress legislated each land swap. It became clear, though, that due to the cumbersome process of land-swap approval before Congress, federal agencies had better control of the minutiae of land swaps and could better handle them. As the Public Land Law Review Commission (PLLRC) reported, cumbersome congressional swaps motivated the eventual passage of the 1922 Act (1970:203).

Despite the impracticality of legislating individual swaps, those congressmen who had survived the scandals of the "in lieu" land section had the issue of fraudulent exchanges still fresh in their minds. Yet, in congressional hearings held in 1920, the legislature debated "whether the [Forest] Service would sacrifice the interests of the government if given the discretion lodged in the General Exchange Act" (PLLRC 1970:203).[9] Eventually, however, the bureaucracy's smooth operation made delegating swap powers to the agency a necessity. With the passage of the GEA, the Forest Service won

---

9 According to the General Exchange Act, "the Secretary of Agriculture is authorized in his discretion to accept on behalf of the United States title to any lands within the exterior boundaries of the national forests which, in his opinion, are chiefly valuable for national-forest purposes . . . in exchange . . ." 16 U.S.C. § 485 (March 20, 1922, ch. 105, § 1, 42 Stat. 465).

the battle over whether to confer discretionary authority on the executive branch to expedite the consolidation of forestlands.

The power of the Forest Service to swap lands was limited. Power was delegated to the Forest Service only for the exchange of national forest lands. "Though the General Exchange Act on its face appear[ed] to permit exchange of national forest lands of any type," the U.S. Attorney General thought differently (PLLRC 1970:204). In an opinion issued on March 21, 1924, he "held that the General Exchange Act was intended to apply only to public land forests and not to acquired national forest lands" (PLLRC 1970:234). Therefore, he excluded from the coverage of the Act those lands acquired under the provisions of the Weeks Act of 1911. This opinion prompted the USDA to request specific legislation that would confer on the Forest Service the power to swap parcels of in-held land in national forests that were acquired through the Weeks Act. A year later, this wish became law with the passage of the Weeks Exchange Act.

Both the GEA and the Weeks Exchange Act required that the lands transferred by the Forest Service and the lands surrendered by the private party be located in the same state. In addition, as explained above, both statutes required that the lands exchanged be of equal value. Two other requirements were present in both pieces of legislation. Not only should any Forest Service exchange be finalized according to the public interest, but such swaps should also lead to the acquisition of lands mainly valuable for forest purposes.

There was a safeguard against fraud included in Weeks Exchange Act that was not present in the GEA. All the exchanges proposed under the Act of March 3, 1925, needed the approval of the National Forest Reservation Commission, a body composed of three members of the executive branch and four members of Congress, whose duty is to safeguard the public interest in the swap. Unlike the Weeks Act exchanges, "the Secretary of Agriculture is lodged with sole discretion to make this determination" of public interest in the land swaps conducted under the GEA (PLLRC 1970:214). The House Committee on Agriculture introduced this important safeguard in order to protect those governmental interests abused by the fraudulent schemes under the "in lieu" section between 1897 and 1905. Unfortunately, this safeguard protects mostly eastern forestlands that historically have not been part of fraudulent transactions.

The Taylor Grazing Act of 1934

The era of disposition of the public domain ended in 1934 with the passage of the Taylor Grazing Act (1934). This law was named after Representative Edward Taylor of Colorado, who had sponsored the original House bill. With this statute, Congress enacted a new policy of retention and management of the lands that remained in the public domain as unentered under the administration of the Grazing Service, a newly created agency. Thus the process of conserving federal lands, which began in the late nineteenth

century with the creation of forest reserves, continued with this new legislation. However, this legislation most importantly regulated the rangelands by
creating grazing districts that were administered by Advisory Boards composed of ranchers (Laitos, Zellmer, Wood, and Cole 2006). In 1946, a new
agency took charge of the management of these lands – the BLM, replacing
the GLO and the Grazing Service.[10]

The public domain lands of the early 1930s were mainly lands left unoc-
cupied by homesteaders. They were used by the livestock industry and subdivided into major grazing districts. Thus Secretary of the Interior Ickes
supported a bill that would conserve those lands by providing for their development while halting further damage from overgrazing (Dana and Fairfax
1980:161). The purpose of the resulting Taylor Grazing Act was immediately
to curtail free access to the public domain and regulate the management of
the newly reserved federal lands. However, the livestock industry soon challenged the DOI. According to Dana and Fairfax, "those operators who had
come to dominate the industry in a period of might makes right were not
inclined to give up 'their' land or prerogatives under a federal regulatory
scheme" (1980:162). The elites of the grazing (livestock) business were successful in their ability "to define [the statute's] implementation to their own
advantage" (Dana and Fairfax 1980:163).[11] They argued that land swap
should be examined according to the nature of the statute. Thus, since "this is
a grazing act . . . [the] purpose is to provide for orderly administration of the
public domain and to stabilize the livestock industry" (Moran 1964:28). As
a result, for the first three decades the political leverage of ranchers captured
the control of policymaking on the public domain (Weaver 2003:359).[12]

By the letter of the law, the Taylor Grazing Act "provided the Secretary with general power to exchange lands under his jurisdiction for either
state or private lands, principally to serve rangeland needs" (Anderson
1979:661). Section 8 of the Act allowed the exchange of federal for private
lands that carried a public use value,[13] but immediately after its signing, it
was reinterpreted by the federal government as a mandate to create compact
grazing districts.[14]

10 The Executive Reorganization No. 3 of June 6, 1946, successfully merged the two agencies
into the Bureau of Land Management.
11 On this point, see William Rowley (1985). The author confirms the "desire to have the
new agency more under the control of stockmen" (Rowley 1985:152).
12 In 1950, Marion Clawson, director of the BLM said, "It is doubtful if today any public
land policy could be adopted which was unitedly and strongly opposed by the range livestock industry" (Clawson 1979:381–382).
13 Section 8 recognizes the discretionary power of the Secretary of the Interior to exchange
lands with private parties after the determination is made that the land swap is in the public interest, the value of the lands selected and offered is equal, and the lands are both in
the same state or no distant more than 50 miles from the adjoining state.
14 The section allowed equal value land swaps each time "public interests will be benefitted
[sic] thereby." 43 U.S.C. § 315(g) (1970).

Hearings held before the House of Representatives in 1933 discussed "the possibility that the [bill's] provisions would permit the perpetration of fraud on the government, that is, the exchange of poorer land for better land achieved by misrepresenting the condition or value of the land to the government" (PLLRC 1970:7). Nevertheless, the House Committee on Public Lands kept the original language of the bill requiring the exchange to be conducted on an equal value basis. Missing was any standard for determining the value of private lands. At the time of the House debate in 1934, only Representative White of Idaho discussed "the exchange feature of this bill" (PLLRC 1970:7–8).[15] He worried that the bill, as written, allowed swapping valueless private lands for valuable federal holdings despite the law's requirement of equal value exchanges. Rep. White thought fraud might occur whenever a private party may "have secret information as to the . . . value of the land" (U.S. House 1934:6361). According to him, calculated speculation could lead to defrauding the government, as long as the public interest was invoked by the private party proposing the trade (U.S. House 1934:6361). Indeed, for both the Senate and the House, the terminology stressed the necessity of a "mutual benefit" or "mutual advantage" for the parties to the exchange, without clearly defining the public interest.

In 1936, an amendment to the Taylor Grazing Act "authorized the Secretary [of the Interior] to exchange for private lands lying inside or outside the boundaries of a grazing district" (Anderson 1979:662) as long as the "public interest" would benefit. The law still contained no definition of the public interest. Deciding whether a land exchange were in the public interest was in the discretion of local land offices and such "determination[s] will, of course, be affected by considerations related to land and range management and grazing and the livestock industry" (Moran 1964:50).

However, soon enough an answer to the issue concerning the public interest of a land swap was on its way. In 1948, the DOI decided an appeal by Elbert O. Jensen of the rejection of his proposal to swap selected grazing lands in exchange for his land, which was within the boundaries of the Cache National Forest. The BLM had rejected his application because his lands were not in the same grazing district as the public lands, and thus the swap would not benefit the public interest under Section 8(b) of the Taylor Grazing Act. In disagreement with the BLM's position, Solicitor White argued instead that "the 'public interests' mentioned in section 8(b) of the Taylor Grazing Act may encompass interests outside the particular grazing district involved in the exchange" (*Jensen* 1948:231–232). Accordingly, the decision stated that "the prospect of improving the administration of a national forest might . . . warrant a finding that the 'public interests will be benefited' by an exchange . . . of public land within a grazing district for

---

15   See in particular 78 Cong. Rec. 6361 (1934).

privately owned land within the boundaries of the national forest" (*Jensen* 1948:232).

Years later, in 1963, the U.S. Court of Appeals for the District of Columbia reexamined and reinterpreted the term "public interests" in Section 8 of the Taylor Grazing Act. According to that section,

> When public interests will be benefited thereby the Secretary is authorized to accept on the behalf of the United States title to any privately owned lands within or without the boundaries of a grazing district, and in exchange therefor to issue patent for not to exceed an equal value of surveyed grazing district land or of unreserved surveyed public land in the same State . . .
>
> (Taylor Grazing Act 1934:98)

The appellants, operators of a cattle ranch, owned land acquired through nineteenth century railroad grants. They claimed that the BLM was authorized to swap "publicly owned grazing lands for privately owned lands only when the public interests in grazing on the public range and in conservation will be benefited thereby" (*LaRue* 1963:430). Thus the issue posed before the court was "whether or not such an acquisition under the exchange provisions . . . requires a determination that the net effect of the exchange will benefit public grazing interests" (*LaRue* 1963:435).

The court concluded that the public interest "encompasses all the potential value of multiple use management, not just public grazing interests" (Coggins and Glicksman 2007:13–67). In support of its decision, the majority cited an opinion released by the Secretary of the Interior construing Section 8(b) and its term "public interests" as embracing multiple use management. According to that opinion,

> The benefit to the public interests, which is the criterion of the statute, need not be related exclusively to conservation of Federal grazing resources nor need it be shown that a proposed exchange will promote range management . . . The Taylor Grazing Act is a multiple purpose act and while its chief immediate purpose was to stop injury to the public domain by unregulated grazing and to promote the stabliization [sic] of the livestock industry, section 1 of the act authorizes the Secretary of the Interior to establish grazing districts in order to promote the highest use of the public domain.
>
> (*LaRue* 1963:430)

The court reasoned that the statute failed to limit "public interests" to exchanges seeking grazing rights (Quarles and Lundquist 1984:381). Thus, wider discretion should have been accorded to the agency (Coggins and Lindeberg-Johnson 1982:77). The court held that public interests should be evaluated according to the "net result" (Coggins and Nagel 1990:501).

The BLM's duty was to compare "the advantages which the offered land would bring to conservation and the grazing industry with any disadvantage to those interests which might result to them from the withdrawal of the selected lands from a grazing district" (*LaRue* 1963:431). Since the net result was to facilitate the public interest determination in the management of the public domain, the court held that the BLM's action in this instance was well within its "wide area of discretion" (*LaRue* 1963:432).

Even with decisions at hand which helped flesh out the meaning of public interest, the interpretation of the element of equal value was left unresolved. Aside from the phrase "fair market value," interpretive tools were still absent from the bill. The element of equal value was applied as a standard procedure without considering the influence of market forces (PLLRC 1970:2). In the 1960 annual report, the Secretary of the Interior recognized that under the language of Section 8, as adopted by the BLM, the private parties were acquiring public lands at below-market value.[16] This process allowed speculators to obtain "windfall profits" just before the BLM launched its "anti-speculation policy, in a two decade delay" (DOI 1960:241). Up to 1960, public lands had been acquired at prices below market value because the BLM was approving swaps of lands "in areas where the real estate market [wa]s so unstable or uncertain that values [could] not be established with confidence" (DOI 1960:241).[17] Besides, speculators obtained windfall profits when the BLM would approve swaps even when "a marked dissimilarity in location or character of the offered and selected lands" was present (DOI 1960:241). Per the report, "marked dissimilarity works against equating of values" (DOI 1960:241).

In response to the new anti-speculation policy, in 1964 Moran stressed the importance of "standardization of practices" in order to give agencies ample discretion in their duties. Moran highlighted the "increasing need for closer contact between the administering officials and the representatives of private interests and an understanding by each of the problems of the other" (1964:50). This legal scholar knew that no exchange procedure could succeed without cooperation. Land exchanges, according to Moran, were created to facilitate private acquisition of public lands.

Over a decade later, the mineral development industry complained about the problem of federal officials being overly reluctant to approve swaps. According to one author, this complaint "stems from a fear that if the applicant ends up with a better deal in the trade than the government, charges of fraud or malfeasance could be brought against them. . . . All parties who

16 A report issued by the DOI Office of Survey and Review in 1956 had just exposed the failures of the appraisal process within the different agencies of the department.
17 Herein lays the conundrum embodied in land exchanges. Equality of exchanges is determined on market rates but the process is complicated by private interests, which, often successfully, seek to inflate their land values.

seek to effect an exchange for Federal lands must recognize this as a serious problem" (Eliason 1976:629). The requirement of completing a land
exchange in the public interest, or a peculiar interpretation of this requirement, had become standard practice in DOI directives and regulations under
the Act. Solicitor General Margold had issued an opinion in 1934 interpreting the exchange section of the Act to mean that the implementation of public
interest evaluations was to be "strictly limited to procuring exchanges for
the implementation of grazing policy" (as cited in PLLRC 1970:19). However,
the Secretary of the Interior hinted at implementing land swaps in furtherance
of resource conservation goals in the 1960 departmental anti-speculation
policy. Only in 1963 did the DOI reverse the Margold interpretation and
become open to any swaps that would "further any land management policy
without regard to whether it was tied to grazing or range stabilization purposes" (PLLRC 1970:19; *LaRue* 1963). A definite change of direction was
in the making.

Further modifications were made to national policies regarding public
land management after the passage of the 1964 Federal Classification and
Multiple Use Act (CMUA). These modifications occurred in order to expand
the possible uses of public domain lands. While the CMUA reaffirmed the
retention policies in the Taylor Grazing Act, it also required the BLM to
adopt a multiple use paradigm when designating administered lands, and
one year later the BLM issued conforming regulations. The CMUA specified
that "all present and potential uses and users of the lands will be taken into
consideration. All other things being equal, land classifications will attempt
to achieve maximum future uses and minimum disturbance to or disloca-
tion of existing users."[18] Also in 1964, the BLM made changes to the BLM
Manual to reflect the multiple use provisions of the CMUA. The Manual
recognized varied uses including range administration, public recreation
development, forest management, and watershed protection (BLM Manual,
1964:part 2.15.20). Land swaps were now to be conducted to further these
interests and not merely grazing interests.

Shortly thereafter, in 1968, the Secretary of the Interior tried to streamline
the land-swap process by amending its regulations.[19] While recognizing the
discretion of officials considering land swaps, Secretary Udall expanded the
understanding of land value and the goals of swaps. The regulations listed
uses including consolidation of governmental land-holdings, establishment
of land ownership in order to reach an efficient administration of federal
lands, protection of community and business interests linked to uses of public lands, and implementation of the multiple use principle. Federal lands

18 43 C.F.R. § 2410.1(b).
19 The same year, the DOI Office of Survey and Review had published a scathing report on
    the appraisal practices of the departmental agencies and suggested the creation of a sepa-
    rate office that would oversee land-swap evaluations.

could "be used or disposed of in such a way as to promote their multiple use, sustained yield and highest and best usage" (PLLRC 1970:53).

The 1964 PLLRC

On September 19, 1964, Congress passed a bill creating the Public Land Law Review Commission (PLLRC) to study existing public land laws, regulations, policies, and practices in order to recommend reforms. The intention of such reforms was to improve the management of public lands. Among other recommendations, the Commission suggested modifications to statutes regarding "the exchange of the public lands . . . necessary to assure that the public lands of the United States shall be retained and managed, or disposed of in a manner to provide the maximum benefit for the general public" (PLLRC 1970:2). After extensive analysis, the Commission released a report prepared by private contractors that described problems common to land swaps.

The first problem, according to the report, was the fact that "Congress . . . ha[d] simply been unable to decide what limits to place on the delegation of its acquisition authority in order to protect the public interest" (PLLRC 1970:S-17). The Commission recommended that Congress limit the administrative agencies' authority to use land swaps to cases in which the acquisition would lead to better management of federal lands.

The second problem pertained to an extensive lack of uniformity across agency processes for the exchange of federal lands. The Commission viewed the existing discretion in acquisition procedures as more vice than virtue. The Commission felt that uniformly and fairly treating private parties involved in land swaps was of the utmost importance. Therefore, it recommended standardizing acquisition practices to prevent federal officials from abusing their power during negotiations (PLLRC 1970:S-17). Notably, however, the Commission's Advisory Council, composed of federal agency officials and representatives of major citizen groups, failed to represent any environmental organizations. The Council, instead, was replete with numerous representatives of business groups interested in developing the federal lands.

It is worthwhile to remember that Wayne Aspinall established the Council. Aspinall, a conservative, pro-private property, pro-industry Colorado congressman, specifically hoped the result of the Commission's work would be to facilitate more private development on public lands (Sturgeon 2002:153). Thus the third problem reflected the interests of the Advisory Council's constituency. Accordingly, the procedures for completing land swaps were being blamed for process failures in the protection of property owners (PLLRC 1970:S-17). Here, the Commission thought that private property owners were being slighted rather than the government being defrauded in land swaps!

The Commission evaluated each of the private contractors' suggestions to remedy these problems. First, the Commission suggested that Congress establish an independent committee charged with oversight of land swaps by all agencies. An alternative would be to send to the courts "any impasse as the valuation of lands which are the subject or object of an exchange" (PLLRC 1970:S-19). A third remedy dealt with the issue of uniformity by proposing a single acquisition system to be implemented by all agencies. Each of the proposed alternatives carried potential disadvantages. For instance, the proposal to defer the valuation of lands to the court system would create "all the disadvantages in time and money . . . of a regular condemnation proceeding" (PLLRC 1970:455). Further, if federal lands were appraised before any negotiations took place, the federal agency would lose any power of negotiation, thus obliterating any chance for private "property [to] be acquired at less than the appraisal value" (PLLRC 1970:461). Ironically, the Commission considered disadvantageous any practice that would subvert fairness in dealings with private owners. Thus the Commission recommended "that representatives of the government should never use their positions of power to take advantage of those with whom they have dealings" (PLLRC 1970:273).

The real concerns for the Commission were the practices of different federal agencies. The Commission's recommendations hinted at furthering the protection of private parties' interests in dealing with federal agencies. But while the Commission interpreted the failure to standardize acquisition procedures as an obstacle to fair treatment of the public, the report authors had meant somewhat the opposite in the draft document. They were particularly puzzled by specific facts surrounding various swaps conducted by the BLM. They specifically studied two particular land swaps. In the first, the review office in Denver had overridden an appraisal previously accepted by the local office in Phoenix. Afterwards, each newly proposed appraisal of the same federal land was rejected. An independent appraiser was eventually contracted by the office in Phoenix and his appraisal showed a difference of over $1 million between the values of the offered and the selected lands.[20] The private party tried to pressure the appraiser into accepting the original appraisal of the selected lands by filing a complaint against him with the local chapter of his licensing board. On February 12, 1969, the Chief of the Branch of Land Appeals of the BLM's Office of Appeals and Hearings rejected the swap proposal due to the differing values of the offered and selected lands (PLLRC 1970:197).

A more troubling case involved divergent appraisals of selected lands in a proposed exchange under the jurisdiction of both the BLM and the National Park Service (NPS). In this instance, the discrepancy between the appraisal

---

20 According to regulatory terminology, while offered lands are private, selected lands belong to the public domain.

by the BLM and that by the NPS was over $1.5 million. Any loss would have been borne by the government had the swap been completed. The PLLRC adopted the report's conclusion that the deficiencies of the BLM cruise system were to blame for the overvaluation in the Bureau's appraisal. In its response, the "BLM attributed the discrepancy in its cruises to inexperienced cruisers" (PLLRC 1970:339).[21] The report submitted to the PLLRC suggested serious alternatives to the existing land-swap process because of these negative findings; however, the Commission still failed to establish a new inter-departmental office in charge of evaluating each agency's appraisal techniques, as previously requested by the DOI Office of Survey and Review (OSR) (DOI 1968).

The new era of land exchanges: the FLPMA

A few years later, in 1976, Congress passed the Federal Land Policy Management Act (FLPMA), which reestablished a policy of federal land retention and multiple-use management of the public domain under the control of the BLM. Under the FLPMA, the public domain was officially renamed "public lands" and the BLM was authorized, as an agency, to manage these retained assets.[22] Through this new legislation the agency finally found both a mission and an organic act. The mandate was for the BLM to "manage the public lands on a "[sic] multiple use-sustained yield basis" (Dana and Fairfax 1980:340).

In the same legislation, Congress gave the USFS new authority in land swaps (§§ 205–206).[23] Congress was acting on a suggestion from the PLLRC regarding uniformity of procedures for acquisition and swap of public lands. Through this legislation, the two agencies, both subject to the mandate of conservation of public lands, were to have identical procedures for land swaps. According to the PLLRC, "land exchange authority should [have] be[en] used primarily to block up existing Federal holdings" (1970:270), with the only goal in mind being the improved management of public lands. In practice, however, natural resources lawyers saw at the time and later that "pursuing exchanges purely for land consolidation benefits ma[de] little sense for the BLM" (Quarles and Lundquist 1984:414).

21 The BLM still referred to the obsolete GLO terminology of cruises and cruisers, which are today synonymous with appraisal reports and appraisers.
22 Public lands are defined as any land and interest in land owned by the United States within the several States and administered by the Secretary of the Interior through the BLM. See 43 U.S.C. § 1702(e).
23 The regulations to implement FLPMA in Forest Service exchanges were codified under 36 C.F.R. Part 254. The Forest Service's statutory and management mandate had been entirely redefined in the 1974 Resources Planning Act and the 1976 National Forest Management Act.

Indeed, the FLPMA still allowed some disposition of public lands when it provided that "a tract of public land or interests therein may be disposed of by exchanges by the Secretary under this Act" (§ 206). It required that both the offered and the selected lands be of equal value. Appraisal became necessary in order to verify the equality in value and that appraisal had to conform to the Department of Justice Uniform Appraisal Standards for Federal Land Acquisitions (UASFLA). In addition, regulations passed by the Forest Service and the BLM required a review of the appraisal by the lead state appraiser or the state director at the agency's state office (Regulations Relating to Public Lands, § 2201.3–4; Regulations Relating to Forest Service, § 254.9(d)). This required the drafting of a review report and analyzing, approving, or adjusting the market value appraisal according to the highest and best use of the selected land.

According to the claims of legal scholars Quarles and Lundquist, "the federal government, in turn, has employed complex exchange evaluation procedures, involving numerous subjective and often undisclosed assumptions, which critics suggest frequently overstate federal land values and understate the market value of private lands" (1984:373).[24] The law recognizes only the "standard of the market value" (Regulations Relating to Public Lands, § 2200.0–5(n); Regulations Relating to Forest Service, § 254.2)[25] of the lands and this value "must be based upon a determination of the 'highest and best use' of the property. 'Highest and best use' is defined as the 'most probable use' of the property, based on market evidence as of the date of valuation" (Kitchens Jones 1996:21). However, in the absence of market information, it could be difficult to determine the fair market value (FMV) of any land. As Anderson believes, the "final determination of FMV may largely be the result of the talent of parties to a transaction to juggle hypotheses, exaggerate the significance of scarce data, and infer value from prospecting and other development expenditures . . . all combin[ing] to undermine the FMV" (1979:686–687). Simply put, all these operations are antithetical to a common calculation of the FMV, and they could mislead rather than help in a final determination of value.

According to Frank Gregg, director of the BLM under the Carter administration, "further problems are created by differences of opinion and professional appraisers' findings regarding the value of specific tracts. Differences in valuation methodologies . . . and allocating the costs of the time consuming value determinations further complicate the process" (1982:518).

---

24 No data are offered by the authors in support of this statement.
25 Both the regulations for the Forest Service and the BLM define market value as "the most probable price in cash . . . that lands or interests in lands should bring in a competitive and open market under all conditions requisite to a fair sale, where the buyer and seller each acts prudently and knowledgeably, and the price is not affected by undue influence." See 43 C.F.R. § 2200.0–5(n); 36 C.F.R. § 254.2.

Director Gregg, however, failed to mention that deliberate undervaluation of public lands could be the problem, as pointed out by a 1956 DOI committee and a 1968 OSR report.

Ironically, Steven Quarles and Thomas Lundquist comment that they were "aware of only one case in which the assertion has been made that equal value was not received in an exchange. . . . [In that instance] environmental plaintiffs raised equal value concerns in an effort to halt a Forest Service exchange that would have aided the proposed Big Sky recreational development in Montana" (1984:380).[26] Quarles and Lundquist, two legal practitioners working for the Endangered Species Coordinating Council (ESCC), a coalition of more than 200 resource development companies, were not necessarily unbiased. Their assertion that public domain lands had been undervalued in just a single swap was contradicted by data collected since the Oregon land fraud trial of 1903 in a recent investigation in 1987 by the GAO (1987:1). In addition, we cannot forget that past and present judicial deference to agency discretion has meant that cases of undervaluation may not have been subject to public scrutiny!

Furthermore, we should address the other aspect of concern relative to land swaps as illustrated by GAO reports. In the present U.S. public lands policy, FLPMA is also important for its attempt to ensure that swaps further a public interest. According to Dana and Fairfax (1980), the provisions of FLPMA must be interpreted in the context of other statutes such as the National Forest Management Act (NFMA) and the Multiple Use Sustained Yield Act (MUSYA). In this new framework, "all real estate transactions must be evaluated in the land use planning process and must protect the multiple-use value of the land" (Dana and Fairfax 1980:340). However, reports are particularly skeptical of the implementation of the BLM mandate as far as it concerns "the public interest" in multiple-use, especially when the law requires that the public interest be "well served." As a matter of fact, the law fails to specify how and to what degree an interest is "well served." Section 206 provides that in order to determine the public interest involved in a swap, either the agencies "shall give full consideration to better federal land management and the needs of state and local people, including needs for lands for the economy, community expansion, recreation areas, food, fiber, minerals, and fish and wildlife."[27]

26 Quarles and Lundquist are referring to the claims raised by a group of recreational users of public forestlands in southwest Montana and decided by the Ninth Circuit Court of Appeals in *National Forest Pres. Grp. v. Butz*, 485 F2d 408 (9th Cir. 1973).
27 Both the Forest Service and the BLM act under regulations that prescribe the securing of public objectives such as: protection of fish and wildlife habitats, cultural resources, watersheds, wilderness and aesthetic values; enhancement of recreation opportunities and public access; consolidation of lands; expansion of communities and promotion of multiple-use values. See 43 C.F.R. § 2200.0–6(b); 36 C.F.R. § 254.3(b).

Ultimately, it is a matter of interpretation of the law, and the federal court system has usually given carte blanche to the agency's determination of the public interest. The problem is that in practice the public interest is subordinated to the interests of private parties. In fact, according to a district court in Colorado, "Section 1716(a) requires merely that the agency consider and weigh the factors which are listed. . . . It does not give the factors any particular priority, nor does it require the agency to do so" (*Lodge Tower* 1995:1380).

In addition, there are dangers stemming from such a non-specific term as "public interest" (Brown 2000:15). The legislation provides that both parties involved in a land exchange can "mutually agree" to absorb the entire costs related to the exchange (FLPMA, § 206). This would include "the cost of appraisals and other reports that are contracted out, including the environmental assessment or impact statement, for both the offered and selected lands" (Kitchens Jones 1996:22–15). The danger is apparent that each agency might develop a practice of looking favorably on the willingness of a private party to conduct a swap and pay for the expenses of the transaction, not to benefit the government but rather to achieve a favorable valuation. Indeed, it is now common for private parties to closely participate in the appraisal process. Pro-development lawyer Kitchens Jones recommends to her clients that they become pro-active in conveying information to, and sharing conclusions with, the federal appraiser. She suggests: "These efforts should be undertaken with the attitude of assisting the agency in making a sound decision on the exchange; the proponent must not be perceived by staff as trying to unduly influence or interfere with their responsibilities" (Kitchens Jones 1996:22–30).

Confirming the worries of preservationists and legal practitioners, in 1987 the GAO reviewed the exchange programs as actually implemented. In fact, agencies had resorted to increased use of swaps to eliminate in-holdings – islands of private lands interspersed within federal land areas. The study commissioned by the Senate was to inquire about the land-swap process and make recommendations for improvement. The results of the study were indeed perplexing. The study conducted by the GAO found several instances where the BLM and the Forest Service had failed to attain equal value in federal land exchanges with private parties (GAO 2000:3).

FLEFA in 1988

In 1988, in direct response to the GAO study, Congress passed the Federal Land Exchanges Facilitation Act (FLEFA), which introduced a system of bargaining and arbitration for land-swap disputes. "In fact, exchanges became so popular that in 1988 their proponents pushed through a bill to streamline the process. They complained that land exchanges took too long, that the Forest Service and BLM had vastly different processes . . . and that there was no way to settle differences over appraisal values" (Bama 1999:para. 27).[28] According to Congress, the Act was passed "to facilitate and expedite land exchanges . . . by providing more uniform rules and regulations" (FLEFA 1988). The statute acknowledged the importance of land swaps for the consolidation of federal landholdings in order to achieve better management, protect natural and recreational resources, and promote the multiple-use principle. Several voices rose against the possible misuse of the new law. Among others, Rep. Ron Marlenee, a conservative pro-privatization congressman from Montana, opposed the bill. During hearings Rep. Marlenee sought to protect the everyday recreationist's and hunter's use of federal lands. Not only did he highlight the risk of possibly trading those very same lands out of federal ownership, but he also objected that the bill raised several issues concerning the possibility of misusing federal lands to compensate private parties for assuming the administrative costs of a swap. Rep. Marlenee's ultimate fear was the untimely "giving away or selling off federal lands to a vested few, those who are involved in the exchange rather than identifying land and opening it up to sale to the general public" (U.S. House 1986:20608).

The FLEFA set up a process of arbitration and negotiation if the two swapping parties could not agree on the valuation of the lands involved. It allowed adjusting the land valuations to compensate a party for costs incurred. But the BLM's implementing regulations led to loss of value for the government (TAF 2002).[29] The agency placed its appraisal reviews with its own realty division, an office that promotes swaps. The realty division frequently approved undervaluation of federal lands (Draffan and Blaeloch 2000).

On October 2, 1991, the USDA, in accordance with FLEFA, issued a draft rule for implementation procedures for land swaps. On March 8, 1994, the final rule was issued. The final rule was intended to clarify issues such as determining the public interest in a land swap. Under the final rule, the Forest Service officer is to reach a determination whether the public interest is served by giving "full consideration to the opportunity to achieve better management of Federal lands and resources, to meet the needs of State and local residents and their economies" (36 C.F.R. § 254.3(b)(1)). Contrary to previous land exchange regulations, the officer must now consider fish and wildlife habitat, cultural resources, watersheds, aesthetic value, the consolidation of lands for proper management and development, and the promotion of multiple-use values. The officer must base the decision on

---

28 The increased popularity of land exchanges was due to the nature of this policy tool. Since FLPMA establishes a policy of federal land retention, an exception to this policy, which allows the transfer of public lands to private ownership is through the completion of federal agency exchanges.

29 Regulations concerning the BLM implementing FLEFA were passed in 1993 and were codified at 43 C.F.R. Part 2200.

factors that entail more than economic considerations. In addition, the same innovative Forest Service regulations require that the officer's findings be documented in the administrative record (36 C.F.R. § 254.3(b)(3)).

The final rule adopted specific requirements regarding land appraisers. The appraiser must be "an individual agreeable to all parties and approved by the authorized officer, who is competent, reputable, impartial, and has training and experience in appraising property similar to the property involved in the appraisal assignment" (36 C.F.R. § 254.9(a)(1)). In addition, the regulations require that each appraiser meet certain state regulatory standards as set forth by Title XI of the Financial Institutions Reform, Recovery, and Enforcement Act (FIRREA).

The regulations require that the appraiser estimate the value of the land by its "highest and best use" (59 Fed. Reg. 10,871; 36 C.F.R. § 254.9(b)(1)(i)). This is defined as "the most probable and legal use of a property, based on market evidence, as of the date of valuation" (59 Fed. Reg. 10,868; 36 C.F.R. § 254.2). The appraiser's "highest and best use" determination becomes part of the appraisal report. In addition, the appraiser has to certify that he or she "has no present or prospective interest in the properties appraised, and has not received any compensation contingent upon the conclusions of the report" (Blando 1994:332). A qualified review appraiser then evaluates the report in order to determine whether it is "complete, logical, consistent, and supported by market analysis" (36 C.F.R. § 254.9(d)(2)(i)). The review appraisers are required to set forth their conclusions in a separate review report.

After FLEFA

The Clinton administration embraced the goals of the FLPMA and sought to restore the previous consolidation of public lands by reversing the checkerboard pattern. However, since this was done to achieve environmental preservation, it immediately evoked the ire of private developers (Leshy 2001:220). Lobbyists went on the offensive to state publicly that "the administration's process is at odds with the FLPMA model for environmental evaluation and public interest consideration" (Feldman 1997:2–39) because its officials dared to propose acquiring environmentally sensitive private lands in exchange for public lands. Clinton's opponents argued that swaps should be more "traditional." This position reflected an ideological objection to the government pursuing land protection initiatives rather than the traditional, privately proposed trades. Accordingly, only a "traditional" land swap would allow "a truly open, collaborative decision making process" (Feldman 1997:2–40), where, of course, resource development would take priority over environmental factors.

The crux of the matter is the different interpretation that private interests give to the statutorily mandated "public interest" (Blaeloch 2001). Private interests that pursued resource production saw the Clinton administration as failing to prioritize their interests. Their critique was that "the exchanges dedicate large land areas, at great public expense, to a single set of dominant uses by precluding all resource development activity" (Feldman 1997:2–41). Pro-development lawyers clearly defined the controversy: "land exchanges present the only viable means of acquiring the federal land, and thus, eliminating the federal government, from the midst of a private development project" (Feldman 1997:2–6).

In such circumstances, it is easy to understand how private business might receive preferential treatment from federal agencies (Draffan and Blaeloch 2000). After all, as pro-development lawyer Kitchens Jones concludes in her review of land swaps, the secret to success is in "maintaining the interest and support of the federal land management agency. When the agency and the proponent cooperate and coordinate their efforts, a land exchange represents a win-win situation for all parties" (as cited in Feldman 1997:2–51). An unsophisticated reader might misinterpret this passage by Kitchens Jones as an obvious statement, but a more critical reading reveals what lies beneath the façade of obviousness. She merely restates the same terminology and arguments proposed a year earlier by Dave Cavanaugh, the then Senior Specialist for the BLM appraisal process (Kitchens Jones 1996:10). Cavanaugh had just launched an alternative approach to BLM land swaps, and his activities were investigated promptly, leading to his reassignment by the Office of the Inspector General.

Policy scholar Cass Sunstein describes how the framers of the Constitution created a government that would supposedly safeguard our nation against the evil of "self-interested representation by government officials" (1993:25). They envisioned this "underlying evil: the distribution of resources or opportunities to one group . . . [as] a violation of the impartiality requirement – a naked preference" (Sunstein 1993:25). These naked preferences, reflective of interest group politics, lead agency officials who are amenable to the privatization of public lands into developing working relationships with land developers. Without securing the keys to the castle first, how then could the distribution of resources to one person or group be preserved in violation of the impartiality requirement?

To no surprise, in 2000 the GAO confirmed this distribution of resources. The new report found that the BLM and USFS continued to overvalue offered private lands and undervalue selected federal lands. Data showed both agencies had established a practice of disapproving land appraisals when they were considered unsatisfactory by proponents. New appraisals would then be prepared to accommodate the proponents. In addition, since 2006 discomforting signs have appeared in successive governmental studies.

Conclusion

In chronicling the history of federal land swaps, this chapter has followed a process that demonstrates the trial and error of diverse interests in regards to land swaps. Our first conclusion confirms the fears expressed in the environmental activist literature (Draffan and Blaeloch 2000) that the use of swaps has been and continues to be a disaster (GAO 2000).[30]

A review of the historical literature confirms that the public interest of the community at large has taken a backseat to private interests which support the economic development of public lands. Because no law or judicial precedent on swaps favors economic over other interests, multiple interests should properly be the basis of the agencies' decision-making. Notwithstanding that, recent studies conducted by investigative federal agencies have, indeed, confirmed Gonzalez's key of interpretation: conservationist policies of the Roosevelt administration have maintained a patrimony of natural resources that are being squandered in ill-advised land exchanges (GAO 2000). However, those very same conservationist policies have been subject to criticism by political conservatives. Policies enacted by Congress since 1897 directed at the reacquisition of land in-holdings have been poorly implemented and have mainly failed, according to some conservative authors (Feldman 1997; Kitchens Jones 1996), in their goal of rebuilding a more manageable public domain. So, is the solution to the problems a fire sale of the national forestlands, as advocated by Nelson (1995)?

Unlike this market-efficient solution, answers could be found by searching the true intentions of misbehaving individuals. What if the culprit of this centennial controversy is traceable to simple self-interest? Let us not forget that corruption has always been present among government officers, appraisers, and politicians (Blaeloch 2001). A century ago, people were charged with conspiracy to defraud the government of the public domain, while presently less environmentally protective administrations only threaten criminal investigations. For example, in 2002, in the proposed San Rafael Swell Exchange, the State of Utah offered state lands for federal lands ripe with oil, gas, and shale deposits. Although there was a difference in value (over $117 million), "cooked" appraisals devalued federal lands and overvalued state lands (St. Clair 2003). In its audit of these practices, The Appraisal Foundation requested, to no avail, a criminal probe by the DOJ.

Finally, the term "public interest" has remained undefined. In the 1930s the term meant "mutual benefit" or "mutual advantage." Over 80 years later, statutes still provide no precise definition. This has fostered complaints by both private and environmental interests. Depending on the party complaining, the federal agency is tagged as either reluctant to complete land swaps (Feldman 1997) or as too cozy with the resource development industry (Brown 2000).

In its 1970 report, the PLLRC suggested that judicial action be one of the means used by government agencies to achieve a proper valuation of lands. Over 40 years later this suggestion still has not been implemented.

---

30 The GAO found that both "agencies have given more than fair market value for nonfederal land they acquired and accepted less than fair market value for federal lands they conveyed" in violation of the public interest at large (2000:4).

Notwithstanding the unresponsive approach to the Commission's suggestions by both the executive and legislative branches, the Ninth Circuit Court is finally adopting it. There is still a long way to go before judicial action will help sort out claims of corruption of individual agency officers. After all, in 1997 in the Zephyr Cove Exchange (Lake Tahoe Basin), while the private party profited over $10 million by completing the land swap, the Forest Service employee who "exceeded his authority, withheld information from the Federal staffs normally overseeing land exchanges, failed to inform a FS appraiser about the total acreage . . . and, misled the FS appraiser about the future uses to which the land would be put" faced no criminal charges (USDA 2000, 9–10).

Table of Cases

Greer Coal., Inc. v. U.S. Forest Serv., 65 ERC 1658 (2007)
Elbert O. Jensen, 60 I.D. 231 (1948)
LaRue v. Udall, 324 F.2d 428 (D.C. Cir. 1963)
Lodge Tower Condominium Ass'n v. Lodge Props., Inc., 880 F. Supp. 1370 (D. Colo. 1995)
National Forest Pres. Grp. v. Butz, 485 F.2d 408 (9th Cir. 1973)

References

Acts of Mar. 1, 1911, ch. 186, Stat. 961.
Anderson, F. R. (1979). Public Land Exchanges, Sales, and Purchases Under the Federal Land Policy and Management Act of 1976. *Public Land Management, 4*, 657–700.
Bama, L. (1999, March 29). Wheeling and Dealing. *High Country News*, http://www.hcn.org/servlets/hcn.Article?article_id=4889 (accessed November 12, 2014).
Blaeloch, J. (2001). *The Citizens' Guide to Federal Land Exchanges: A Manual for Public Lands Advocates*. Seattle, WA: Western Land Exchange Project.
Blando, M. (1994). Land Exchanges Under the Federal Land Facilitation Act Department of Agriculture Forest Service. *Environmental Lawyer, 1*, 327–339.
Brown, S.J.M. (2000). David and Goliath: Reformulating the Definition of "the Public Interest" and the Future of Land Swaps After the Interstate 90 Land Exchange. *Journal of Environmental Law and Litigation, 15*, 235–293.
Burton, L. (2002). *Worship and Wilderness: Culture, Religion, and Law in the Management of Public Lands and Resources*. Madison: University of Wisconsin Press.
Cavanaugh, D. (1999, May/June). A Successful Approach to Voluntary Land Acquisitions, *Right of Way*, 8–13.
Cheney, B. & Cheney, L.V. (1983). *Kings of the Hill: Power and Personality in the House of Representatives*. New York, NY: Continuum.
Clawson, M. (1979). *The Western Range Livestock Industry: The Management of Public Lands in the United States*. New York: NY: Arno Press.
Coggins, G. C. & Glicksman, R. L. (2007). *Public Natural Resources Law*. New York, NY: C. Boardman.
Coggins, G. C. & Lindeberg-Johnson, M. (1982). The Law of Public Rangeland Management II: The Commons and the Taylor Act. *Environmental Law, 13*, 1–101.

Coggins, G. C. & Nagel, D. K. (1990). Nothing Beside Remains: The Legal Legacy of James G. Watt's Tenure as Secretary of the Interior on Federal Land Law and Policy. *Boston College Environmental Affairs Law Review, 17*(3), 473–550.

Culhane, P. J. (1981). *Public Lands Politics: Interest Group Influence on the Forest Service and the Bureau of Land Management.* Baltimore, MD: Johns Hopkins University Press.

Dana, S. T. & Fairfax, S. K. (1980). *Forest and Range Policy: Its Development in the United States.* New York, NY: McGraw-Hill.

Draffan, G. & Blaeloch, J. (2000). *Commons or Commodity? The Dilemma of Federal Land Exchanges.* Seattle, WA: Western Land Exchange Project.

Eliason, M. D. (1976). Land Exchanges and State In-Lieu Selections as They Affect Mineral Resource Development. *Rocky Mountain Mineral Law Institute, 21*, 617–655.

Federal Land Exchanges Facilitation Act of 1988, Pub. L. No. 100-409, 102 Stat. 1086 (August 20, 1988).

Feldman, M. D. (1997). The New Public Land Exchanges: Trading Development Rights in One Area for Public Resources in Another, *Rocky Mountain Mineral Law Institute, 43*, 2-1-45.

Foss, P. O. (1960). *Politics and Grass: The Administration of Grazing on the Public Domain.* Seattle: University of Washington Press.

Gates, P. W. (1968). *History of Public Land Development.* Washington, DC: U.S. Government Printing Office.

Gonzalez, G. A. (2001). *Corporate Power and the Environment: The Political Economy of U.S. Environmental Policy.* Oxford: Rowman & Littlefield.

Gregg, F. (1982). Federal Land Transfers in the West Under the Federal Land Policy and Management Act. *Utah Law Review, 3*, 499–524.

Ise, J. (1920). *The United States Forest Policy.* New Haven, CT: Yale University Press.

Kaufman, H. (1960). *The Forest Ranger: A Study in Administrative Behavior.* Baltimore, MD: Johns Hopkins Press.

Kitchens Jones, E. (1996). Acquiring Federal and State Land Through Land Exchanges. *Utah Bar Journal, 9*, 19–22.

Laitos, J., Zellmer, S. B., Wood, M. C. & Cole, D. H. (2006). *Natural Resources Law.* Eagan, MN: Thomson West.

Leshy, J. D. (2001). The Babbitt Legacy at the Department of the Interior. *Environmental Law, 31*, 199–227.

Moran, R. L. (1964). Sales and Exchanges of Public Lands. *Rocky Mountain Mineral Law Institute, 15*, 25–50.

Nelson, R. H. (1995). *Public Lands and Private Rights: The Failure of Scientific Management.* Lanham, MD: Rowman & Littlefield.

Pettigrew, R. F. (1970). *Imperial Washington: The Story of American Public Life From 1870–1920.* New York, NY: Arno Press.

Pinchot, G. (1947). *Breaking New Ground.* New York, NY: Harcourt Brace.

Public Land Law Review Commission. (1970). *Final Report of Study of Appraisal Techniques and Procedures Utilized in Connection With Action Related to Federal Public Lands.* Sacramento, CA: Kronick, Moskovitz, Tiedmann and Girard.

Puter, S.A.D. (1908). *Looters of the Public Domain.* Portland: OR: Portland Printing House.

Quarles, S. P. & Lundquist, T. R. (1984). Federal Land Exchanges and Mineral Development. *Rocky Mountain Mineral Law Institute, 29*, 367–420.

Roth, D. & Williams, G. (2003). *The Forest Service in 1905.* Washington, DC: U.S. Department of Agriculture. Online at http://www.fs.fed.us/newcentury/1905-Renaming-the-Forest-Service.doc (last visited January 26, 2015).

Rowley, W. (1985). *U.S. Forest Services Grazing and Rangelands: A History.* College Station: Texas A&M University Press.

St. Clair, J. (2003). Giving the West Away. *Progressive, 65,* 29–32.

Sturgeon, S. C. (2002). *The Politics of American Water.* Tucson: University of Arizona.

Sunstein, C. R. (1993). *The Partial Constitution.* Cambridge, MA: Harvard University Press.

The Appraisal Foundation. (2002). *Evaluation of the Appraisal Organizations of the Department of Interior Bureau of Land Management: Including a Special Evaluation of an Alternative Approach Used in St. George, Utah.* Washington, DC: Author.

U.S. Department of Agriculture. (2000). *Audit Report: Zephyr Cove Land Exchange* (USDA Report No. 08003–6-SF). South Lake Tahoe, CA: Lake Tahoe Basin Management Unit.

U.S. Department of the Interior. (1904). *Annual Report of the Secretary of Interior.* Washington, DC: U.S. Government Printing Office.

U.S. Department of the Interior. (1960). *Annual Report of the Secretary of Interior.* Washington, DC: U.S. Government Printing Office.

U.S. Department of the Interior. (1964). *BLM Manual.* Washington, DC: U.S. Government Printing Office.

U.S. Department of the Interior. (1968). *Audit Operations.* Washington, DC: U.S. Government Printing Office.

U.S. General Accounting Office. (1987). *Federal Land Acquisition: Land Exchange Process Working But Can Be Improved.* Washington, DC: U.S. Government Printing Office.

U.S. General Accounting Office. (2000). *BLM and the Forest Service: Land Exchanges Need to Reflect Appropriate Value and Serve the Public Interest.* Washington, DC: U.S. Government Printing Office.

U.S. House of Representatives. (1934). *Congressional Record: The Taylor Grazing Act of 1934: H.R. No. 6462.* Washington, DC: U.S. Government Printing Office.

U.S. House of Representatives. (1986). *Congressional Record: Federal Land Exchange Facilitation of 1986: H.R. No. 4814.* Washington, DC: U.S. Government Printing Office.

U.S. Senate. (1900, May 31). Cong. Record, 56th Cong., 1st Sess., 6288.

Weaver, J. C. (2003). *The Great Land Rush and the Making of the Modern World, 1650–1900.* Montreal: McGill Queens University Press.

White, R. (1991). *A New History of the American West, "It's Your Misfortune and None of My Own."* Norman: University of Oklahoma Press.

Wilkinson, C. F. (1992). *Crossing the Next Meridian: Land, Water, and the Future of the West.* Washington, DC: Island Press.

4   Federal land exchanges and the law

In July 2001, the OIG for the DOI released its investigation of exchanges conducted by the BLM in Washington County, Utah. The final report concluded that the "BLM may have compromised the integrity of its appraisal process, a key control in ensuring the integrity of public land transactions and valuations" (DOI 2001:i). According to the OIG, the BLM had failed to demonstrate the independence and objectivity of the appraisers and the appraisal reviews. The BLM had created an "alternative approach" to the appraisal process because local landowners were vehemently opposed to the agency's Utah regional appraisal staff and their appraisals. In direct response to these local complaints, the BLM had transferred responsibility for reviewing Washington County appraisals to its Senior Specialist for Appraisal in the Washington, DC, office. The Senior Appraiser quickly developed an "alternative approach" that allowed local landowners to participate in the appraisal and its review.

After studying appraisals and reviews approved through this approach, the OIG found "that the alternative approach did not separate the appraisal process from price negotiations" (DOI 2001:ii). The OIG concluded that these practices could not guarantee the integrity of the appraisal process and had modified appropriate land values at the expense of the public interest.

The controversy arose when landowners in Washington County had collectively opposed appraisals conducted by the agency regional staff. That prompted the BLM's Utah State Director to remove its appraisal staff from responsibility and request the BLM's Washington Office Senior Specialist for Appraisal to review land valuations in the county. The approach created by the Senior Specialist "opened up the appraisal process to involve landowners" (DOI 2001:2). This approach violated the independence and objectivity of the appraisers and reviewers. As the OIG suggested, the independence and objectivity of appraisers are the "critical factors in ensuring the acquisition or exchange of land based on fair market value and in precluding the appearance of conflict of interest or wrongdoing" (DOI 2001:4).

The OIG reviewed 10 out of 22 land exchanges concluded between June 1996 and June 1999 by the BLM's St. George Field Office in Washington County. Of those 10, the OIG selected eight appraisal review reports completed by the Senior Specialist. The OIG concluded that the alternative approach had failed to ensure that the lands be exchanged at fair market value. The OIG stated that the "use of this approach increased the appearance of conflict of interest and wrongdoing and brought the integrity of BLM's land acquisition program into question" (DOI 2001:5). According to the report, the alternative approach was based on the interests of the local landowner. The Senior Specialist

> shared appraisal reports with the landowner and then met with the landowner . . . to identify and resolve any disagreements the landowner might have with the appraiser . . . . When agreement was reached on an appraised value satisfactory to the landowner, the Senior Specialist finalized a review report.
>
> (DOI 2001:5)

The Senior Specialist believed that the federal appraisal process was "outmoded" and needed to be replaced with an approach that let the property owner be involved. The Senior Specialist's rationalizations notwithstanding, the OIG found that the alternative approach "diminished the objectivity of the process and appeared to adjust the appraised value to the landowner's desired selling/exchange values" (DOI 2001:6).

The audit cited an exchange in which the Senior Specialist admitted that he had approved a lesser value of the selected lands because the private parties were "apprehensive" about the higher value in a different appraisal. In another transaction, the Senior Specialist gave instructions to the appraiser to reappraise the federal lands which were eventually devalued by 27% without an adequate explanation. In a third transaction, the Senior Specialist asked the appraiser to use an appraisal addendum and increase the value of the offered lands by 12%. In this land exchange, the OIG "found that the appraisal addendum did not reconcile the new, higher value estimate to the lower comparable sales approach value the appraiser estimated in his original appraisal report" (DOI 2001:7). In a fourth transaction, the Senior Specialist approved an appraisal that was 30% higher than even the value proposed by the proponent.

Introduction

This previous investigation illustrates how key positions in a federal agency could sidestep the legal process and infuse their practices with behavior that favors interest groups over the general public. Some agency officials could derail the public interest of a land transaction to favor private groups of landowners and speculators. To make better sense of how this behavior and practices become "normalized" by a federal bureaucracy, this chapter provides a description of present policy on federal land exchanges. This section also describes the stages of a swap, including the proposal, the NEPA process, and the final approval of the transaction by the agency. An overview of the specific technical terms used at each stage completes the first section, setting the stage for an analysis of judicial interpretations of those terms.

The passage of FLPMA in 1976[1] conferred upon the BLM a mandate and organizational structure with clear directives for multiple-use management, meaning the retention of public lands for multiple purposes, including the expansion of communities, economic development, recreation, and aesthetic value. Congress enunciated a new mode of management for the public domain, expressly declaring "it is the policy of the United States that . . . the public lands be retained in federal ownership."[2] According to two scholars, "Congress . . . adopted a comprehensive land-use planning and management system designed to ensure that the remaining unreserved public lands would be managed more coherently as national resource" (Palma and Kite 1995:371). However, FLPMA also required the BLM to identify any public lands[3] suitable for sale, exchange, or transfer, if "as a result of the land use planning procedure provided for in the Act, it is determined that disposal of a particular parcel will serve the national interest."[4] According to the Act's policy statement, "the national interest [would] be best realized if the public lands and their resources [were] periodically and systematically inventoried and their present and future use [were] projected through a land use planning process coordinated with other Federal and State planning efforts."[5] Section 1713 authorized the BLM to dispose of lands that were difficult and uneconomical to manage or when important public objectives would be better served by transfer than by retention.

The FLPMA requires that the USFS and the BLM exchange lands only if the lands to be swapped are located in the same state, are of equal value, and the swap serves the public interest.[6] When making the public interest determination, the agency must consider whether the swap would provide better management of public lands, meet the needs of local communities, or other purposes of multiple-use management. The intrastate requirement, which was originally part of the Taylor Grazing Act (§ 8), is explained by the fact that western states want to maintain the feasibility of recreational benefits when federal agencies acquire private lands in their territory (Palma and Kite 1995:372).

Section 1715 of FLPMA authorizes the BLM and the USFS to acquire private lands through two alternatives: outright purchases and land swaps.

1   Pub. L. No. 94–579, 90 Stat. 2743.
2   43 U.S.C. § 1701(a)(1).
3   Public lands are defined as any land and interest in land owned by the United States within the several States and administered by the Secretary of the Interior through the BLM (43 U.S.C. § 1702(e)).
4   43 U.S.C. § 1701(a)(1).
5   43 U.S.C. § 1701(a)(2).
6   43 U.S.C. § 1716(b).

According to Section 1716(a) of FLPMA, federal agencies may enter into any land exchange they determine to be in the public interest. For a land swap to be in the public interest, the test is whether "the values and objectives which Federal lands or interests to be conveyed may serve if retained in Federal ownership are not more than the values of the nonfederal lands or interests and the public objective they could serve if acquired."[7]

Once a swap is determined to satisfy the public interest in terms of bettering management of public lands, meeting the needs of state and local residents and their economies, protecting fish and wildlife habitat, cultural resources, watersheds, wilderness and aesthetic values, consolidating lands for more efficient management, or expanding communities (Blaeloch 2001:34),[8] the next requirement is showing that the lands to be exchanged are of equal market value.[9] Both agencies have promulgated regulations defining market value as "the most probable price in cash, which lands or interests should bring in a competitive and open market . . . where the buyer and seller each acts prudently and knowledgeably, and the price is not affected by undue influence."[10]

This definition allows agencies to exercise discretion while using private appraisers (Coggins and Glicksman 2007:13–72). This compounds the problem "that land values are subjective" (Draffan and Blaeloch 2000:32). Appraisers work under the directives of the Uniform Appraisal Standards for Federal Land Acquisitions (UASFLA), formulated in 1992 by the DOJ, and the Uniform Standards of Professional Appraisal Practice (USPAP).[11] Under these directives "the appraiser must determine the highest and best use of the property being appraised" (Coggins and Glicksman 2007:13–75). This provision introduces unpredictability to the process because the appraiser attaches value to a property only in terms of a dollar value (Coggins and Glicksman 2007:13–72). The provision for "highest and best use" is an "economic construct" that allows some elements to be overvalued (e.g. the presence of roads) or undervalued (e.g. wildlife habitat) (Draffan and Blaeloch 2000).

Overview of land exchange procedures

A land swap is usually processed in three distinct phases: the land exchange proposal, the NEPA[12] phase, and the final appraisal. The first phase includes

---

7   See for the BLM 43 C.F.R. § 2200.0–6(b)(1); see for the Forest Service 36 C.F.R. § 254.3(b)(2)(i).
8   See for the BLM 43 C.F.R. § 2200.0–6(b); see for the Forest Service 36 C.F.R. § 254.3(b).
9   43 U.S.C. § 1716(b).
10 36 C.F.R. § 254.2. A similar provision is found in BLM regulations, see 43 C.F.R. § 2201.3–2.
11 See for the BLM 43 C.F.R. § 2201.3–1(a); see for the Forest Service 36 C.F.R. § 254.9(a)(1).
12 For the purpose of NEPA, see 42 U.S.C. § 4321.

an exchange proposal, negotiations, a minimum appraisal stage coupled with a feasibility study, the signing of a statement of intent, and the preparation of environmental reports. The first phase starts with the exchange proposal. Usually, a private landowner proposes a land swap once the federal lands to be exchanged are identified in the agencies' management plans. The formal proposal is addressed to the agency official in charge of managing the lands proposed for the swap,[13] usually the local District (USFS) or Field Office (BLM). After submission of the exchange proposal, that office prepares a feasibility report.[14] This report will usually include the following:

- a description of the offered and selected lands;
- the major resource values involved, e.g. endangered species habitat, aesthetic value, public recreation, etc.;
- a determination of whether the proposal conforms to the agency's existing land management plans or whether a plan amendment would be required;
- the future use of the lands to be exchanged;
- a discussion of foreseeable conflicts or problems, such as public opposition, and whether or not local governments support the proposed exchange; and
- a preliminary estimate of value, if available, and title information, such as a title report prepared by a title company (Kitchens 2000:22–18).

Once the State Office Director prepares and approves the feasibility report, the proponent and the District Manager will work out the details of a non-binding Agreement to Initiate (ATI).[15] According to the law, if a consensus is reached, the "parties must execute a nonbinding agreement to initiate the exchange" (Coggins and Glicksman 2007:13–63).[16] Once the agreement is completed, the agency "must publish appropriate notification in newspapers of general circulation in the counties in which the affected lands are located. The notice should include an invitation for written public comments" (Coggins and Glicksman 2007:13–64).[17] This form of publication is also known as a Notice of Exchange Proposal (NOEP) and it "describes the land exchange proposal, including the lands to be exchanged,

---

13 See for the BLM 43 C.F.R. § 2201.1(a); see for the Forest Service 36 C.F.R. § 254.4(a).
14 See for the BLM 43 C.F.R. § 2201.1(b); see for the Forest Service 36 C.F.R. § 254.4(b).
15 See for the BLM 43 C.F.R. § 2201.1(c); see for the Forest Service 36 C.F.R. § 254.4(f).
16 The entry into an exchange agreement will not bind either party to consummate the proposed land swap, see for the BLM 43 C.F.R. § 2201.7–2; see for the Forest Service 36 C.F.R. § 254.4(f).
17 See for the BLM 43 C.F.R. § 2207.7–1; see for the Forest Service 43 C.F.R. § 254.8(a) and (b). Unlike the Forest Service, according to the IBLA, the BLM is not required by its regulations to hold a public meeting for each land swap proposal, see *Charles W. Nolen*, 166 IBLA 197 (2005).

the proponent, and the benefits to the public" (Kitchens 2000:22–20–21).[18] Upon completion of the public comment phase, the agency initiates an environmental analysis of the offered and selected lands.

The NEPA[19] process begins after completion of the environmental reports that conclude the first stage. This process begins with the agency determining environmental issues and drafting an environmental assessment (EA) or environmental impact statement (EIS)[20] and concludes with a final (EA) EIS and the agency's record of decision (ROD). The "NEPA analysis must address the environmental consequences of the private development that will occur after the exchange, since the agency's decision to complete the exchange allows that development to occur" (Palma and Kite 1995:378).

In this process "private consultants prepare the NEPA document, subject to review by the agency" (Kitchens 2000:22–36–37). The environmental analysis, either in the form of an EA or EIS, should review all foreseeable impacts of the swap. This includes whether and how water resources, wildlife, endangered species, cultural resources, recreation, and local economies may be negatively affected. The analysis will incorporate cultural resource inventories "conducted on the offered and selected lands to determine the presence of sites that may be eligible for the National Register of Historic Places pursuant to the National Historic Preservation Act" (Kitchens 2000:22–38).[21] The analysis will include any wildlife surveys conducted to determine whether the swap could affect any species protected under the Endangered Species Act.[22]

In accordance with the UASFLA, the third phase starts with the final appraisal of the lands by the agency's regional offices.[23] This phase includes the equalization of the land values, the signing of a swap agreement, the clearing of title, the approval of the transaction by the Office of General Counsel (OGC), and conveyance of the deeds.

The most important part of this phase is the determination by the agency "whether to approve an exchange proposal based on the public interest standard" (Coggins and Glicksman 2007:13–64). The agency must publish a notice of decision "authorizing completion of the exchange or stating that the exchange will not be allowed" (Beaudoin 2000:238). If the swap is approved, the agency District Manager must explain the decision-making process in a Notice of Decision (NOD) and demonstrate how the public interest is served by the exchange.[24] An administrative challenge to the

18 See for the BLM 43 C.F.R. § 2201.2; see for the Forest Service 36 C.F.R. § 254.8.
19 42 U.S.C. §§ 4321–4347.
20 See for the BLM 43 C.F.R. § 2200.0–6(h); see for the Forest Service 36 C.F.R. § 254.3(g).
21 16 U.S.C. §§ 470–470(s).
22 16 U.S.C. §§ 1531–1543.
23 See for the BLM 43 C.F.R. § 2201.3; see for the Forest Service 36 C.F.R. § 254.9.
24 See for the BLM 43 C.F.R. § 2201.7–1(a); see for the Forest Service 36 C.F.R. § 254.13(a).

decision may be filed with the Realty Specialist within 45 days of publication.[25] The challenge can be based on issues arising out of the appraisal, the review report, the EA or the EIS, all of which are made available for public review after issuance of the NOD.

If the agency decides to proceed with the swap and the State Director approves the agreement upon consulting with the Regional Solicitor, an exchange agreement is signed by the parties.[26] This agreement is binding on the parties but can be terminated by a reversal of the approval decision or by mutual consent of the parties involved.[27] In a completed land swap, "title to both the federal and non-federal lands pass simultaneously and are deemed accepted by the parties when the documents of conveyance are recorded in the local recording office" (Coggins and Glicksman 2007:13–65–66).[28] As an example of a transaction completed in accordance with these federal policies, the BLM has proffered the Professor Valley Land Exchange.

The Professor Valley Land Exchange

This specific land exchange is a model for an uncontested land swap. On August 9, 1996, a private party submitted a proposal to the local office of the BLM in Utah for a land swap on behalf of Professor Valley Ranch (PVR). His proposal was to swap 17.86 acres of federal lands in Moab, Utah, already leased to the company for ranching purposes, for development rights (through a conservation easement) on 32.10 acres of PVR's privately owned lands. After following the lengthy required procedures, the BLM notified the public on March 8, 2001, of the planned preparation of an EA of the proposed swap. Immediately afterwards, the agency started the process of collecting the necessary documentation. From March 14 through April 17, 2001, the BLM collected reports on air and water quality, cultural and paleontological surveys, and consultations regarding Native American concerns.

The resulting assessment was made available for public comment from July 21 to August 19, 2005. Due to the fact that land values in the area of the proposed exchange had risen consistently from the 1980s through 2004, the divergence in the valuation of the selected and the offered lands had grown wider. A new appraisal completed in July 2006 emphasized the necessity of eliminating 14.84 acres of the offered lands from the exchange proposal in order to reach equal value. On December 6, 2006, a new appraisal confirmed the correctness of that calculation. The EA was completed on August 2007. The BLM and the PVR executed the ATI the day after the NOEP was

25 See for the BLM 43 C.F.R. § 2201.7–1(b); see for the Forest Service 36 C.F.R. § 254.13(b).
26 See for the BLM 43 C.F.R. § 2201.7–2; see for the Forest Service 36 C.F.R. § 254.14(a).
27 See 36 C.F.R. § 254.14(b).
28 See 36 C.F.R. § 254.16(b).

published on April 3, 2008. On May 2, 2008, the BLM completed the new supplemental EA and released it the following month. On July 21, 2008, the Appraisal Services Directorate (ASD) approved the BLM's valuation of the selected and offered lands. On February 10, 2009, the BLM approved the land exchange with PVR, acquiring in fee the 17.26 acres of privately owned lands and transferring the 17.86 acres of selected land to PVR.

This exchange exemplifies the goals of transactions with private owners of lands adjacent to public lands. The acquisition of the offered lands allows them to remain undeveloped along with adjoining BLM-administered lands. The acquisition of the 17.26 acres of the offered lands allows the protection of the scenic qualities of the Professor Valley and ensures habitat for a sensitive plant species, the Dolores rushpink. As the agency concluded, "The opportunity to protect the scenic values and sensitive plant habitat associated with the non-Federal lands is of greater value to the public than continued management of the 17.86 acres of Federal lands that . . . continue to be utilized primarily for agricultural and ranching purposes" (DOI 2009:4).

Case law on federal land exchanges

Unfortunately, uncontested land swaps like the Professor Valley represent only one aspect of land exchange practices. Contested land swaps are becoming more the norm. Case law on federal land exchanges was sparse until the 1980s, when various parties began challenging agency practices (Coggins and Glicksman 2007:13–53). Since then, the major issues raised by plaintiffs have concerned the agencies' interpretations of legal terms such as equal value, market value, correct appraisal of the exchanged lands, and the public interest. In 2000 the Ninth Circuit, in the *Desert Citizens* case, issued the preeminent opinion on the undervaluation of federal lands selected for exchange. Before reaching this pivotal case, this chapter provides a historical overview of the case law, both judicial and administrative, on federal land swaps.

In 1922, the General Exchange Act (GEA) was passed, mandating the USFS to acquire private offered lands as long as they were located within the boundaries of a national forest. The agency was to determine both that such lands were valuable mainly for national forest purposes and that the public interest would benefit. The offered and the selected lands were to be of equal value (16 U.S.C. § 485). This changed the previous practice of swaps based on equal acreage (Paul 2006:112). In 1934 Congress passed the Taylor Grazing Act; Section 8 of this statute extended the power to complete land exchanges to the Grazing Service (which would become the BLM) within the DOI. Thus, the Bureau could exchange lands of equal value as long as the public interest benefited.

Until 1976, the BLM and the USFS used the Taylor Grazing Act and the GEA, respectively. The FLPMA provided a uniform set of procedures for both agencies. Although FLPMA repealed the Taylor Grazing Act, the GEA

remains valid. The unified procedure requires that both agencies complete
a land exchange as long as they determine that the transaction will benefit
the public interest. The Secretary makes this determination by giving "full
consideration to better Federal land management and the needs of state and
local people, including needs for lands for the economy, community expansion, recreation areas, food, fiber, minerals, fish and wildlife." This standard requires the federal agency "to balance the various uses of the public
land . . . whether or not an exchange proposal benefits the public interest
may depend upon which of the multiple uses of public land is perceived
as more valuable by the agency" (Jones 1996:21). Although "the agency
is tasked with making the consideration of these factors part of their [sic]
record of decisions . . . the statute does not assign any weight or relative
rank to the factors" (Paul 2006:121).

As Brown pointedly remarked, "while many of the foregoing statutes
and regulations refer to the 'public interest,' none of them define the term"
(2000:247). As the federal agency "allegedly 'understands' and protects the
public interest in a land exchange . . . there are no objective standards by
which the public may judge whether the agency in fact has the best interests
of the public in mind" whenever it completes a swap (Brown 2000:247). She
believes that if Congress defined local community interest as a major com-
ponent of the general public interest determination, it should place on an
equal footing the rights of American Indians, environmentalists, and loggers,
notwithstanding their historically diverse claims to the land in question.

More importantly, FLPMA still requires that the lands be of equal value.
Under the agencies' regulations, equal value is determined according to the
highest and best use of a property, as determined under its most probable
use, "as if it were private and marketable" (Ragsdale 1999:13). The issue
of equal value was debated in the first case examined in this section. In this
case, an administrative court was asked by the plaintiffs to set aside the
BLM appraisal of the offered and selected lands (*Kellerblock* 1978). As this
case indicates, the equal value of the lands in the transaction is one of the
most common issues in current federal land exchange litigation.

Another important case follows the coverage of these cases, the DeMars/
Bold Land Exchange. Here, the IBLA was twice faced with a public interest
determination by the BLM State Director. The deciding factor in the two
decisions was that in the first the BLM challenged only the plaintiff's standing while in the second the agency, confronted with more damning evidence,
had to fight on the merits. In other words, the BLM, as long as it proffered
an interpretation, even an implausible one, was bound to prevail (*National
Wildlife Federation* 1985).

In another case, the IBLA was asked to evaluate the public interest in
a land transaction in New Mexico. The court recognized that the BLM
had properly considered the public interest in the land swap because it had
determined the maximization of the resource values of the lands involved
(*City of Santa Fe* 1991).

In the 1991 *McGregor* case, the IBLA held that as long as the value of the selected lands was not more than that of the offered lands, the decision of the federal agency would stand. The administrative panel rejected the plaintiffs' challenge because they had failed to provide an alternative independent appraisal in support of their claim. In another case before the administrative court, the plaintiffs submitted an appraisal which they believed showed the BLM had accepted an overvaluation of the offered lands (*Wells* 1992). Despite the agency's original failure to submit its own appraisals, the court ruled the plaintiffs' appraisal to be inadequate.

In the next case, plaintiffs challenged a USFS land exchange within the city of Boulder, Colorado (*Lodge Tower* 1995). The plaintiffs challenged the agency's determinations both on the public interest and the equal value. The district court found the administrative record supported the agency's determinations. The court held that as long as the agency considered and weighed the factors listed by FLPMA, it is free to give more weight to some factors over others. On the issue of the value determination, the district judge dismissed the claim. The plaintiffs had no prospect of success on the merits because so long as the appraiser follows the instructions given by the USFS, no challenge to the appraisal is possible.

In another case, in 1998, the IBLA decided a challenge brought by an avid environmentalist against the completion of a land swap in Wyoming (*Jolley* 1998). This panel not only found that the plaintiff had standing but also that he had proved that the appraiser used by the BLM was not impartial. The panel set aside the land exchange and remanded the matter to the BLM to hire an impartial appraiser.

Two years later, the Ninth Circuit Court decided the most important litigation in the arena of land swaps, the *Desert Citizens* case. In this instance, first the IBLA, then a federal district court, and later on a circuit court had to decide a case brought as an environmental groups' challenge to a land exchange in California. The appellate court found that the environmentalists' recreational and aesthetic enjoyment of federal lands were legally protected interests that created standing. The court also held that the appraisal adopted by the BLM was outdated and based on an erroneous assessment of the highest and best use of the selected lands (*Desert Citizens* 2000).[29]

Paul Kellerblock (IBLA)

On December 5, 1978, the IBLA heard a challenge brought by Paul Kellerblock, a private proponent of a land swap with the USFS. Kellerblock's land was located within the boundaries of the Toiyabe National Forest, but he wanted BLM land in exchange. In this swap, the USFS would have

---

29 This legal precedent was affirmed nine years later in *National Parks & Conservation Ass'n v. Bureau of Land Mgmt.* (2010).

acquired lands adjacent to the Toiyabe National Forest and then transferred
to Kellerblock BLM lands just southwest of Las Vegas, Nevada. Originally,
the USFS had advised Kellerblock that the swap could be completed in
conformity with his land valuations. However, the BLM rejected the USFS
appraisal reports because of technical inadequacies. "The Director, Denver
Service Center, BLM, advised the Nevada State Director that the appraisal
'subtly favored the private landowner, perhaps in an unconscious effort to
facilitate the exchange'" (*Kellerblock* 1978:161).

Due to its ownership of the selected public lands, the BLM commissioned
several appraisals of the offered and selected lands. "It is interesting to note
that in each appraisal other than the initial study by the Forest Service, the
selected lands were shown to have a much higher value than the offered
lands" (*Kellerblock* 1978:161). Eventually, on September 19, 1977, the
BLM invited Kellerblock to "amend his application by elimination of the
least desirable tracts so as to equalize the values between the offered and
the selected lands" (*Kellerblock* 1978:162).

A challenge ensued in which Kellerblock claimed that the BLM's appraisals failed to reflect the values of both the offered and the selected lands. The
IBLA argued that the substance of the complaint, based on the valuation
distinguishing between retail and wholesale purchase prices, was simply
explained "by the differing character of the lands in question" (*Kellerblock*
1978:163). As the Board explained,

> The disparity reflects simple market forces at work in that the selected
> lands are in an area which has become increasingly developed as the city
> of Las Vegas in recent years has grown toward and around it. Subdivi-
> sion expansion coupled with residential and commercial construction
> has created a brisk, present market for retail land sales . . . The offered
> lands, in contrast, lie in an area where real estate activity has been rela-
> tively slow, indeed, virtually dormant.
>
> (*Kellerblock* 1978:163)

The Board found that the "disparity is the result of a retail demand forcing the selected lands values toward a sort of economic maturation, while
the highest use of the offered lands remains a subject for wholesale speculation" (*Kellerblock* 1978:164). Thus, the BLM's decision was affirmed
because the Board viewed this valuation approach to be consonant with
Section 102(a)(9) of FLPMA, which mandated that federal agencies receive
fair market value in the swap of public lands.

The DeMars/Bold Exchange: *National Wildlife Federation* (IBLA 84–505)

On September 5, 1984, the IBLA decided a challenge brought by the National
Wildlife Federation (NWF) against a decision by the BLM to complete a land

swap. The original exchange proposal involved 1,430.59 acres of BLM land to be swapped for 241.1 acres of offered lands in Fergus County, Montana. The NWF submitted comments to the BLM's Notice of Realty Action (NORA). Six days later, the BLM responded by readjusting the acreage of the selected lands by removing 20 acres. The selected lands were now appraised at $181,000, which was $45,000 more than the value of the offered lands. This new appraisal would meet the limit of a 25% cash differential in accordance with the provisions of FLPMA Section 1716(b). The NWF took this decision before the IBLA by challenging the EA, which it called insufficient.

An issue addressed by the IBLA was whether the agency had adequately assessed impacts on wildlife. The Board was puzzled by the BLM's decision to pursue the land swap since it was based "at least in part . . . on assurances from the 'potential owner' of the public land that future management of those lands would ensure wildlife habitat" (*NWF* 1984:313). The NWF's challenge forced the judges to evaluate whether the BLM had considered reasonable alternatives to the proposed swap in its EA, such as protecting public values through a covenant. The IBLA pointed out that 43 C.F.R. § 2200.1(c)(4) provides that a swap may involve the use of "reservations, terms, covenants and conditions necessary to insure [sic] proper land use and protection of the public interest" (*NWF* 1984:313–314).

In addition, the Board appropriately investigated the "potential owner" of the selected lands since that person must guarantee the future protection of wildlife habitats once the swap is completed. The Board found that "the BLM in this case shows that Tom DeMars and his wife will receive title to the selected land . . . (but) NWF continually refers to [Robert] Bold as the potential owner of the land" (*NWF* 1984:314). The IBLA was puzzled by the allegations "that Bold has been actively involved in various sodbusting [converting wildlife lands into agricultural use] situations," and by the fact "that assurances from the 'prospective owner,' relied on by the State Director, are not binding and do not guarantee protection of the wildlife habitat or soil stability" (*ibid.*).

Confronted with these findings, the IBLA opined, "the failure to discuss the possibility of sodbusting and the lack of consideration of protective covenants are serious deficiencies in the evaluation of this proposed land exchange" (*NWF* 1984:315). The Board was not satisfied with the EA since "the intentions of the potential owner, whoever that might be, do not ensure proper land use and protection of the public interest" (*ibid.*). Thus, the IBLA held that the BLM should adopt a covenant which would safeguard recreational and wildlife values in the selected lands.

Therefore, the IBLA vacated the BLM's decision to pursue the land exchange and remanded the case to the agency. The IBLA ordered the BLM to address any concerns over whether "Bold is an actual participant in the exchange itself" (*NWF* 1984:316). In addition, since "neither the land report, EA, nor the notice states a cash payment to equalize value is involved in this exchange . . . [and] regulations require that the notice contain the terms and conditions of the exchange" (*ibid.*), the BLM was found in violation of this requirement.

National Wildlife Federation (IBLA 85–482)

A year later the same parties squared off before the IBLA. By this time, the "BLM [had] reviewed the case and determined to modify the proposed exchange so that only 1,160.59 acres of public land would be exchanged for 241.1 acres of private land . . . [so] there would be no [need for an] equalization payment" (*NWF* 1985:272). The appellants challenged the inadequacy of the EA since it failed to give due consideration to a conservation easement. Accordingly, the appellants argued that "this failur [sic] [exhibited] a lack of good faith on the part of BLM in its evaluation of the easement alternative" (*ibid.*). On this challenge, the IBLA agreed with the BLM that any alternative conditions or covenants which would guarantee the protection of the wildlife and recreational values in the selected lands to be "a hardship on the exchange proponent (Tom DeMars) and the potential landowner (Robert Bold) by restricting opportunities for future management of the land" (*NWF* 1985:280). Since "Tom DeMars ha[d] verbally indicated that he [would] not consider this alternative," (*ibid.*) both the BLM and IBLA agreed that no covenants should be attached to the exchange.

The IBLA also disregarded the appellants' claim that the land swap did not serve the public interest. The Board accepted, as proof of the public interest involved, "copies of letters from the Fergus County Conservation District and the Montana Public Council [two business organizations] evidencing support for the exchange" (*NWF* 1985:277). The IBLA cited a written statement by the NWF's Regional Director: "We believe this acquisition would be very much in the public interest" (*ibid.*). However, a more accurate reading of the statement in context would have revealed that the NWF's Regional Director was recognizing that the "acquisition" of the offered lands was in the public interest, but he was against the completion of the land swap because he knew that the selected lands would be converted to agricultural use. Finally, the Board cited the BLM's EA in its conclusions as evidence that the swap was in the public interest. Actually, the six reasons used by the BLM were all describing the acquisition of the offered lands and never discussed whether the overall transfer would serve the public interest!

City of Santa Fe et al. (IBLA)

On August 15, 1988, the IBLA decided a challenge brought by the City of Santa Fe, New Mexico, against a proposed land swap between Louis Menyhert, owner of private lands in Taos County, and the BLM, which managed a 280-acre parcel just west of Santa Fe. The NORA published by the BLM stated "that the Federal parcel had a high value for residential development but only a limited potential for public use, and that the Taos lands had high values for wildlife habitat, livestock grazing, and public recreation" (*Santa Fe* 1988:398). The BLM had approved the swap after the parties amended the offer to include 1,740 acres of Menyhert's land to reach equal value.

The City of Santa Fe appealed to the IBLA. The city argued that the swap "would result in a loss of open space and recreational utility . . . [and] the . . . action was undertaken without regard for the interests of local property owners and . . . the City . . . result[ing ultimately] in chaotic urban sprawl" (*Santa Fe* 1988:399). The city challenged the public interest determination. The Board found that the purpose of a land swap is "to maximize resource values for the public through a rational, consistently applied set of regulations . . . which promote the concept of multiple use management" (43 C.F.R. § 1601.0–2). Since the administrative record showed that the selected lands were already zoned as rural residential and the County of Santa Fe "ha[d already] expressed that it ha[d] no objection to the exchange . . . and any proposed development," (*Santa Fe* 1988:401) the Board found no evidence there was a danger of urban sprawl and denied the challenge.

City of Santa Fe et al. (district court)

Less than a month later, on September 8, 1988, the BLM and Louis Menyhert exchanged warranty deeds and completed the swap. However, litigation was far from over. On September 26, 1988, Antonio J. Baca, a party to the prior litigation and a grazing lease holder of lands involved in the swap, challenged the IBLA decision in the U.S. District Court for the District of New Mexico. He challenged the appraisals adopted by the BLM. On March 27, 1990, the court remanded the case to the IBLA for reconsideration. Specifically, the district court judge ordered the Board to assess "whether a degree of fluctuation in the specific terms of this transaction as great as that disclosed in the sequence of land appraisals . . . is contemplated by the statutory exchange program" (*Santa Fe* 1991:309). The court expressed surprise about the different valuations of the selected federal lands, which had been appraised by the BLM on July 28, 1988, at $700,000 but were valued by "the 1990 Santa Fe County Tax Assessor's Notice of property tax valuation . . . to [be worth] $1,484,000" (*Santa Fe* 1991:315).

Thus, the parties were again before the IBLA. The plaintiffs offered into evidence the different valuations of the offered and selected lands. In 1985 and 1986 the offered lands had been appraised by a BLM appraiser at $966,000. However, two years later, using more recent comparable sales, two different appraisers, citing fluctuations in the value of properties in the area, appraised the same lands at $825,000 (on February 18, 1988) and $837,000 (on May 17, 1988). On July 28, 1988, the BLM elected to use the former appraisal. New appraisals had been requested for the selected 280 acres of federal lands due to alleged fluctuations in value. While those lands had been appraised in 1985 at $980,000 ($3,500 per acre), three years later, two updated appraisals were prepared. On February 18, 1988, the BLM appraised the lands at $700,000 ($2,500 per acre). On July 1, 1988, another appraisal commissioned by the BLM appraised them at $784,000 ($2,800 per acre). Both appraisals "determined that the Federal tract was inferior to comparables sold at $3,500 . . . and $3,100 per acre" (*Santa Fe* 1991:314–315). On July 28, 1988, the BLM elected to use the appraisal of $2,500 per acre.

The plaintiff proffered first to the district court and then to the IBLA a 1990 notice from the Santa Fe tax assessor, asserting the value of the selected lands transferred by the BLM to Menyhert to be $1,484,000. Unlike the district court, the IBLA was unmoved by this evidence. The IBLA held that "neither Baca nor any party ha[d] submitted evidence to this board that would support a finding that the tax assessor's notices were based on an appraisal or appraisals conducted in a manner meeting the Uniform Standards" (*Santa Fe* 1991:315). In addition, the Board found, "Baca ha[d] failed to show error in either of the 1988 appraisals, [or to] show that BLM . . . failed to conduct those appraisals in conformance with the Uniform Standards, or submit a verifiable appraisal contradicting the 1988 appraisals" (*ibid.*).

The IBLA referred to precedent for the rule "that absent showing error in the appraisal method by a preponderance of the evidence, the agency's appraisal generally may be rebutted only by another appraisal" (*Santa Fe* 1991:315). The Board found that even with the evidence proffered by Baca, it was "unable to determine whether the Santa Fe County Tax Assessor had arrived at the figure quoted by Baca by projecting from an earlier year or by conducting a comparable sales analysis" (*ibid.*). Thus, the IBLA agreed with the BLM that the different appraisals reflected fluctuations in the value of the land. Since the value adjustments approved by the BLM were consistent with appraisal updates that were themselves consistent with the Uniform Standards, the Board affirmed its prior decision.

Burton A. & Mary H. McGregor et al. (IBLA)

On April 15, 1991, the IBLA decided a challenge brought by Burton and Mary McGregor against a land exchange proposed by the Colorado State Office of the BLM. This challenge concerned a land swap between the BLM and Everett Randleman, the owner of ranch land in Colorado. In the proposed swap, Randleman would transfer 640 acres of land for 951 acres of public land.

The challengers contended that the BLM had violated Section 206(b) by pursuing the land exchange even though the values of the lands were unequal. The BLM had approved the appraisals of the offered and selected lands on September 8, 1988, concluding, "at that time . . . the parcels had the same highest and best use, i.e., assemblage for livestock production" (*McGregor* 1991:104). The McGregors challenged the determination of the highest and best use of the selected lands. They cited an internal memo to the BLM District Manager from the Acting Chief State Appraiser, who argued that the selected lands' highest and best use was actually recreational development. The McGregors also argued that by using comparable sales in the area the selected lands should have been valued at between $1,000 to $3,000 per acre rather than the much lower value reached by the BLM's retained appraiser. They, therefore, challenged the land swap under Section 206(b), since "the per acre value of those parcels of land differ[ed] by as much as 1,500 percent" (*ibid.*). The administrative judges remained unimpressed because the McGregors failed to submit an alternative independent appraisal report to substantiate their claims. The Board consequently decided to accept the BLM's valuations of the offered lands ($160,000) and the selected lands ($163,000).

Ultimately, however, the IBLA halted the exchange because new appraisals were now necessary for both the offered and the selected lands since the previous appraisal reports were almost three years old. At this juncture, the Board stressed that BLM regulations introduced after the exchange proposal made the appraisals binding on the exchanging parties for only one year after calculations of the value of the lands.[30]

W.J. & Betty Lo Wells (IBLA)

On February 28, 1992, the IBLA decided a challenge brought by W.J. and Betty Lo Wells against a proposed swap of lands between Wayne and Sheree Pitrat and the BLM. The proponents had offered 236 acres of their lands for 586 acres of public lands near Prescott, Arizona. The Wellses, who were the Pitrats's neighbors, argued that "the value of the land [selected] significantly exceed[ed] that of the property for which it was exchanged" (*Wells* 1992:251). In support of their claim "the Wells submitted appraisals stating the Pitrats' land was worth nearly $100,000 less than the value determined in BLM's appraisal" (*ibid.*). Following a request of the IBLA, the BLM submitted its appraisals, which valued the offered lands at $350,000 and the selected lands at $351,504.

The administrative panel acknowledged the attempt by the Wells to prove their claim by submitting their own appraisal reports prepared and signed by Warren Henry, an independent appraiser. However, the judges found the appraisal reports "inadequate." The administrative board declared that "the Henry appraisal [was] based on an inspection of the Pitrats' property 'from the hills above the subject's south boundary,' rather than on-the-ground inspection such as BLM conducted" (*Wells* 1992:253). In addition, the IBLA reasoned that the "Henry Appraisal, by focusing on the value of the 'depreciated improvements and other amenities' of [the Pitrats']

---

30 43 CFR 2201.2–2(f) published in 54 FR 34387 (Aug. 18, 1989).

property, significantly understate[d] the value of land . . . at only $1,120 per acre" (*Wells* 1992:253–254). The judges believed that such miscalculations accounted for the differences and concluded that the claimants had failed to demonstrate that the BLM had committed error in its appraisal.

Lodge Tower Condominium Ass'n v. Lodge Properties, Inc. (district court)

On March 31, 1995, the U.S. District Court for the District of Colorado decided a challenge brought by the Lodge Tower Condominium Association, an unincorporated association representing owners of condominiums that were adjacent to a two-acre parcel of land which had been transferred to a private party in a land swap by the USFS. Lodge Properties, Inc., a private corporation and purchaser of the federal land, intended to develop the land, located within the boundaries of the town of Vail, Colorado (Coggins and Glicksman 2007:13–70). Lodge Properties had previously acquired a 385-acre parcel of land within the Eagle Nest Wilderness Area and then offered to exchange it to the USFS to acquire the developable parcel in Vail. The Association argued that the land exchange was in violation of the public interest provisions of FLPMA Section 1716(a) and Section 485 of the GEA. Both provisions required the USFS to exchange public lands only after determining that the public interest would benefit (Coggins and Glicksman 2007:13–70). Factors to be considered were the betterment of federal land management, recreational concerns, and the consideration of state and local needs.

The first issue before the court was whether the agency had weighed those factors. The court concluded that the administrative record showed the agency had decided to pursue the land exchange in order to better federal land management (Ragsdale 1999:31). In addition, the district court reached the same conclusions as the USFS on the swap's furtherance of other two factors: recreation and wilderness.

The court had a much more difficult time explaining how the land swap would satisfy the public interest by benefiting the needs of state or local people. The court looked at the administrative record and found that it was still unclear whether the selected land was going to be developed as a hotel site or as low-density residences. However, the court concluded that although only the development of the site as a hotel could be described as a potential benefit for the local people and economy, the public interest determination made by the agency was not necessarily erroneous. The court reasoned that "section 1716(a) requires merely that the agency consider and weigh the factors which are listed in the section. It does not give the factors any particular priority, nor does it require the agency to do so" (*Lodge Tower* 1995:1380). The court concluded that Section 1716(a) should be interpreted only as a list of factors to be considered by the agency; ultimately the USFS was free to choose and give importance to some factors over others (Coggins and

Glicksman 2007:13–71). In this case "the agency did not fail or refuse to consider the needs of local people or local economic impact . . . . It simply attached much less importance to these factors than it did to the other ones" (*Lodge Tower* 1995:1380).

Next was the Association's argument that the USFS had violated the FLPMA requirement of equal value. The plaintiffs argued "that the lodge parcel ceded by the United States was more valuable than indicated by the agency's appraisal . . . [and] the agency's appraisal used an improper local zoning classification, which had the effect of depressing the value of the lodge parcel" (*Lodge Tower* 1995:1381). This argument was based on the premise that the appraisal of the federal land had not been based on the highest and best use standard as required by the USFS Appraisal Handbook and the DOJ's UASLFA (Ragsdale 1999:13). According to the Association, "the appraiser considered the land as if it were zoned for 'primary/secondary residential,' [but] . . . it should have been considered as 'commercial core 1 district'" (*Lodge Tower* 1995:1381). Although the administrative record contained evidence that this was correct, the court turned down the Association's challenge (Ragsdale 1999:32). The judge accepted the assertion of the USFS that the selected land was not going to be rezoned after the swap. Since the appraiser had followed the instructions given to him by the USFS and those instructions assumed the zoning of the property as "primary/secondary residential," the court rejected the challenge to the appraisal.

Finally, the court turned to the Association's claim that the USFS had violated its guidelines in the appraisal process. The claimants argued that both offered and selected lands should have been reappraised. This argument was based on a USFS guideline which stated that an appraised value is only valid for one year. Since the USFS, after an administrative appeal, had required a reappraisal of the selected land, the claimants argued for a reappraisal of the offered land, too. However, the court interpreted the agency's guideline as limited exclusively to reappraisal of selected lands.

John R. Jolley (IBLA)

On July 2, 1998, the IBLA decided a challenge brought by John Jolley, an avid outdoorsman, against a BLM exchange of land in Washakie County, Wyoming. In the proposed swap, known as the Great Western Land Exchange, a limited liability corporation created by two land developers, Neal Hilston and John D. Sloan, had offered to swap 2,379 acres of land for 6,934 acres of land managed by the BLM. Jolley challenged the swap by arguing the appraiser used by the BLM had not been impartial.

According to BLM regulations, a land swap appraisal must be conducted by a "qualified appraiser . . . who is competent, reputable, impartial, and has training and experience in appraising property similar to the properties involved in the appraisal assignment" (43 C.F.R. § 2202.3–1a). The BLM's appraiser was Neal Hilston, who was a partner of the swap proponent. The Board became concerned about the appearance of partiality. For the Board, "impartiality" implies that the person be "disinterested" in the land swap. This further implies that the appraiser could not hold any financial interest in the lands to be swapped. Yet Hilston was "one of the two principals who created GWLE . . . Hilston signed GWLE's 'Agreement to Initiate a Land Exchange'" with BLM. The Agreement identifie[d] GWLE as the proponent of the swap and 'certifie[d]' that the proponent ha[d] 'legal ownership or control of the non-Federal lands'" (*Jolley* 1998:42–43). Thus the record showed that Hilston could not have been impartial (Coggins and Glicksman 2007:13–72).

The Board found against the BLM because "Hilston's status as a corporate officer of GWLE [gave] him a stake in the outcome of the exchange . . . that preclude[d] him from being 'impartial' under any recognized definition of that term so that he [could] not perform the appraisal in addition to his other functions in facilitating the exchange" (*Jolley* 1998:43–44). The Board found that the BLM had relied on Hilston's appraisal documents, which were not official appraisals, in violation of its own regulations. According to those regulations, an appraisal is "a written statement independently and impartially prepared."[31] Since the exchange was based on an improper appraisal, performed by a person who was not impartial, the Board remanded the case to the agency, cautioning it to retain an appraiser qualified under its regulations.

The Mesquite Regional Landfill Exchange: *Donna Charpied* et al. (IBLA)

On November 14, 1996, the IBLA decided consolidated challenges of environmental groups against the BLM's decision to enter into a land swap with the Gold Fields Mining Corp. and its subsidiary, Arid Operations, Inc. On February 14, 1996, the BLM had approved the Mesquite Regional Landfill land exchange, which would allow Gold Fields to operate "a regional solid waste disposal facility . . . adjacent to the existing Mesquite Mine" (*Charpied* 1996:46–47). This swap would have exchanged 2,640 acres of private land for 1,750 acres of BLM land.

The challengers argued that the appraisal approved by the BLM had failed to consider that the selected parcel was proposed to be used "as a landfill . . . as a result the land should [have] be[en] appraised as 'a highly desirable landfill location' and valued in comparison to landfill sites, instead of being treated as mine support lands, an action that greatly undervalues the Federal property" (*Charpied* 1996:48). In addition, the challengers claimed that the valuation used by the BLM had expired due to

31 43 C.F.R. § 2200.0–5(c).

Section H-2200–1 of the BLM Manual, which presumes the validity of an appraisal for a period of six months. The appraisal had been released by the firm of Nichols and Gaston on August 1, 1994, but the land swap was approved on February 14, 1996.

As to the claim of undervaluation of the selected lands, notwithstanding that the challengers proffered a valuation of a comparable site used as a landfill and appraised by the tax county assessor at $45,737 per acre, the IBLA accepted the Nichols and Gaston appraisal of $350 per acre. The IBLA acknowledged that "there are plans for the mine to become part of a major landfill facility" (*Charpied* 1996:50) but refused to accept the challengers' argument that the future use of the selected lands required a higher appraisal. This was despite the transaction being named the "Mesquite Regional Landfill Exchange."

The argument that the appraisal had expired went no better for the challengers. The IBLA held that the BLM Manual "states that 'shelf life is an administrative, agency determination'" (*Charpied* 1996:49). Thus, it interpreted the six-month period of validity as "a matter of some flexibility, depending upon the circumstances of the appraisal itself" (*ibid.*). The Board concluded that the challengers had failed to show that the BLM had been in error when it approved "the appraisal reports . . . [as] a valid guide to valuation of the exchanged lands" (*Charpied* 1996:50). Thus the Board affirmed the BLM's decision.

Desert Citizens Against Pollution v. Bisson (district court)

In a continuation of the previous land swap, on January 30, 1997, the U.S. District Court for the Southern District of California decided a new challenge brought by environmentalists against the Mesquite Regional Landfill Exchange. The challengers asked the court to grant an injunction to halt the swap pending the outcome of litigation.

The challengers had made two substantive claims on the merits. First, they "claim[ed] that the agency fail[ed] to consider the possibility that the selected lands could be most valuable for use as a landfill when determining the highest and best use of the selected lands" (*Desert Citizens* 1997:1436). The second claim was based on the six-month validity period for appraisals. This claim asked the court "to consider whether the appraisal of the selected lands should be updated given the fact the appraisal of the selected lands was prepared in August 1994 and BLM's approval did not come until February 1996" (*ibid.*).

As to the first claim, the court addressed whether the appraisal conformed to statutory and regulatory provisions in accordance with FLPMA. Section 206(d) of FLPMA directs the agency to obtain an appraisal of the market values of the lands to be swapped. "That appraisal must determine the 'market value' of the affected lands, based on the 'highest and best use' of the appraised property, and estimate its market value 'as if in private ownership and available for sale in the open market.'"[32] The challengers attacked the highest and best use determination of the appraiser (Kitchens 2000:22–24). Nichols and Gaston "analyzed the highest and best use of the lands and found that at the time of the appraisal 'the subject lands . . . [were] considered to have a highest and best use for utilization in conjunction with the . . . mining operation of Gold Fields'" (*Desert Citizens* 1997:1438). Under BLM regulations and UASFLA, the highest and best use is "the most probable legal use of a property, based on market evidence as of the date of valuation" (43 C.F.R. § 2200.0–5(k)). The UASFLA, in addition, requires that "the appraiser must consider whether the use is 'physically possible, legally permissible, financially feasible, and results in the highest value'" (*ibid.*).

Therefore, the challengers attacked the appraiser's failure to address use as a landfill as a physically possible, legally permissible, and financially feasible use of the selected lands (Kitchens 2000:22–24). However, the court disagreed. Evaluating the administrative record, the court found that "there was no general market use of the land as a landfill" (*Desert Citizens* 1997:1438). The court explained that both the appraising firm and the BLM "were under no obligation to consider and discredit unmeritorious uses, they needed only to consider those uses that are legally, physically, and financially feasible, and a landfill [did] not fall within that definition" (*ibid.*).

The court then moved on to the second substantive claim that "the Nichols & Gaston appraisal of the selected lands was conducted in June 1994 but the ROD was not issued until February 1996, and therefore, the BLM should not have relied on the allegedly outdated appraisals" (*Desert Citizens* 1997:1439). This claim was based on the BLM Manual, which recognized the validity of an appraisal for a period of six months. In rejecting this argument the court accepted the interpretation of the BLM appraiser, who "declared the valuations valid for a period of one year unless the market showed significant changes before that time" (*ibid.*). Therefore, the court looked at the administrative record and determined that, since no showing had been made of a significant change in the circumstances of the market, the expiration of the six-month period had not invalidated the BLM's equal value determination (Kitchens 2000:22–31). Thus, the court concluded, "as there is no regulation that sets a mandatory shelf life for appraisals, the BLM did not act in excess of its statutory authority" (*Desert Citizens* 1997:1440).

Finally, the court looked at the entire project of which the land swap was a part and found it to have considerable value for the public at large. The court believed the project would represent a significant source of revenue and employment for the local county and added that such "an

---

32 *Desert Citizens Against Pollution v. Bisson*, 954 F. Supp. 1430, 1433 (S.D. Cal. 1997). See 43 C.F.R. § 2201.3–2(a)(1)-(2).

environmentally safe landfill [would] serve the needs of millions in Southern California, as well as produce millions of dollars in host fees, taxes, and wages" (*Desert Citizens* 1997:1440). Contradicting itself, however, the court also held that "based on the evidence presented in the papers and at the hearing . . . there was no general market use of the land as a landfill" (*Desert Citizens* 1997:1438).

Desert Citizens Against Pollution v. Bisson (circuit court)

On November 6, 2000, the U.S. Court of Appeals for the Ninth Circuit reviewed the district court ruling on the challenge raised against the Mesquite Regional Landfill Exchange. The circuit court held in favor of the appellants and reversed the lower court's decision (Stengel 2001:583).

The Ninth Circuit first addressed the issue of standing. The environmental groups, alleged that their "members currently use and enjoy the federal lands at the proposed landfill site for recreational, aesthetic, and scientific purposes. Desert Citizens contend that the land exchange [would] prevent them from using and enjoying these lands" (*Desert Citizens* 2000:1176). The appellate judges found that the plaintiffs did have standing (Stengel 2001:584). The court held that "the recreational or aesthetic enjoyment of federal lands is a legally protected interest whose impairment constitutes an actual, particularized harm sufficient to create an injury in fact for purposes of standing" (*ibid.*). The court evaluated the policy behind FLPMA and found the preservation of natural resources to be one of its main goals (Siegel 2004:367).

The lower court had found the environmental groups' alleged injury to be the same as that of the public at large (Stengel 2001:584). The appellate court disagreed:

> The present challenge to FLPMA's equal-value requirement is not merely a generalized allegation of federal revenue loss at taxpayers' expense. Rather, it is an effort by land users to ensure appropriate federal guardianship of the public lands [,] which they frequent. If, by exchange, public lands are lost to those who use and enjoy the land, they are entitled . . . to file suit to assure that no exchange takes place unless the governing federal statutes . . . are followed, including the requirement that the land exchanged is properly valued by the agency.
> (*Desert Citizens* 2000:1177)

Therefore, by looking at the policy behind FLPMA, which requires the protection of aesthetic and recreational interests, the court found that the Desert Citizens group's interest in challenging an alleged unlawful swap of public land established standing.

The court then turned to the merits. Desert Citizens alleged that the BLM had failed to comply with FLPMA by relying on an outdated appraisal that undervalued the federal lands (Coggins and Glicksman 2007:13–75). There-fore, the BLM was in violation of Section 206(b), the equal value require-ment. This argument was based on the claim that the outdated appraisal was predicated on the erroneous highest and best use of the property as a mining operation rather than a landfill. The Court of Appeals found, on this issue, that the lower court had erred. In fact "evidence available prior to 1994 indicated that the selected lands were expected to be used for landfill pur-poses, and the existence of other landfill proposals in the region indicated a general market for landfill development" (*Desert Citizens* 2000:1181).

In addition, the court wrote, "the appraiser well knew that Gold Fields and the BLM fully intended to utilize the land for the Mesquite Regional land-fill, and had taken substantial steps to do so" (*Desert Citizens* 2000:1182). From the evidence in the administrative record, the court concluded that the specific intent of the land swap was to facilitate the construction of the Mesquite Regional Landfill. "There [was] no principled reason why the BLM, or any federal agency, should remain willfully blind to the value of federal lands by acting contrary to the most elementary principles of real estate transactions" (*Desert Citizens* 2000:1184). The court held that the appraisal should have considered landfill use to be the highest and best use of the public lands. In fact, evidence available to the appraiser showed that use of the public land as a landfill was physically possible, legally permis-sible, and financially feasible in accordance with UASFLA (Coggins and Glicksman 2007:13–76).

The court next considered the appellants' challenge to the BLM's use of an outdated appraisal. According to the BLM Handbook Manual "approved values are valid for 6 months but this may vary by state or individual cir-cumstances . . . Appraisal updates should be requested as the appraisal approaches the end of its shelf life, or if significant local events warrant a re-examination."[33] The court held that "even under the California State Office's unwritten policy of presuming appraisals to be valid for a year, the Nichols & Gaston appraisal would have expired in June, 1995, eight months before it was used by BLM as the basis for the ROD" (*Desert Citi-zens* 2000:1185). The shelf life of the appraisal had expired and "significant local events" had made the landfill use even more possible, permissible, and feasible (Coggins and Glicksman 2007:13–76). Despite this evidence being present in the administrative record, neither the appraisal reviewer nor the BLM ever considered a reexamination of the appraisal. The appellate court also noted that the lower court had failed to take notice of the "significant changes in pertinent laws or zoning or other events which . . . substantially affect the value of a parcel of property. These would include the zoning change and other enactments associated with Imperial County" (*Desert Citizens* 2000:1186).

33 BLM Handbook Manual H-2200–1, Chapter VII(J).

Therefore, the Ninth Circuit reversed the lower court's decision and set aside the land swap because of the failure of the appraiser and the BLM to consider landfill use as the highest and best use (Coggins and Glicksman 2007:13–75). The court wrote:

> The difference between $46,000 an acre for a landfill site, and the $350 an acre for . . . mine support, is evidence that the value of the land if appraised for a landfill would be much higher. The government must not wear blinders when it participates in a real estate transaction, particularly if the result . . . is the transfer of a flagrantly undervalued parcel of federal land to a private party.
>
> (*Desert Citizens* 2000:1187)

Case law analysis

Federal statutes, beginning with the GEA of 1922, have mandated that agencies make public interest determinations before any land exchange can be completed. Section 315g of the Taylor Grazing Act allowed federal land swaps only if the public interest were benefited (Coggins and Glicksman 2007:13–66). Originally, "public interest" was interpreted[34] "provid[ing] for orderly administration of the public domain and to stabilize the livestock industry" (Moran 1964:28).[35] Later, in 1963, a federal Court of Appeals in *LaRue v. Udall* broadened the term "public interest" to "encompass all the potential values of multiple use management, not just public grazing interests" (Coggins and Glicksman 2007:13–67).

In 1976, FLPMA replaced the provision related to land exchanges (Coggins and Glicksman 2007:13–66). It required the public interest "decision to be formal and written, and perhaps made on the basis of a record of sorts" (Coggins and Glicksman, 2007:13–67–68). Accordingly, the IBLA held in *Nevada Power Co.*[36] that "the BLM . . . must explain fully its public interest determination" (Coggins and Glicksman 2007:13–68). The IBLA has held that the agency has to evaluate the public interest in an exchange before concluding it.[37] However, as commentators have pointed out, "judicial review of public interest determinations are by nature so multi-faceted and 'spongy' that a secretarial public interest determination will be overturned only in the most egregious circumstances" (Quarles and Lundquist 1984:381).[38]

---

34 *Red Canyon Sheep Co. v. Ickes*, 98 F.2d 308 (D.C. Cir. 1938).
35 Although, in 1948, the Department of Interior in the *Jensen* case had already interpreted the public interest of a land swap as encompassing federal interests outside the grazing district involved in the transaction.
36 *Nevada Power Co.*, 137 IBLA 328 (1997).
37 See *Swanson-Superior Forest Prods., Inc.*, 127 IBLA 379 (1993).
38 In the *National Wildlife Federation* case, the IBLA ruled that as long as the BLM proffered an interpretation of the public interest determination, its interpretation was bound to prevail.

One example of "egregious circumstances" occurred in the public inter-est determination in a swap conducted by the BLM under the provisions of the Alaska National Interest Lands Conservation Act (ANILCA) of 1980. In the St. Matthew Island Exchange, a federal court in Alaska set aside the swap because the Secretary of the Interior had failed to demonstrate the public interest would benefit.[39] Secretary James Gaius Watt had tried "to assist private resource development at the expense of wilderness values, but the federal court for the District of Alaska ruled that the Watt conception of the public interest differed radically from what Congress had in mind" (Coggins and Nagel 1990:499). In other words, "an outrageous or literal misstatement" should not receive deference, in interpreting the meaning pf public interest (Ragsdale 1999:33).

The court found that "the Secretary overstated the benefits that would accrue for wildlife protection while understating the probable damage to the wildlife habitat of the island" (Coggins and Glicksman 2007:13–82). The court stated that the term "public interest" should not be interpreted as an undefined promotion of the general welfare, but rather in the con-text of the policies and purposes of the underlying legislation (Coggins and Glicksman 2007:1383). The judge concluded that in this swap "the interests acquired were redundant, that the interests conveyed by the United States would be subject to serious environmental impacts and that, even under a deferential standard, the exchange could not be considered in the public interest" (Ragsdale 1999:33). This case stands for the proposition that any federal agency should support a public interest determination with data in the administrative record (Brown 2000:278). This failed swap had impor-tant repercussions. According to Coggins and Nagel,

> the St. Matthew Island case apparently is the first instance in which a court has reviewed in depth a formal public interest determination necessary to perform an otherwise discretionary function by the Secre-tary and found the determination to be so lacking in substance as to be arbitrary and capricious.
>
> (1990:501)

Years later, in the Circle West Coal Exchange,[40] a federal court in Mon-tana "ruled that the BLM was not required to consider effects on competi-tion because that element was not included in the statutory list of factors and that the Secretary had adequately considered the required factors" (Coggins and Glicksman 2007:13–70). In affirming this ruling, the appel-late court considered the way the Secretary had reached his public interest

39 *National Audubon Soc'y v. Hodel*, 606 F. Supp. 825 (D. Alaska 1984).
40 *National Coal Ass'n v. Hodel*, 675 F. Supp. 1231 (D. Mont. 1987), *aff'd*, 874 F.2d 661 (9th Cir. 1989).

determination and concluded that whichever factors were deemed preeminent, their relative weights were left to the agency.

A few years later, the USFS completed a land exchange in Vail, Colorado. An association of local landowners challenged the public interest determination made by the USFS. The district court was affirmed by the Tenth Circuit[41] in finding that Section 1716(a) of FLPMA "requires merely that the agency consider and weigh the factors which are listed in the section. It does not give the factors any particular priority, nor does it require that the agency do so" (*Lodge Tower* 1995:1380).[42] The plaintiffs had challenged the public interest determination, disputing the priority given by the agency to some of the factors listed by FLPMA (Coggins and Glicksman 2007:13–70). However, some authors believe that "for a system of land exchanges to maximize public benefits, it must involve the steady disposition of relatively small parcels of high value, typically where federal lands abut cities" (Heisel 1998:308). The court eventually found that the USFS had not abused its discretion in giving more weight to the interests of improving federal land management and natural resources protection over the interests of the local community, which wanted to protect a small parcel of forest land within Vail. As Ragsdale surmised, the "public interest might also include a number of . . . resource management or protection issues . . . deemed of primary significance even if in conflict with the local public needs" (1999:31).

A later case in the same circuit expanded the agency's discretion to determine the public interest. The court held that "the agency need only demonstrate that it considered relevant factors and alternatives after a full ventilation of issues and that the choice it made was reasonable based on that consideration" (*Thomas Brooks* 1990:643).[43] However, practically simultaneously, the IBLA reached a completely different decision on an exchange in New Mexico.[44] The Board "overturned [the] land exchange because the BLM [had] failed to consider the extent to which the anticipated development on the public lands that would be passed out of federal ownership would adversely affect the public interest" (Palma and Kite 1995:373). In this case, the agency had failed to demonstrate that the exchange would benefit the public interest. The BLM assessment of the public interest must include "any adverse impact resulting from the exchange, including determining the possible consequences of future development of the public land" (Fried 1998:504).

Similarly, in *Center for Biological Diversity* the Ninth Circuit held that the public interest determination in the Ray Land Exchange had been arbitrary

41 *Lodge Tower Condominium Ass'n v. Lodge Props., Inc.*, 880 F. Supp. 1370 (D. Colo. 1995), *aff'd*, 85 F.3d 476 (10th Cir. 1996).
42 See also *Shasta Coal. for the Pres. of Pub. Land*, 172 IBLA 333 (2007).
43 *Thomas Brooks Chartered v. Burnett*, 920 F.2d 634, 643 (10th Cir. 1990).
44 *City of Santa Fe et al.*, 103 IBLA 397 (1988).

and capricious (2010). The BLM had concluded that the "proposed land exchange would be in the public interest and that mining and related activity was likely to occur on the land to be sold to a private mining company regardless of whether the exchange took place or not" (Coggins and Glicksman 2007:13–68). The court held that without an accurate determination of environmental consequences, the BLM could not make the public interest determination.

In addition to a public interest determination, Section 1716(b) of FLPMA requires that land exchanges be completed on the basis of equal value.[45] Federal courts have "simply assumed that FLPMA's equal value requirement did not give rise to an independent cause of action to enforce the statute" (Kite and Black 1992:6–29). Therefore, courts have held that private parties could not challenge agency decision-making based exclusively on a violation of the equal value determination because they could not establish a particularized "injury in fact." For example, in *National Coal Ass'n,*[46] the district court "held that the plaintiffs lacked standing to challenge [the BLM]'s equal value determination because they failed to allege any injury to themselves" (Kite and Black 1992:6–29). Since the environmentalists based their claim to standing exclusively on their status as taxpayers, the court rejected their suit. As Stengel explains, any

> challenge to FLPMA's equal-value requirement is not merely a generalized allegation of federal revenue loss at taxpayer's expense. Rather, it is an effort by land users to ensure appropriate federal guardianship of the public lands which they frequent.
>
> (2001:590)

Under current case law, equal value means equal monetary value.[47] It has been the practice of the agencies, and the administrative or judicial courts supervising them, to accept the appraisals of official appraisers notwithstanding the fact that parties may have challenged their valuations (*Greer Coalition* 2012:635).[48] In *Greer Coalition* (2007), the court required that an

45 In the *Kellerblock* case, the IBLA established that in order to challenge an appraisal the appellant must show by clear and precise evidence that errors were made in the land valuation (see also the *Nolen* case). In the *Fallon Ice* case, the board found that the appellants had submitted sufficient evidence to question whether the BLM's appraisal accurately determined the value of the selected lands (*Fallon Ice & Cold Storage Co.*, 85 IBLA 224, 225 (1985)).

46 *National Coal Ass'n v. Hodel*, 675 F. Supp. 1231 (D. Mont. 1987).

47 See *Brent Hansen*, 128 IBLA 250 (1993).

48 *Greer Coal., Inc. v. U.S. Forest Serv.*, 470 Fed. App'x 630, 635 (2012). See also *W.J. & Betty Lo Wells*, 122 IBLA 250 (1992); *City of Santa Fe et al.*, 120 IBLA 308 (1991); *Desert Citizens Against Pollution v. Bisson*, 954 F. Supp. 1430 (S.D. Cal. 1997); *Charles W. Nolen*, 166 IBLA 197 (1990); *Shasta Coal. for the Pres. of Pub. Land*, 172 IBLA 333 (2007).

agency provide a reasonable explanation for its acceptance of the appraiser's valuation.[49] Thus the *Jolley* court set aside the exchange and remanded the matter to the BLM because the appraiser was found to lack impartiality.[50]

Another requirement for determining equal value is that the highest and best use of the federal land be determined by the agency. According to Ragsdale, "the regulations call for an appraisal, under uniform standards, to determine the highest and best (and most profitable) use of the federal property, as if it were private and marketable" (Ragsdale 1999:13). However, in *Lodge Tower*,[51] the district court upheld the exchange. The USFS had not considered the highest and best use of the federal lands, which depended on the possibility of rezoning that the USFS had not instructed its appraiser to consider. Ragsdale stresses the deference given by courts to the specific use of the land at issue as established by the administrative agency, which gives the agencies wide discretion to determine the value of federal lands (*Lapis* 2009).[52]

However, in *Desert Citizens* (2000), the Ninth Circuit held that the agency had failed to find the highest and best use for the swapped lands.[53] The Ninth Circuit "argued that the construction of landfill was reasonably probable and should have been considered" (Stengel 2001:587). The lower court had held, much as in *Lodge Tower*, that the agency could permissibly be mistaken about the highest and best use, since at "the time of the appraisal, the landfill project was too tenuous . . . not legally, physically, or financially feasible" (Kitchens 2000:22–24). Contrarily, the circuit court found that that information had been available at the time of the appraisal and a much more probable and profitable use raised the value of the federal land (Coggins and Glicksman 2007:13–75).[54]

According to Stengel "stringent application of the 'highest and best use' standard is imperative in light of the fact that both the BLM and the Forest Service consistently undervalue federal lands at the expense of the taxpayer" (2001:590–591). The appellate court in *Desert Citizens* "held that the plaintiffs' challenge of the appraisal was not a generalized grievance affecting all taxpayers but rather, 'an effort by land users to ensure appropriate federal guardianship of the public lands which they frequent'" (Stengel 2001:585). This conferred on the organization standing to challenge the swap. The "decision in *Desert Citizens* illustrates the importance of an open

---

49 *Greer Coal., Inc. v. U.S. Forest Serv.*, 65 ERC 1658 (2007).
50 *John R. Jolley*, 145 IBLA 34 (1998).
51 *Lodge Tower Condominium Ass'n v. Lodge Props., Inc.*, 880 F. Supp. 1370 (D. Colo. 1995).
52 *Ted Lapis*, 178 IBLA 62 (2009).
53 See also *National Parks & Conservation Ass'n v. Bureau of Land Mgmt.*, 606 F.3d 1058 (9th Cir. 2010).
54 See also *National Parks & Conservation Ass'n v. Bureau of Land Mgmt.*, 606 F.3d 1058 (9th Cir. 2010).

and honest appraisal of public lands as well as the need for a forum in which citizens can challenge land trades when they contradict the public interest" (Stengel 2001:596).

Another issue raised in this case was a BLM regulation[55] providing, "The appraisal must take into account historic, wildlife, recreation, wilderness, scenic, cultural, or other resource values and amenities" (Coggins and Glicksman 2007:13–61). According to the plaintiffs, the appraisal failed to reflect the potential of the land for development. Draffan and Blaeloch believe that, under normal circumstances, the treatment of the concept of "equal value is exacerbated by the continued belief that land is not worth anything until it is developed" (2000:32).

Accordingly, what is usually lost in the appraisal is the fact that wildlife habitat or cultural resources are not conducive to traditional economic valuation. It is important to highlight that even though federal directives provide for the consideration of non-monetary values of resources attached to the land, in reality, these resources are insignificant in the final appraisal. According to Blaeloch, "the appraisal community has largely rejected the idea of attaching 'public interest value' to lands, largely because this creates a leveraging opportunity for private owners to jack up the . . . exchange price for lands that have little market value" (2001:37). Therefore, the "highest and best use"[56] of the property is based exclusively on a market value that considers only the monetary value of resources, be they timber or minerals (Coggins and Glicksman 2007:13–61).

This failure to acknowledge the "public interest value" of land creates a paradox in cases such as the Huckleberry Mountain Exchange, where the lands initially conveyed by the USFS contained sections of the Huckleberry Divide Trail, which were appraised for their economic timber value and not for their cultural/historic values. According to Blaeloch, a case like this creates "a two-edged sword, because the same public land that fetches the highest value in a trade may also be land that should not be exchanged because of its [cultural or historic] value" (2001:37). Where the USFS, after court injunction, repurchased the same land from the timber company, the agency ended up paying for the newly increased value. This new valuation was in accordance with a more recent appraisal which reflected the importance of the preservation of the cultural/historic value of the Divide Trail. This was notwithstanding the fact that "the appraisal community has largely rejected the idea of attaching 'public interest value' to lands, . . . because this creates a leveraging opportunity for private owners to jack up the sale or exchange price" (Blaeloch 2001:37).

55   36 C.F.R. § 254.9(a)(1).
56   See for the BLM 43 C.F.R. § 2201.3–3; see for the Forest Service 36 C.F.R. § 254.9.

Conclusions

Under current case law, the term "public interest" allows the agencies ample discretion (Coggins and Glicksman 2007:13–68). Some authors have suggested that only in egregious circumstances would a court overturn an agency's public interest determination (Quarles and Lundquist 1984).[57] Thus when the BLM acknowledged in its directives a multiple use of its lands, "public interest" was taken to encompass any potential use recognized by the agency. A court looked at the net result of the land swap, and as long as the advantages shown by the agency outweighed the costs, the public interest determination was not to be touched (*LaRue*). This line of reasoning was further confirmed, even under new legislation (FLPMA), in *McGregor* and *Shasta Coalition*.

Because FLPMA contains specific factors to be considered in a public interest determination, the work of the courts and the agencies has become even more streamlined since the agency is only required to justify the exchange under one of the multiple factors (*National Coal Ass'n*).[58] As long as the determination follows the purposes of the legislation, the agency's determination is unchallengeable (*Shasta Coalition*).

Similarly, courts have been reluctant to overturn agencies' decisions concerning a standard such as equal valuation reflected in the land appraisal (*National Coal Ass'n*). Whenever this standard becomes "variegated," "non-prioritized" and "malleable" (Ragsdale 1999:43), vulnerability to extortion in strong-arm negotiations increases considerably. However, according to Ragsdale (1999), the courts would overturn only an outrageous misstatement of valuations.[59] For example, the IBLA rejected the plaintiffs' claim for failing to submit an alternative appraisal to challenge the agency's (*McGregor*).[60] In another case, the court rejected the appraisal proffered by the claimants as "inadequate" to challenge an agency's decision (*Wells*). In a third case, the court, rather than accept the appraisal of the plaintiff, held the issue of valuation "premature" and remanded to the agency for a new appraisal (*Swanson-Superior*).

Courts are more likely to order new appraisals when a considerable length of time elapses between the appraisal and the judicial opinion (*Fallon Ice*). The Ninth Circuit Court even chastised the BLM for accepting an outdated appraisal and its "willful blindness" that was contrary to elementary principles of real estate transactions (*Desert Citizens*). In another case, the court

---

57 The egregious example is provided by the St. Matthew Island Exchange, where the court found the agency's decision arbitrary and capricious.

58 For a similar decision regarding the USFS see the *Lodge Tower* case.

59 In accordance with this statement see the opposing decisions in the *Desert Citizens* case in the original trial and its appeal; while the district judge failed to find the outrageous behavior of the BLM, the Ninth Circuit Court scolded the agency for its willful blindness.

60 In the same case, the administrative panel condoned the practice of the agency to waive the equalization payment required by law.

was receptive of challenges to an appraisal. In this case, evidence was proffered that the appraiser was not impartial because he had a profit interest linked to the completion of the land swap. Since he was not "disinterested" in the swap, the panel set aside the approval of it (*Jolley*).

However, the courts have rejected the idea of attaching the "public interest value" to the valuation of lands involved in a swap. This failure to acknowledge the "public interest value" of land might create a paradox (*Muckleshoot Indian Tribe* 1999). There, when the lands were initially conveyed to a timber company, they were appraised for their economic timber value and not for their cultural/historic values. However, when the agency, upon court injunction, repurchased the same land from the timber company, it paid for an increased value reflecting the importance of those cultural/historic values.

Finally, as far as the issue of standing to challenge agencies' decisions, the courts have rejected the theory that private parties may claim an injury in fact when they base their challenge only on their status as taxpayers (*National Coal Ass'n*). According to the Ninth Circuit, it would be different if the plaintiffs were acting to ensure federal guardianship of the federal lands (*Desert Citizens*). On the other hand, when plaintiffs show an adverse effect on a cognizable interest in the land to be transferred, the courts have recognized standing (*Jolley*).[61]

Table of Cases

Center for Biological Diversity v. Dep't of Interior, 623 F.3d 633 (9th Cir. 2010)

Donna Charpied et al., 137 IBLA 45 (1996)

City of Santa Fe et al., 103 IBLA 397 (1988)

City of Santa Fe, 120 IBLA 308 (1991)

Desert Citizens Against Pollution v. Bisson, 954 F. Supp. 1430 (S.D. Cal. 1997)

Desert Citizens Against Pollution v. Bisson, 231 F.3d 1172 (9th Cir. 2000)

Fallon Ice & Cold Storage Co., 85 IBLA 224 (1985)

Greer Coal., Inc. v. U.S. Forest Serv., 65 ERC 1658 (2007)

Greer Coal., Inc. v. U.S. Forest Serv., 470 F. App'x 630 (9th Cir. 2012)

Brent Hansen, 128 IBLA 250 (1993)

John R. Jolley, 145 IBLA 34 (1998)

Paul Kellerblock, 38 IBLA 160 (1978)

Ted Lapis, 178 IBLA 62 (2009)

LaRue v. Udall, 324 F.2d 428 (D.C. Cir. 1963)

Lodge Tower Condominium Ass'n v. Lodge Props., Inc., 880 F. Supp. 1370 (D. Colo. 1995)

61 See also the Ninth Circuit Court decision in the Desert Citizens case.

Burton A. & Mary H. McGregor et al., 119 IBLA 95 (1991)

Muckleshoot Indian Tribe v. U.S. Forest Serv., 177 F.3d 800 (9th Cir. 1999)

National Audubon Soc'y v. Hodel, 606 F. Supp. 825 (D. Alaska 1984)

National Coal Ass'n v. Hodel, 675 F. Supp. 1231 (D. Mont. 1987)

National Parks & Conservation Ass'n v. Bureau of Land Mgmt., 606 F.3d 1058 (9th Cir. 2010)

National Wildlife Fed'n, 82 IBLA 303 (1984)

National Wildlife Fed'n, 87 IBLA 271 (1985)

Nevada Power Co., 137 IBLA 328 (1997)

Charles W. Nolen, 166 IBLA 197 (2005)

Red Canyon Sheep Co. v. Ickes, 98 F.2d 308 (D.C. Cir. 1938)

Shasta Coal. for the Preservation of Public Land, 172 IBLA 333 (2007)

Swanson-Superior Forest Prods., Inc., 127 IBLA 379 (1993)

Thomas Brooks Chartered v. Burnett, 920 F.2d 634 (10th Cir. 1990)

W.J. & Betty Lo Wells, 122 IBLA 250 (1992)

References

Beaudoin, R. M. (2000, Spring/Summer). Federal Ownership and Management of America's Public Lands Through Land Exchanges. *Great Plains Natural Resources Journal*, 229–299.

Blaeloch, J. (2001). *The Citizens' Guide to Federal Land Exchanges: A Manual for Public Lands Advocates*. Seattle, WA: Western Land Exchange Project.

Brown, S.J.M. (2000). David and Goliath: Reformulating the Definition of "the Public Interest" and the Future of Land Swaps After the Interstate 90 Land Exchange. *Journal of Environmental Law and Litigation, 15*, 235–293.

Coggins, G. C. & Glicksman, R. L. (2007). *Public Natural Resources Law*. New York, NY: C. Boardman.

Coggins, G. C. & Nagel, D. K. (1990). Nothing Beside Remains: The Legal Legacy of James G. Watt's Tenure as Secretary of the Interior on Federal Land Law and Policy. *Boston College Environmental Affairs Law Review, 17*(3), 473–550.

Draffan, G. & Blaeloch, J. (2000). *Commons or Commodity? The Dilemma of Federal Land Exchanges*. Seattle, WA: Western Land Exchange Project.

Fried, J. (1998). The Grand Staircase-Escalante National Monument: A Case Study in Western Land Management. *Virginia Environmental Law Journal, 17*(4), 477–530.

Heisel, E. J. (1998). Biodiversity and Federal Land Ownership: Mapping a Strategy for the Future. *Ecology Law Quarterly, 25*, 229–312.

Jones, E. K. (1996, June/July). Acquiring Federal and State Land Through Land Exchanges. *Utah Bar Journal, 9*, 19–22.

Kitchens, E. (2000). Federal Land Exchanges: Securing the Keys to the Castle. *Rocky Mountain Mineral Law Institute, 46*, 22–1–51.

Kite, M. S. & Black, S. W. (1992). Land Exchanges With the Federal Government: Mineral Law Series. *Rocky Mountain Mineral Law Foundation, 4*(6), 1–44.

Moran, R. L. (1964). Sales and Exchanges of Public Lands. *Rocky Mountain Mineral Law Institute, 15*, 25–50.

Palma, J. D. & Kite, M. S. (1995). Roadless Lands and Wilderness Planning: A History and Overview. In R. J. Fink (Ed.), *The Natural Resources Law Manual* (pp. 370–381). Chicago, IL: Section of Natural Resources, Energy, and Environmental Law, American Bar Association.

Paul, B. (2006). Statutory Land Exchanges That Reflect "Appropriate" Value and "Well Serve" the Public Interest. *Public Land & Resources Law Review, 27,* 107–129.

Quarles, S. P. & Lundquist, T. R. (1984). Federal Land Exchanges and Mineral Development. *Rocky Mountain Mineral Law Institute, 29,* 367–420.

Ragsdale, J. W. (1999). National Forest Land Exchanges and the Growth of Vail and Other Gateway Communities. *Urban Lawyer, 31,* 1–45.

Siegel, J. R. (2004). Zone of Interests. *Georgetown Law Journal, 92,* 317–368.

Stengel, A. (2001). Insider's Game or Valuable Land Management Tool? *Tulane Environmental Law Journal, 14,* 567–596.

U.S. Department of the Interior. (2001). *Land Exchanges and Acquisitions* (USDI Report No. 2001-I-413). Sacramento, CA: Author.

U.S. Department of the Interior. (2009). Record of Decision, Professor Valley Exchange. Moab, UT: Author.

5   Analyzing governmental studies

In 1989, Kaiser Eagle Mountain, Inc. (KEM), proposed to the BLM a swap in order to facilitate KEM's "construction and operation of the Eagle Mountain Landfill and Recycling Center Project . . . an enormous solid waste municipal landfill . . . approximately 1–1/2 miles from the Joshua Tree National Park" (*Charpied* 1999:316–317).

KEM and its partner, Mine Reclamation Center (MRC), planned to use an unreclaimed open pit iron mine to pursue the acquisition of federal lands to complete the construction of the largest landfill in the country. On September 25, 1997, the BLM announced its approval of the exchange. On December 9, 1998, the BLM denied all administrative challenges to the swap and "cleared the way for the exchange of approximately 3,481 acres of public land . . . (selected public lands) . . . in return for 10 [scattered] parcels owned by KEM totaling approximately 2,846 (offered private lands) plus a cash payment of $20,100" (*Charpied* 1999:318).

Over 10 years later, on November 10, 2009, the Ninth Circuit released its own decision on the litigation over this swap (Eagle Mountain Landfill and Recycling Center Exchange). The case reached the Ninth Circuit after the district court had reversed a previous IBLA decision and ruled in favor of the environmental plaintiffs. The appellate court set aside the swap because the agency's appraisal did not consider a landfill as the "highest and best use" of the selected lands. This appraisal had "found that the 'highest and best use' of the public lands in question was 'holding for speculative investment.'" (*NPCA* 2009:739). The BLM's "appraisal explicitly stated that it did 'not take into consideration any aspects of the proposed landfill project'" (*ibid.*).

The court cited its own decision in *Desert Citizens*, where it had "examined a highest and best use claim almost identical to that presented in the instant case" (*NPCA* 2009:743). Under *Desert Citizens*, "uses that are reasonably probable must be analyzed as a necessary part of the highest and best use determination. This analysis must have due regard for . . . such needs as may be reasonably expected to develop in the near future" (*Desert Citizens* 2000:1181). *Desert Citizens* was particularly on point because the selected lands were being traded to be used as a landfill. In addition, "because the 'existence of other landfill proposals in the region indicated a general market for landfill development,' landfill use was reasonably probable and must 'at the very least' have been considered in the highest and best use analysis" (*NPCA* 2009:743). In fact, the *Desert Citizens* court had "relied upon as evidence of market demand the 'Eagle Mountain Regional Landfill proposed by Kaiser'" (*ibid.*). Thus, the court argued, "The facts of *Desert Citizens* are virtually identical to the facts . . . in the instant case" (*ibid.*).

Moreover, "the [BLM] appraisal was clearly cognizant of Kaiser's proposal, yet explicitly stated that it was not taking 'into consideration any aspect of the proposed landfill project.' [Yet] Kaiser and the BLM do not contest the physical or legal feasibility of constructing a landfill at the Eagle Mountain site" (*NPCA* 2009:743–744). The court added that as held in *Desert Citizens*, "the presence of competing proposals alone is sufficient to establish market demand and financial feasibility" (*NPCA* 2009:744). Therefore, "if the Kaiser landfill proposal was sufficient to establish a reasonable probability of the Mesquite Landfill's financial feasibility, the Mesquite Landfill and other proposals must demonstrate similar feasibility of the Kaiser project" (*ibid.*).

The Ninth Circuit concluded that "the use of the land as a landfill was not only reasonable, it was the specific intent of the exchange" (*NPCA* 2009:745). As in *Desert Citizens*, "there is no principled reason why the BLM, or any federal agency, should remain willfully blind to the value of federal lands by acting contrary to the most elementary principles of real estate transactions" (*ibid.*).

Introduction

This chapter tries to provide an answer to that question. Why is it that federal agencies "remain willfully blind" to the value of the selected lands? To help answering this question, this chapter analyzes investigations conducted by GAO, a nonpartisan branch of Congress; The Appraisal Foundation (TAF), a private organization that certifies land appraisers and drafts of land appraisal standards; and the USDA and DOI OIGs, which oversee the legality of the land transactions of the USFS and the BLM. These investigations overlap to some degree. Although this creates redundancy in the data, it is noteworthy that they produced similar conclusions.

In 1985, the U.S. Senate requested the GAO to review the exchange programs as actually implemented. The results of the study were somewhat perplexing. By 1987 (the year of the report publication) it had become clear that both the BLM and the USFS were inconsistent in their attempts to adjust unequal values and were waiving equalization payments in violation of the law. In practice, this rounding-off meant offering federal lands at below their appraised values (GAO 1987). These practices were in violation of the equal value requirement of FLPMA.

In 1991, the DOI OIG conducted a thorough review of the appraisals of lands exchanged by the BLM. The OIG hired an outside reviewer to analyze the data. The reviewer confirmed that inadequate appraisal reviews were being accepted by the agency. In 1996, the same OIG audited BLM land exchanges in Nevada. This audit confirmed that the local state office had failed to obtain equal value in three of the four exchanges examined. The Nevada state director of the BLM had been giving in to pressure from proponents unhappy with agency appraisals. The OIG concluded that there was a lack of accountability throughout the office.

A few years later (1998), the OIG for the USDA issued a report concerning a USFS land exchange in Nevada. The USDA OIG found inappropriate pressure employed by the private party. The OIG questioned the integrity of a USFS lands and realty manager and two other staff managers who had a serious conflict of interest regarding land exchanges in the district. In 1999, the USDA OIG examined another USFS land exchange in Nevada. In this instance, the USFS lands and realty staff had compromised the valuation process, justifying their actions as "a gesture of good faith" toward the private proponent. Evidence showed that the private party had been pressuring the lands staff into completing the exchange.

In March 2000, TAF issued its first report evaluating the appraisal organization of the USFS; TAF decided to forgo an examination of the agency's appraisal reports. Although that examination could possibly have uncovered undervaluation of federal lands, TAF instead concentrated its interviews of agency employees on the issue of inappropriate influence of private parties over USFS staff. The data showed that the agency was allowing such influence over appraisers in order to achieve "acceptable" results for proponents (TAF 2000). Furthermore, the land management line officer was compromising the independence of appraisers. The same year, the GAO issued a report on BLM and USFS land exchange practices. This report found that both agencies had overvalued private lands and undervalued federal lands. Both agencies had disapproved appraisals considered unsatisfactory by the private parties. New appraisals would then be prepared to satisfy private proponents (GAO 2000).

Immediately after publication of the GAO's report, the DOI OIG released a report on the BLM's Utah state office land exchange practices. This study uncovered the so-called "alternative approach" devised by the BLM (DOI 2001). This approach was used to complete land swaps and lessen the pressure tactics of private proponents. In this exchange, the BLM Senior Specialist (Chief Appraiser) had arbitrarily taken over the duty of reviewing appraisals in Utah. The BLM's Acting Assistant Secretary defended this action by stating that the Senior Specialist had used his influence "to facilitate" exchanges in Utah (DOI 2001).

Finally, in 2002, TAF issued its latest report, this time concerning the BLM's appraisal organization. The report confirmed previous findings of inappropriate pressure exercised by private parties over staff appraisers.

This pressure, according to TAF, was political in nature and had clouded the objectivity of the appraisers. Specifically, instances of improper political influence were shown to be present wherever a BLM state director had been a political appointee. In this climate, the agency had favored private over public interests. The report concluded that the result had been the completion of land swaps that were unwise and unsupported by evidence. After this brief summary, we move on to take a closer look at each of these studies.

GAO 1987 report: land exchange process working but can be improved

In April 1985, Congress asked the GAO to review BLM and USFS land exchange practices, in particular "the application of the equal value criteria for any assets [and] the use of cash equalization payments to make up the difference in value" (GAO 1987:48). Between April 1985 and May 1986, the GAO investigated some of the 706 exchanges conducted by the two agencies between October 1981 and March 1985.

The major flaws in the practices of the agencies, as reported by the GAO, were the BLM's waivers of cash equalization payments and the both agencies' adjustments of unequal values, with both practices leading to failures to obtain equal value. Of the 706 swaps, 217 required a cash equalization payment. In 29 of the exchanges, equal value was not obtained. In three exchanges, the BLM waived the equalization payments in violation of FLPMA. In 26 exchanges, both the BLM and the USFS adjusted the appraised values, in effect waiving the equalization payment. These practices violated FLPMA, which does not allow federal agencies to "round off" appraised values.

For its study, the GAO selected 16 test cases plus a random sample of 61 BLM exchanges (out of 183) and 90 USFS swaps (out of 532). These sample cases were used to determine whether the agencies received equal value. Unfortunately, in this particular study the GAO did not conduct an independent review of the appraisal reports.

In 10 of the 16 cases, equal value was achieved either by adjustment of acreage (three cases) or by cash equalization payments. In the cases of cash equalization, though, the agencies chose to either adjust appraisal values or waive the payments. These practices were in violation of FLPMA. In addition, the GAO found that in three of the 61 BLM exchanges, the agency had waived the cash equalization payment. A BLM Deputy Director of Operations issued a memo in March 1986 prohibiting the waiver of cash payments. Ironically, however, he also gave "instructions in the memorandum allow[ing] district managers the discretion to declare unequal appraised values to be 'equal' on the basis of . . . nonquantifiable considerations" (GAO 1987:33) such as aesthetics, riparian rights, and wildlife habitat. That instruction was in violation of FLPMA.

The report found that both the BLM and the USFS had rounded appraisals before the appraisal report had been submitted for review. The GAO found that out of the 16 test cases and the 61 sampled cases, the agencies had adjusted the appraisals in 26 exchanges, in some cases for thousands of dollars. In 16 out of the 26 cases, both the private and federal land appraisals were adjusted. The USFS's Pacific Southwest Region was involved in 15 of those 26 cases. In each case, "the result of the rounding was to lower the value of the federal parcel and make it equivalent to the appraised value of the nonfederal land" (GAO 1987:35). In another USFS region the GAO found inconsistent practices, too. Out of 12 cases, the agency required cash equalization payments in only seven. In the remaining five cases the federal land values were adjusted downward without explanation.

OIG audit report on land exchange activities, BLM

In June 1991, the DOI OIG released an audit report on BLM land swaps. The audit investigated whether fair value was received in land swaps completed by the BLM. The OIG reviewed 78 land appraisals completed by staff or fee appraisers. An external review appraiser from the U.S. Army Corps of Engineers analyzed 34 of the 78 appraisals. The OIG found that the BLM had failed to receive fair value in these land transactions and saw two causes. First, the BLM had failed to effectively review the land appraisals. Second, the BLM had allowed unauthorized staff to make value changes after the local State Chief Appraiser had approved the valuations.

The OIG investigation had been launched to respond to criticism about the practices of the BLM. Thus, the review appraiser was retained by the OIG "(1) to determine whether the estimated fair market value of the land was supported by the appraisal data and (2) to determine whether any identified deficiencies in following appraisal standards were sufficient to question the estimated fair market value" (DOI 1991:3). In order to complete his duties, the review appraiser examined the appraisals and visited the lands transferred in the swaps. His conclusions were that "(1) inadequate reviews of the appraisals [were] used to establish the fair market value of the land, [and] (2) land value adjustments [were] made without proper approval" (DOI 1991:3).

The findings of the study confirmed the charges of critics that the federal government was not receiving equal value in land swaps. According to the OIG, "responsible Bureau personnel did not effectively review land appraisals or properly prepare the required documentation on 71 of the 78 appraisals . . . reviewed" (DOI 1991:5). In 31 of the 78 appraisals, no review had even been completed. Of the remaining 47 appraisals, at least 40 had deficiencies related to lack of effective review or failure to prepare required documentation. In addition, 17 out of the 34 appraisals reviewed by the Corps of Engineers appraiser were considered to be "substandard." The reviewer found that unauthorized agency personnel had changed valuations in previously approved appraisals in order to reach equal value on paper, in violation of FLPMA.

In an example used in the report concerning a land swap in Arizona, the contract appraiser had made an upward adjustment in the value of the offered lands but failed to do the same for the federal lands. According to the OIG, "the use of an upward price adjustment only for the private party may have resulted in the Government's losing about $1 million on this exchange" (DOI 1991:7). In the same transaction, the appraiser reached a higher value for three parcels in the offered lands on the conclusion that the highest and best use of the property was commercial development. The OIG review appraiser found this to be inaccurate because the property had inadequate access for commercial development. This cost the government about $400,000. In a land swap in California, a contract appraiser valued the offered lands at $102,500, although the private party had optioned to purchase the same property for $75,000. In this case, the private property was overvalued by 37% or $27,500.

In a third land exchange in Arizona, a contract appraiser had valued offered lands in Elgin at the same value as a similar property in Tucson. But in another land exchange, the same contract appraiser had justified a higher valuation of two parcels of private lands in Tucson because comparatively to Elgin their location was "superior." In the latter exchange, the OIG review appraiser estimated that the overvaluation of offered lands had cost the government approximately $841,000.

OIG audit report on Nevada land exchange activities, BLM

In July 1996, the DOI OIG released an audit report on the BLM's Nevada State Office's land exchange practices. The major findings were that the office had failed to follow statutory and regulatory provisions and had failed to obtain equal value in three out of four land swaps.

The first swap, the Oliver Ranch Exchange, was valued at over $8 million and involved a 591-acre plot of federal land subject to a private easement over 220 acres. The audit found that the government's interests had not been fully protected. The Bureau's office had failed to properly evaluate the importance of the easement. The state office appraised the encumbered land at 10% of its potential value. The report concluded that if the Nevada office had fully evaluated the easement and reached an agreement to relinquish the easement rights over 189 out of the 220 original acres, as the new proprietor did, the Bureau would have saved $4.2 million. The "State Office management was aware that such a loss to the Government was possible but decided that the 'benefits' of acquiring the Oliver Ranch warranted the expeditious transfer of the land to private ownership" (DOI 1996:5–6). As the report concluded, the Nevada State Office's action was completely unjustified.

The Red Rock Exchange was also valued at over $8 million. In this exchange the Bureau "increased the established fair market value for some of the exchanged private land from $1.5 million to $2.7 million without a documented rationale to substantiate that action" (DOI 1996:6). Thus, the agency overvalued the offered lands by $1.2 million. The federal government lost an additional $157,000 because the proponent of the exchange received an unjustified discount. The report concluded that the lands acquired by the federal government were not particularly needed, and at the very most only 120 out of the over 2,000 acres acquired were considered an area of critical environmental concern. About 420 acres were part of the riverbed!

The OIG was puzzled by the failure to attain equal value in this exchange. In July 1994, the Chief Appraiser of the Bureau's Arizona State Office had conducted a review of a fee appraisal of the private lands. However, the Nevada State Director declined to use the approved land values in the review report and requested that a staff appraiser conduct the review. Responding to the request, the Nevada Chief Appraiser selected a member of the staff who approved a higher valuation.

The Nevada State Office then acquired the offered parcels at an increased value of $1.2 million. No additional documentation was provided to support the increase. In addition, the Nevada Chief Appraiser granted a $157,000 discount on the federal lands. The Nevada Chief Appraiser failed to document or to justify this discount. In this exchange, clearly the Nevada State Director, acting under the pressure of an "unhappy" proponent, accommodated the proponent through questionable means.

The third major swap was the Galena Resort Exchange, valued at over $35 million. In this case, the state office again lost assets without receiving equal value. The state office completed the first phase of the swap on August 12, 1994, without reaching equal value. The lands and realty managers were acting under pressure from the proponent. The Bureau failed to use the Nevada Chief Appraiser's review of the values identified by the original appraiser and, instead, overvalued and paid over $107,000 for two private parcels. At the completion of the first phase, the Bureau had transferred too much federal land without receiving adequate value in return. The private proponent consequently owed the government over $9 million!

The fourth land exchange, the Tonopah Exchange, was conducted by the Bureau's Battle Mountain District Manager, who swapped 25 acres of Bureau land in Las Vegas to acquire a defunct bowling alley in Tonopah, Nevada. The goal was to convert the bowling alley into a new administrative complex for the Tonopah Resource Area. As established by the OIG report, the BLM "expect[ed] to spend about $2.1 million to renovate the property acquired, which is over $1.5 million more than the amount currently appropriated for the Bureau to construct a Tonopah administrative complex" (DOI 1996:25). The OIG concluded that the swap was not in the public interest because rather than acquiring natural resources it was an acquisition of an administrative facility.[1]

---

1 The BLM Director did not challenge these conclusions.

The OIG then reviewed the land documents at the Office of the Assessor and Recorder for Clark County, Nevada. This review "indicated that land exchange proponents have been very successful in realizing sizeable gains by selling land received from the Bureau in smaller parcels shortly after title to the land was transferred" (DOI 1996:11). The report cited an example of 70 acres of BLM selected lands that were exchanged at a $763,000 value and then resold the same day for $4.6 million. In another instance, 40 acres of federal lands previously valued at $504,000 were resold on the day of exchange for $1 million. Finally, in a third instance, 25 acres of former BLM lands valued at $909,000 were resold two months later for $1.6 million.

OIG 1998 advisory report on the BLM Del Webb Land Exchange in Nevada

In March 1998, the OIG issued its final report on a review of the BLM's Nevada State Office. In this report, the OIG expressed concern about the interference of the BLM's Washington Office with the appraisal of federal lands in the Del Webb Exchange.

The Del Webb Exchange was put in motion after Del Webb submitted to the BLM an exchange proposal concerning 4,975 acres of the agency's lands in Nevada. Del Webb wished to turn those lands into a retirement community. On November 27, 1995, the Nevada State Office selected a contract appraiser. However, the BLM's Washington Office overrode that decision and allowed Del Webb, after the corporation had expressed its displeasure, to use its own appraiser to value the selected lands. The state office in Nevada, in direct violation of regular practice, accepted the new appraiser. Of the four land exchanges completed in Nevada by the BLM between June 1995 and August 1997, the Del Webb Exchange was the only one where the appraisal of selected lands was conducted by an appraiser selected by the proponent. According to the Nevada State Director and the Associate State Director, the BLM's Deputy Director made the decision to allow the proponent to choose its own appraiser. However, the Deputy Director stated that the Nevada State office had made that decision on its own. Unfortunately for the Deputy Director, a subsequent letter written by the CEO of Del Webb made express reference to the acts of the Deputy Director to get the Nevada State Office to change its decision.

Once completed, the first appraisal valued the 4,776 acres of selected lands at $43 million by using the unauthorized development-based method. In this particular method of appraisal, speculation replaces the real value of the property, thus a valuation "reflects the highest price a proponent of a land exchange could afford to pay for the lands and still earn its desired profit" (DOI 1998:6). According to the UASFLA, the appraiser should have used the fair market value method because the development approach is both "prone to error" and does not reflect the highest price of the property. On March 5, 1996, the Nevada State Chief Appraiser informed Del Webb of his concerns over the method used by the appraiser. His office requested a new appraisal, which valued the lands at $52.1 million, creating a difference between the appraisals of $9.1 million. The new appraisal confirmed the fears expressed by the Nevada State Chief Appraiser over the valuation approach of the first appraiser.

At that point, the BLM's Deputy Director replaced the State Chief Appraiser in his review of the Del Webb appraisal. The State Chief Appraiser was relieved of duty because the Washington Office felt that he had nurtured his own "preconceived opinion of value" (DOI 1998:6), which was prejudicial to the appraisal review process.[2] The Washington Office Chief Appraiser then contracted with a firm, nominated by Del Webb, to conduct the review appraisal. The Washington Office Chief Appraiser later explained that the decision to contract with a private firm was motivated by a desire "to avoid greater expense to the United States" (1998:7). He failed to submit any documentation to support his claim. The only justification found was "that the contractor was selected because the firm was experienced 'in appraising master planned communities'" (1998:7). As pointed out in the report, the contractor was especially experienced in appraising retirement communities built by Del Webb!

The OIG then notified the BLM of its intent to perform a new audit of the Nevada land swaps. On January 7, 1997, the OIG informed the BLM that the Del Webb Exchange would be part of the audit. On January 27, 1997, the BLM contracted for a third appraisal of the federal lands. This contract specifically requested that the appraiser use the comparable sales method, which uses the fair market values of the lands. The new appraisal valued the federal lands at $52.1 million. This new appraisal confirmed, "Only the Sales Comparison Approach to value was directly applicable in this analysis" (DOI 1998:8). This valuation was $9.1 million higher than the previous one.

Afterwards, the OIG listed the various deficiencies in the agency's management of land exchanges. The list included the following:

- the Bureau did not comply with appraisal standards;
- the proponent was significantly involved in the decision-making process;
- the Nevada State Chief Appraiser was removed from his appraisal review responsibilities; and
- the Washington Office Chief Appraiser decided to accept the first appraisal and appraisal review, concluded that the $43 million value was reasonable and adequately supported, and recommended . . . that the appraisal be approved (DOI 1998:11–12).

---

2 After the investigation conducted by the OIG, no evidence was found in support of these allegations against the Chief Appraiser. As the OIG report showed, no evidence had been found that would justify the replacement of the Chief Appraiser. Instead, as documented by both the Nevada State Director and the Associate District Manager, the State Chief Appraiser had been adamant in his protection of due compliance with the DOJ's Standards.

The OIG stressed that the decision made on February 2, 1996, by the Washington Office to allow Del Webb to choose its own appraiser of the selected lands "raised concerns that Del Webb was exerting undue influence over the exchange" (DOI 1998:28). The report then analyzed a conference call held on March 25, 1996, between the Nevada State office staff and the BLM's Deputy Director. They discussed Del Webb's request for a new appraiser to conduct the review of the first appraisal report. However, the Nevada Deputy State Director for Resources told the Deputy Director that there was no evidence supporting the allegations made by Del Webb concerning the bias of the Nevada State Chief Appraiser. At that point, a Del Webb representative joined the conference call in the Deputy Director's office. The representative stated that the corporation wanted the Nevada State Chief Appraiser removed from the swap because of bias against the company. He explained that the company did not want another BLM State Chief Appraiser to be designated as reviewer because "Del Webb did not believe that they were qualified to evaluate a complex development approach appraisal" (DOI 1998:30). The Deputy Director concluded the conference call by stating that the BLM would hire a private appraiser.

The following day, Del Webb sent a memo to the Washington Office Chief Appraiser requesting that no communication take place between the new appraisal reviewer and the BLM unless a representative of Del Webb were present. In addition, the memo requested that the Washington Office Chief Appraiser be the only BLM employee allowed to contact the new appraisal reviewer. The Washington Office Chief Appraiser agreed to all these terms. On March 27, 1996, the Washington Office Chief Appraiser conducted five phone interviews with prospective appraisers while Del Webb's representatives listened. The following day the Chief Appraiser selected the one designated by Del Webb.

Later, on July 16, 1996, the Washington Office Chief Appraiser received and approved the appraisal review valuing the federal land at $43 million. He forwarded the appraisal review to the Las Vegas District Manager for approval. Neither the Nevada State Director nor the District Manager ever approved the review.

In a meeting held in October 1996, a Del Webb representative asked both the "Authorized Officer" (the Nevada State Director) and the Washington Office Chief Appraiser whether they agreed to the $43 million valuation. Both BLM agents replied in the affirmative and told the corporation that the terms of the agreement were "firm." This surfaced in a letter, sent in December of 1996 by Del Webb's CEO to Arizona Senator John McCain, in which the CEO complained about excessive delay by the BLM.

In the meantime, the BLM published its Notice of Decision on November 4, 1996, stating that the Del Webb Exchange was in the public interest. The BLM indicated that the agency would accept the value of $43 million. On December 9, 1996, the Washington Office Chief Appraiser, as contracting officer representative, accepted the appraisal review and authorized payment to the reviewing appraisal firm.

A few days later, on December 12, 1996, the OIG notified the Bureau of its intent to conduct a follow-up audit of its land exchanges in Nevada. The next day, the BLM's Deputy Director called the OIG asking whether the audit would include the Del Webb Exchange. The auditor confirmed that it would. On December 16, 1996, Senator McCain sent a letter to the DOI Assistant Secretary for Land and Minerals Management questioning the delay of the Del Webb exchange. Two days later a meeting was held at BLM Headquarters. The BLM's Deputy Director, the Nevada State Director, the Las Vegas District Manager, and the Washington Office Chief Appraiser attended. Several issues were discussed, including the OIG audit and the review of Del Webb's first appraisal. The Chief Appraiser suggested that no decision be made until after the meeting with the OIG auditors. On the same day, Nevada Senator Harry Reid sent a letter to the DOI Assistant Secretary reiterating the questions raised by Senator McCain.

On December 23, 1996, the Chief Appraiser sent an email to the contract review appraiser in which "he stated that he wanted to 'resurrect the appraisal and appraisal review' and that he did 'not want management to be displeased with our efforts and flirt with trashing the whole thing'" (DOI 1998:37). On the same day, the BLM's Deputy Director replied to the letters from Senators McCain and Reid by explaining the process and writing that a possible "factor which may potentially affect the timing of the Del Webb exchange [was] the investigation of land exchange activities in Nevada by the Office of Inspector General" (DOI 1998:37).

On January 7, 1997, the OIG audit team met with BLM officials and explained the terms of its follow-up audit. A week later, the BLM's Deputy Director made the decision to order a new appraisal of the federal land. The decision was made to have the Washington Office Chief Appraiser review the new appraisal. The Chief Appraiser prepared the terms of the new appraisal contract. It required that the new appraisers "consider the results of the previous appraisal and appraisal review" (DOI 1998:39). Later, he met with Del Webb's representatives and "stated that 'the second appraisers would not start with a clean slate, but would be instructed to consider the first appraisal'" (1998:39). Earlier that day, the Chief Appraiser had contacted the Solicitor Office for a legal opinion. A staff attorney had stressed that he disagreed with the instructions to the new appraisers to "consider" the first appraisal. The attorney advised the Deputy Director against using the same appraisal firm for the review.

On March 21, 1997, a new appraiser submitted its report. It valued the federal lands at $52.1 million by using the sales comparison approach. In this appraisal, "the appraisers evaluated and considered the cost development approach from the earlier appraisal 'at the request of the client' . . . [but] they concluded that 'only the Sales Comparison Approach to value was directly applicable in this analysis" (DOI 1998:40). On July 29, 1997, the Del Webb Exchange Phase 1-A was completed with the acceptance of the new appraisal.

USDA OIG 1998 evaluation report on the Zephyr Cove Land Exchange

In August 1998, the USDA OIG released its report on the Zephyr Cove Land Exchange in Nevada and its audit of the USFS activities in that exchange. Despite the legal opinion of the Office of General Counsel (OGC) that the USFS was the sole owner of the offered lands and improvements thereon, the agency continued to acquiesce in a third party's unlawful use of the land acquired by the government. The agency was even contemplating a new land exchange proposed by this party, concerning the six contested acres of the USFS lands.[3]

The trouble began when, in the fall of 1995, Olympic Group, L.L.C., proposed a land exchange to the BLM. It had selected federal lands in the Las Vegas valley and offered in exchange a 46-acre property on Lake Tahoe. That property, the Zephyr Cove estate, was extraordinarily important for the agency's management and preservation of natural resources. This exchange was conducted in two phases. In the first phase, the USFS received 35 acres of the offered private lands, appraised at $24.3 million. In the second phase, the agency acquired the last 11 acres of Zephyr Cove, valued at $13.5 million. At the time of the transfer of deeds, no mention was made of the improvements or encumbrances on the property. This second transaction became the object of the OIG investigation. The OIG based its recommendations on an OGC legal opinion issued in April 1998. According to that opinion, the second phase had concluded with the transfer of deeds on April 25, 1997. Although a valid exchange had been completed, USFS staff continued to accommodate the requests of a third party, Park Cattle Co., which had purportedly received ownership of the improvements built on Zephyr Cove by a private transaction with Olympic Group.

Olympic Group had recorded the first warranty deed in April 1997. This deed contained no reservations for encumbrances on the offered land. On June 25, 1997, it recorded a second warranty deed, which also made no mention of improvements. Finally, on July 11, 1997, Olympic Group recorded a third deed, which included a reservation for the improvements. When the USFS requested a legal opinion from the OGC concerning the legal status of the improvements, the General Counsel (GC) confirmed that title to the offered lands had been conveyed on April 25, 1997. Title to the improvements on those lands had been transferred, at that time, to the

---

3 In 2001, the USFS finally acquired the rights to the mansion built on the contested six acres for $575,000.

USFS. According to FLPMA, the USFS acquired title to this land upon the recording of the deed.

The argument made by the original proponent and Park Cattle Co. was that the proponent and the Lake Tahoe Basin Management Unit (LTBMU) of the USFS had been working since February of 1997 on a transaction that would "sever" the improvements from the 11 acres of Zephyr Cove, which were to be exchanged. On March 5, 1997, the LTBMU and Olympic signed an agreement, drafted by the latter, which would grant Olympic an option either to quitclaim the rights to the improvements to a third private party or convey them to the USFS for no consideration. The LTBMU forest supervisor, without consulting the OGC but under recommendation of a retired USFS lands and realty manager, signed this document.

According to the legal opinion of the OGC, the LTBMU had lacked authority to execute that document because the USFS, at the time, did not yet own the land. Further, even after the recording of the first warranty deed, the LTBMU still lacked authority because by recording the first deed the proponent had lost title to the land and its improvements. Thus, it could not have made any reservations later. According to the evaluation report,

> Any reservations must be stated in the warranty deed when title is conveyed to the USA, and must specify the area to be encumbered by the improvements, the intended use, and the duration of the reservation. Any reservation for such use would require that the appraisal be redone to reflect the effect on the value of the lands being conveyed to the USA.
> (USDA 1998b:7)

Olympic, however, wrote to the acting LTBMU forest supervisor, and, after misrepresenting the terms of the agreement reached in March of 1997, related to him the transfer of the improvements to a private party. The acting forest supervisor, nominated in April 1997, was unfamiliar with the previous agreement. However, the forest supervisor was immediately pressured into a decision. In fact, he had received continuous calls from Olympic, county commissioners, and Park Cattle Co. managers cajoling him to support the land transfer. According to the records of the acting forest supervisor, he had sought advice from a retired USFS manager who had previously worked on the same proposal. With the advice of the retired manager and "as a result of the pressure from the proponent, county commissioners, and the private party, he sent a letter to the proponent . . . acknowledging the proponent's choice to sell the improvements to the private party" (USDA 1998b:8). In a meeting held in August 1998 among OGC legal staff and USFS regional employees, the USFS regional lands director stated that the acting forest supervisor's letter had been "issued in error." In fact, the forest supervisor had lacked authority to make any decision on the Zephyr Cove improvements.

Eventually, on July 11, 1997, Olympic recorded the third warranty deed, which this time contained some vague improvements reservation language.

The OGC opinion, though, confirmed that whenever "significant terms of the reservation, such as the area encumbered by the improvements, purpose of use, and duration are not spelled out, this document is void for vagueness" (USDA 1998b:20). Neither the BLM nor the USFS had any knowledge of this third revised recording. A few days earlier, Olympic had transferred title to the improvements to Park Cattle Co., which then took possession of the 46-acre Zephyr Cove estate and locked the gates to the property.

At the same time, however, the USFS regional lands staff started to negotiate with Park to resolve the issue. By May 1998, the parties had begun negotiations toward the conclusion of a land exchange with Park. Despite receiving the OGC's opinion to the contrary, the USFS had continued negotiations over the contested six acres of Zephyr Cove and was considering providing Park with a parcel necessary to develop a commercial venture on national forest lands. The USFS had already agreed to pay for the appraisal expenses of this proposed swap. At this point, though, concurring with the OGC's opinion that the USFS was the legal owner of Zephyr Cove and its improvements, the OIG recommended that the agency "cease all actions with the private party . . . concerning the future use of Zephyr Cove lands and improvements until the ownership issues relating to the improvements [are] resolved" (USDA 1998b:16).

USDA OIG August 1998 audit report on the Humboldt-Toiyabe National Forest Land Adjustment Program

In August 1998, the USDA OIG released its audit report on the land adjustment program of the Humboldt-Toiyabe National Forest in Nevada. The report found that USFS management had allowed proponents to unduly influence its own employees.

In one instance, the USFS had failed to control one of its bargaining teams in the completion of a land exchange. The team did not follow the Headquarters' or the OGC's guidelines and allowed the proponent to take complete control of the process. It excluded USFS appraisers from the bargaining process but accepted the appraisal of a fee appraiser nominated by the private proponent. This appraisal was based on unsubstantiated assumptions. This particular land exchange cost the government $5.9 million.

The OIG audit found that in three other exchanges, the USFS had accepted appraisals based on assumptions and speculations, leading to overvaluations of offered lands. In these cases, the agency's regional and district management had allowed the proponents to challenge the appraisals of USFS staff appraisers. Thus the agency had compromised the independence of its own staff.

The OIG also found instances where the integrity of agency personnel had been compromised. One USFS manager had received and accepted gifts from an exchange proponent. Evidence showed that two other employees in key management positions had failed to disclose financial information that could demonstrate a conflict of interest. The OIG's audit report was initiated following a May 10, 1996, whistleblower report of improprieties of USFS land swap practices in Nevada. The first major finding of the audit report was related to the improper bargaining process adopted by the regional USFS in its dealings with an exchange proponent and third-party facilitators in a land swap. In this instance, the bargaining team had violated express guidelines provided by the USFS Headquarters and the OGC. The team had allowed the third-party facilitator to assume control of the land exchange and approve a land transaction that caused the federal government to lose up to $5.9 million. The regional USFS staff had approved an appraisal based on uncorroborated assumptions which had overvalued the offered lands.

This land swap, known as the Deer Creek Exchange, had started with the proposal conveyed to the BLM in the fall of 1993 by a third-party facilitator on behalf of an investment group. The proposal was to acquire some of the agency's lands in exchange for 459 acres of private property known as Deer Creek. The previous year the same investment group had acquired Deer Creek for $2 million. Deer Creek was located within a national forest. Therefore, once the exchange was completed, it would have been retransferred by the BLM to the USFS. Since the facilitator was short $8.5 million in her offer of private lands, she added the Deer Creek property to meet the balance. On August 2, 1994, the private party's appraiser valued this property at $12.5 million. The appraiser found a 614% increase in the value of the parcel, which two years earlier had been transferred for $2 million. The USFS appraisers rejected the appraisal because it was in violation of the UASFLA. By the following year, USFS had rejected four other valuations. At this point the USFS Washington Office suggested that the regional staff begin bargaining under FLEFA provisions. The RO created a bargaining team. The USFS Headquarters provided the following specific guidelines for the bargaining team:

- bargaining had to begin from the agency-approved value of $4.6 million;
- any new information presented by the proponents had to be reviewed by the regional appraiser to ensure its relevance;
- divergent values had to be reconciled by the regional appraiser; and
- any bargaining decision that changed the agency-approved value had to be discussed with the regional appraiser before the new value was finalized (USDA 1998a:7–8).

The OGC added other legal requirements according to FLPMA and FLEFA. The GC required that the appraisal be determined according to UASFLA and that only those appraisals in conformance with federal standards be used as a base for negotiation. On March 13, 1996, the same day that the OGC issued its legal opinion, the bargaining team signed an exchange agreement with the proponent.

At the completion of the audit, the OIG found that the USFS bargaining team had violated both the guidelines and the legal opinion "by using invalid appraisals, letting the proponent . . . control the bargaining process, failing to reconcile the differences in the appraisals, and excluding the participation of qualified Federal appraisers to review the new valuation" (USDA 1998a:8). As confirmed by the USFS Chief Appraiser, the team had accepted an appraisal that violated federal appraisal standards. In addition, the bargaining team had failed to follow the legal procedures of FLEFA.

The bargaining process had started in December of 1995. At that time, only one of the previous five land appraisals met federal standards. That appraisal valued the offered land at $4.6 million. All the other appraisals had either become outdated or were void or unusable because of zoning changes. Only appraisals in conformance to federal appraisal standards may be used in the bargaining process. The bargaining team violated regulatory requirements and used three appraisals that violated federal standards. In this instance "the senior member of the FS bargaining team approved the use of these invalid appraisals without consulting the regional appraiser" (USDA 1998a:9).

According to interviews with members of the team, they had shown up at each meeting unprepared. Throughout the process "they simply accepted the proponent's claims that qualified Federal appraisers from both the FS and BLM had undervalued the Deer Creek land" (USDA 1998a:10). The bargaining team had failed to bargain!

Eventually, the appraiser used three different appraisals, all in violation of federal standards, as the basis for the new valuation. On December 8, 1995, the appraiser submitted the new valuation of the Deer Creek land, finding it to be worth $10,520,000. This valuation was invalid because "it was not a reconciliation of appraisals meeting Federal appraisal standards" (USDA 1998a:11). According to the audit report, this valuation was based exclusively on financial data coming from void and outdated appraisals, complemented only by the new appraiser's assumptions. Every member of the bargaining team accepted the new valuation.

At this stage, the bargaining team had requested the fee appraiser to state in a letter that he had conducted an appraisal review, even though he had actually performed an appraisal. Under USFS regulations, in order to use an appraisal to complete a land exchange the valuation must be reviewed for approval. In violation of the USFS Washington Office's guidelines, the bargaining team failed to submit the new valuation to the regional appraiser for review and final approval.

The senior member of the bargaining team was advised by the Washington Office that the new valuation had to be considered a new appraisal and had to be reviewed for approval. Once again, the bargaining team failed to follow the instructions of the Washington Office and signed the bargaining agreement. Later on, a member of the bargaining team told the OIG auditors that she was concerned about the new valuation, but the senior member had overruled her.

On March 13, 1996, each member of the bargaining team signed the acceptance of the new valuation. During that and the following day, the Washington Office Chief Appraiser communicated with one of the members of the bargaining team by email regarding the future review of the appraisal. At no time during these email exchanges did the member ever mention that the team had already signed the bargaining agreement.

The OIG eventually requested a review of the $10.5 million valuation of the offered lands. It was determined that the new valuation was an appraisal and not a review as purported by the bargaining team. The USFS Chief Appraiser conducted the review of the new Deer Creek valuation and concluded that not only it was in violation of federal law, and thus unusable, but that it also overvalued the property by $5 million.

The OIG later requested a legal opinion by the OGC of the actions of the bargaining team and their compliance with the GC's criteria formulated on March 13, 1996. The opinion confirmed that the team had failed to follow the legal criteria and directives of the OGC. According to the legal opinion, the team had failed to act prudently and had not protected the public interest.

The OIG recommended that the USFS consider disciplinary measures against each member of the team. In addition, it recommended that none of the members of the bargaining team be allowed to "participate in future negotiations with proponents and third-party facilitators involving land exchanges" (USDA 1998a:14).

A second finding in the OIG audit was that about 83% of the land swaps conducted by the USFS in the region between 1993 and 1996 had involved the same third-party facilitator. This practice was in violation of a rule in the USFS Handbook (549.13, Section 31.8) which required the agency to negotiate directly with landowners rather than facilitators. According to the Handbook, the use of a facilitator should be restricted to instances where negotiation with a landowner was impossible.

The audit report stressed that six out of seven top priority list swaps, at the time of the audit, had been proposed by the same facilitator. In addition, it found that the RO was still entertaining land transactions with that facilitator, notwithstanding the fact that the same proposals had been previously rejected for failing to protect the public interest. The auditors concluded that the USFS's RO had failed "to maintain an impartial and businesslike relationship with [those] facilitator[s]" (USDA 1998a:17).

The third finding of the audit was that some appraisals of offered lands in the region were based not on credible evidence but on mere assumptions. The OIG found that in three cases the USFS had accepted appraisals that overstated the values of offered lands by $9 million. In these cases the "regional and lands staff compromised the integrity and independence of FS appraisers when dealing with proponents and third-party facilitators" (USDA 1998a:19). The lands staff had "openly criticized the appraisers in front of the proponents and facilitators" (1998a:19).

The report found that "FS regional lands staff allowed exchange proponents to repeatedly challenge federal appraisals until they obtained the values they desired" (USDA 1998a:28). In some instances, regional lands staff "openly questioned the objectivity and competence of their appraisers in front of the proponent" (1998a:29). In certain cases this caused staff appraisers to disapprove their own appraisals, fearing rejection by the private party. In addition, "FS regional management reorganized their appraisers to have them report directly to the regional realty officer, even though she had no training in or knowledge of Federal appraisal standards and was primarily motivated to complete land exchanges" (1998a:28). As the OIG suggested, the agency had eliminated any controls which would have guaranteed the receipt of equal value. When the OIG interviewed the regional land management, their response was that the decision to reorganize the appraisal review had been made "because the regional appraiser was arrogant and a barrier to completing land exchanges" (1998a:29).

In another instance, proponents had challenged four appraisals completed by BLM and USFS staff. The appraisers who had completed the valuations were the USFS regional appraiser and two BLM state chief appraisers, all with senior federal status and years of experience. Nevertheless, the Regional Director of Lands agreed with the proponents, undermining fellow officials. The Regional Director "characterized the Federal appraisers as 'roadblocks in the way' and 'people kicking over every stone'" (USDA 1998a:31–32). This same Director later became the senior member of the bargaining team in the Deer Creek Exchange that cost the government over $5.9 million.

Finally, a very important finding in the OIG audit report was related to the integrity of USFS regional management. This specific audit report stated that "an FS management employee received gifts, gratuities, and entertainment from a third-party facilitator" (USDA 1998a:62). Such conduct had created a conflict of interest. In addition, two other managers in the same lands section of the RO "had not filed financial disclosure statements for the last three years" (1998a:62).

The OIG had started its investigation of a specific management employee when allegations surfaced about his involvement in land dealings with the same third-party facilitator. He subsequently signed a statement "admitting the receipt of gifts, gratuities, and entertainment from third-party facilitators" (USDA 1998a:62). This conduct was in violation of the Standards of Ethical Conduct for Federal Employees, which prohibited any federal official from accepting gifts of monetary value. After the OIG informed the USFS of the employee's misconduct on January 15, 1998, the manager was reassigned to other duties and retired on April 30, 1998. However, no further action was taken.

USDA OIG April 1999 evaluation report of the Forest Service Pacific Southwest Regional Office Land Adjustment Program

In April 1999, the OIG issued its report on the USFS's Thunderbird Lodge Land Exchange at Lake Tahoe, Nevada. The OIG concluded that the acquisition of the Thunderbird Lodge by the USFS "was an inappropriate use of public resources" (USDA 1999:1). The USFS had originally scheduled the exchange for completion in two phases. In the first, the agency acquired 86 acres of private property valued at over $16 million in exchange for BLM lands in the Las Vegas area. In the second phase, the USFS would have received the remaining 54 acres of the same parcel of land encumbered with a reservation over 6.5 acres concerning the Thunderbird Lodge.[4] This second phase of the land swap, including the developed land, had been valued at $24.4 million.

The original plan of the private developer had been to transfer the acres containing the lodge to private organizations, which would have used the lodge either as a research or conference center. Neither of the two original private interested parties, though, had completed purchase of the Thunderbird structures. Therefore, the USFS was in a position to conclude the second phase. However, the exchange violated federal regulations. The USFS was about to conclude a swap of lands "encumbered by reservations or outstanding interests that would unduly interfere with their use and management as part of the National Forest System" (USDA 1999:8).

The OIG auditing team interviewed the USFS Assistant Director of Lands involved in the proposed land exchange. The Assistant Director told the team "that if the FS cannot maintain the Thunderbird structures, it will probably have to board them up" (USDA 1999:10). The auditing team concluded that the agency should not have borne that administrative burden, which failed to promote a public interest.

At this point, the OIG challenged the decision even to consider the second phase of the exchange. In fact while investigating the exchange, the auditing team uncovered some interesting details related to the first phase. Although the entire property had previously carried water rights, the private developer had "withheld the rights and assured the FS lands staff that all of the water rights would be conveyed in Phase 2" (USDA 1999:1). Questioned about the propriety of this action, the USFS lands staff expressed the idea that the agreement "to let the proponent withhold the water rights [w]as a gesture of their good faith" (1999:15).

However, the USFS lands staff had completed the first phase on the assumption that a private party or organization would acquire the Thunderbird Lodge. In fact, at the time of the beginning of the audit, the lands staff had given a verbal guarantee that phase two would not be finalized until the lodge had been transferred to either a university or non-profit organization. Later on, the agency modified its position and contemplated an exchange even though a purchaser had not been found. The USFS lands staff had justified its change of position by explaining that it was trying to engage in "an effort to be fair to the land exchange proponent" (USDA 1999:18).

---

4 In 2009, the Thunderbird Lodge Preservation Society acquired title to the mansion.

GAO 2000 report on BLM and USFS land exchanges

In June 2000, the GAO released its report on BLM and USFS land swap practices. The GAO had evaluated 51 swaps conducted by the agencies between 1989 and 1999. The major finding was that both the BLM and USFS "have given more than fair market value for nonfederal land they acquired and accepted less than fair market value for federal land they conveyed because the appraisals . . . did not always meet federal standards" (GAO 2000:4). The report also showed that both agencies had established a practice of disapproving land appraisals when they were considered unsatisfactory by proponents. New appraisals would then be prepared to accommodate the proponents.

The major concern, as seen by the GAO, was that both agencies had failed to properly value the lands involved. The report evaluated several swaps completed by the agencies. The first example was the DeMar Exchange. In this case there had been a major dispute over the valuation of the private lands. While the proponent's appraisal had valued them at $7,000 per acre, the agency's appraisal had been $1,000 per acre. The parties finally entered into a bargaining process in which the BLM agreed to value the offered lands at $7,440 per acre!

The report discussed three land swaps conducted by the USFS. In the Cashman, Deer Creek and Red Rock II Exchanges, the USFS had overvalued the offered lands by a total of about $9 million. In each instance, the agency had relied on appraisals not adequately supported by credible evidence in violation of federal standards.

The report also found that the BLM had acted in the same improper way when it completed the Zephyr Cove swap. The BLM had overvalued the private offered land by about $10 million. Similarly, in the Red Rock II Exchange, the BLM disapproved its own regional chief appraiser review "because the exchange proponent was 'unhappy' with the appraised value" (GAO 2000:18). The agency had replaced the chief appraiser with another staff appraiser to review the valuation. This time the review had conferred on the offered land a value that was $1.2 million higher than the valuation of the chief appraiser.

The report found that the same improprieties had marred the Del Webb exchange in 1997. In this swap the agency removed the Nevada State Office chief appraiser when he stated that the proponent's appraisal of the offered lands had not been in compliance with federal standards. The agency then hired an appraiser recommended by the private party to conduct the appraisal review. The BLM's Washington Office Chief Appraiser approved the appraisal. The OIG, though, launched an investigation of the swap and the agency quickly backtracked and hired a new fee appraiser for a new appraisal of the offered lands. "Had the Inspector General not intervened . . . the federal land would have been undervalued by more than $9 million" (GAO 2000:19).

USDA OIG July 2000 audit report on the Zephyr Cove Land Exchange

In July 2000, the OIG released its audit report on the Zephyr Cove Land Exchange. This followed a previous report that had focused on the owner-ship of improvements on the Zephyr Cove property. The new report cov-ered each aspect of the Zephyr Cove exchange to determine whether it had been completed in accordance with federal laws, regulations, and policies. The report analyzed both phases of the exchange: the first acquisition by the USFS of 35.4 acres of the property, and the second, in which the agency acquired the remaining 11.8 acres, including a mansion built on the prop-erty. Despite the lengthy nature of the transaction, the USFS had failed to acquire clear title to the entire property and the total cost of the transactions came to $38 million, twice the actual value of the acquired land.

The OIG concluded by summarizing the various improprieties commit-ted by USFS staff in both phases. First, the USFS had failed to oversee the employee designated to complete the exchange. This same employee misled the staff appraiser who conducted the review of the appraisal of the offered lands. This caused the government to lose money through overvaluation of the offered lands. The employee continued to take inappropriate action by drafting a letter, signed by his superior, which allowed the transfer of the mansion to a private party rather than to the USFS. In addition, he created and filed an improvement reservation on the USFS's newly acquired property. This reservation was created after the second phase of the land exchange was complete and allowed the recipients of the mansion to validate their claim.

Second, the report concluded that even the appraisal process in the swap had been questionable. Both the appraisal and its review had failed to com-ply with federal regulations. The staff appraiser had approved a valuation of $38 million, overvaluing the private property acquired by the agency. Overvaluation had already cost the agency over $20 million. The failure of the staff appraiser to follow federal standards in the appraisal process had two consequences. First, the proponent was able to profit from the sale of the property to the USFS, and, later on, another private party was able to do the same.

In its report, the OIG complained that the USFS's RO had failed to moni-tor the conduct of the staff employee who had completed the exchange:

> He exceeded his authority, withheld information from the Federal staffs normally overseeing land exchanges, failed to inform a FS appraiser about the total acreage being acquired in the land exchange and misled the FS appraiser about the future uses to which the land would be put.
>
> (USDA 2000:9–10)

As stated in the audit report, the RO had designated the staff "employee as the primary contact between FS and BLM staffs. [This choice] contributed to the errors in the Zephyr Cove land exchange" (USDA 2000:11). The employee used his position as primary contact to pass inappropriate instructions to the BLM. Originally, the BLM had felt that the specific employee was an appropriate link between the two agencies because of his seven-year seniority in the field. To make matters worse, the USFS had improperly "assumed that the . . . employee would comply with normal FS review and approval procedures and delegations of authority" (2000:11).

Ultimately "the employee took inappropriate and unauthorized actions that benefited Olympic Group, Inc. and did not protect the taxpayer interest" (USDA 2000:16). The employee had taken his actions without specific authority. The forest supervisor had designated him as the contact between the BLM and the USFS and had given him express instructions to inform the RO of any developments. Despite these specific directives, he had failed to communicate with both the BLM and the USFS. According to the audit, the employee had failed to serve the public interest because he:

- withheld information from a FS appraiser that affected the overall value of the property, benefiting the proponent;
- authorized the acquisition of the Zephyr Cove property with the improvements in place, contrary to RO direction;
- overstated the value of the property by avoiding a deed reservation, benefiting the proponent;
- created an agreement with the proponent that was not supported by the law;
- misinformed a FS appraiser about the future use of the Phase 2 property;
- did not review the Zephyr Cove deeds to ensure they did not contain unacceptable easements, benefiting both private parties;
- attempted to significantly modify the Zephyr Cove title documents after the land exchange was complete; and
- allowed the proponent to sell government-owned improvements to Park Cattle Company (USDA 2000:17).

The USFS employee continued his misconduct by "improperly instruct[ing] BLM to proceed with the land exchange even though the improvements on the Zephyr Cove property would remain in place. These actions . . . exceeded the . . . employee's delegated authority" (USDA 2000:19). He drafted an agreement allowing the proponent to retain ownership of the improvements and the option to sell the improvements to a third party. The employee then submitted the agreement for approval to the acting forest supervisor and misrepresented that he had received approval from the RO and the OGC.

Once the forest supervisor had signed this agreement, the staff employee should have mentioned the supposed prior approval of the deed that transferred the second portion of the Zephyr Cove property. Once again, the staff employee violated his delegated authority and failed to add the reservation of the improvements into the deed. This omission caused the $10 million overvaluation of the offered lands. When asked by the OIG team about his failure to add the reservation to the deed, the employee had no explanation but acknowledged that such omission "would impact the appraised value because the presence of the house would affect the new owner's use of the land" (USDA 2000:21). When he claimed a lack of recollection of the events, the employee was confronted with his notes. In fact, he had stated "in an earlier FS document that [the proponent] did not want a reservation" (2000:21).

The employee continued his misconduct when he told the staff appraiser that the improvements would be a USFS concession. The USFS had approved no such concession. However, the staff appraiser relied on this misinformation and, in his review, approved the valuation of the offered lands at $13.5 million. The "employee told the FS appraiser that the [district office] would issue a special-use permit to the private party . . . and allowed the appraiser to believe that the [district office] would collect a concessionaire fee based on a percentage of the land's fair market value" (USDA 2000:24). According to the report, this information was incorrect.

Finally, the employee, once both phases of the swap were complete, had tried to add the Code of Federal Regulations reservation into the second recorded deed. As the OIG report found, the "employee exceeded his delegated authority and took this action without informing or consulting RO staff or OGC and without considering the potential impact to Zephyr Cove's approved value" (2000:25). Two months after the swap, the employee instructed the BLM to insert the CFR reservation into the recorded deed. He explained this change by stating that "after the land exchange was completed, I somehow realized that the CFR's did apply . . . It somehow came to me that occupancy and use had to be specified in the reservation . . . I cannot recall why I reached that conclusion" (USDA 2000:26). Asked about the propriety of his actions, the employee replied "that he knew he did not have the authority to create CFR reservations" (2000:26). When confronted with the possible ramifications of his conduct, he denied any knowledge of the impact of a CFR reservation on the value of the offered lands. However, "This contradicts the . . . employee's earlier statement . . . that he knew the CFR reservation would have reduced the value of the Phase 2 property" (2000:27).

The OIG wrote that "from our conversations with the . . . employee . . . we determined that the improvement reservation was deliberately omitted from the original Zephyr Cove deed, and was not a simple mistake" (USDA 2000:44). It found that the "employee did not act . . . in the public's best interest when he processed the Zephyr Cove land exchange. He took actions that were inappropriate, unauthorized, and irresponsible" (2000:29).

According to the OIG, the review "appraiser allowed the Zephyr Cove property to be appraised as two separate transactions, rather then [sic] as a single piece of property" (USDA 2000:37). This artificial division had overvalued the property by about $8.7 million. The OIG found that "under

FS policy, the FS appraiser could have elected to appraise the entire Zephyr Cove property as one unit, even though Phase 1 of the land exchange had already been completed" (2000:37). By failing to do so, he allowed the value per linear foot to jump from $6,600 to $19,369, a 194% increase in just nine months. The OIG calculated that because of the review appraiser's lack of due care, the offered lands may have been overvalued by over $20 million.

TAF 2002 evaluation of the appraisal organization of the BLM

In August 2002, TAF released its study on the appraisal organization and practices of the BLM, including an audit of the St. George Field Office in Utah. The study was to determine what organizational changes, if any, were needed to guarantee the "protection of the integrity of the appraisal process, ensurance of accountability of appraisers in accordance with industry standards, identification of ways to prevent management interference, and provision of ensurance of separation of negotiations and the appraisal process" (TAF 2002:4). Thus, TAF visited seven western state agency offices to interview staff and examine files. As TAF discovered, despite extensive searches, important files related to swaps completed by the St. George Field Office were missing.

The results of the interviews allowed TAF to conclude that in the appraisal process "the integrity of the BLM and its appraisers is placed in jeopardy when program management, or the malfeasance of individuals, destroys the independence and objectivity that are required of appraisers by law" (2002:7). In particular, TAF found that BLM management in general, and specifically in Utah, felt "that staff appraisers [were] slow, expensive, and/or unresponsive to BLM or project team goals" (2002:7). In addition, managers felt that the appraisers assumed a "biased and obstructionist" stance.

Accordingly, TAF suggested that overall the appraisal process had been clouded by outside political pressures that negatively affected the performance of the appraisers. Because of this pressure, the appraisal function had adopted practices conducive to:

- abuses of the public trust where there is failure to comply with laws or to conduct orderly operations in accordance with written guidance;
- development of a management "culture" that frequently supersedes written guidance and an administration that fosters controversy;
- interference with the technical and administrative functions of BLM appraisal staff, with resulting waste, inefficiency, abuse of law, and loss of federal monetary and natural resources;
- special treatment of non-federal interests;
- confusion over what constitutes "the public interest"; and

- pressure to charge, or to ignore, qualified market value opinions in order to create the erroneous appearance that land exchanges or transactions are conducted at market value (TAF 2002:9).

It was in this context that appraisers faced challenges by private owners over their valuations. This atmosphere, created by BLM management, encouraged criticism of the agency's appraisers, who found themselves caught between BLM management, which was interested in the successful conclusion of swaps, and private landowners, who were interested in obtaining higher values for their offered lands.

TAF started its investigation at the BLM's Headquarters in Washington, DC. The Washington Office staff discussed the concept of "BLM culture." This referred in part to unwritten policies that violated the agency's written organizational rules. Following unwritten policy, the Utah-Washington County Office had failed to keep copies of land acquisitions conducted under the alternative approach. In fact, as determined by TAF, key case file records, appraisals, and appraisal reviews for dozens of transactions in the vicinity of St. George were never found (TAF 2002:18). In addition, BLM culture damaged public trust each time management "cast doubt upon their appraisers' professional competence and independence" (2002:22).

In direct response to the supposed bias of the staff appraisers, the agency headquarters had created an alternative approach under which the interests of the private landowners would be safeguarded. TAF believed that by undermining the credibility of the appraisal staff, BLM had also undermined their independence. By involving the appraisers in the negotiations, the BLM had created a circumstance in which coercion and pressure by private parties dramatically increased.

Another instance where the BLM culture had resurfaced, according to the TAF report, related to the categorization of land exchanges as either "go or no go." According to the report, "those interviewed indicated that lands and realty specialists frequently believed, or were told, that certain exchanges must be completed" (TAF 2002:25). The problem arose when "the exchange [wa]s insisted upon by a BLM staff member, manager, or other person of authority, regardless of the reason or motivation" (2002:25). This would be a clear instruction to the appraiser that accurate valuations were unwelcome because "if an owner wants more, the only way this can be accomplished is by changing the asserted market value of the proponent's lands to a higher number and/or reducing the asserted market value of the BLM's lands" (2002:25).

The "alternative approach" had been specifically created and implemented "to promote the BLM's ability to carry out its policy . . . that owners be able to 'feel comfortable that they are treated fairly avoiding the biases of BLM appraisers'" (TAF 2002:28). According to the report, the purpose of the "alternative approach" was to show deference to the private parties so their views would be reflected in final valuations.

In these circumstances, appraisers felt wary about any pressure placed upon them to be available to proponents. In addition, "By resisting situations that challenge[d] the independence required of appraisers, BLM staff appraisers risk[ed] their jobs and/or their levels of compensation" (TAF 2002:31). When appraisers expressed professional concerns over valuations, they were "criticized with assertions of bias and/or intent to impose their personal views on the BLM" (2002:32). In these cases, whenever management or land specialists and appraisal staff had disagreed over valuations, the former attempted "to educate the appraisers to better understand the importance of a transaction or exchange" (2002:34). This practice compromised the appraisers' independence, which

[wa]s challenged by management and land specialists who place[d] responsibility on the team responsibilities of the appraiser to develop value opinions that will be acceptable to owners and thereby permit[ted] the closing of exchanges or other land transactions. In some instances, private property owners ha[d] been provided continuing direct access to appraisers and their data, and an opportunity to intercede in ongoing appraisal analysis. Owners ha[d] been given assurances of explicit value determinations, or the avoidance of selected BLM appraisers, by land specialists and/ or management prior to the completion and review of qualified appraisals.

(TAF 2002:34)

Finally, TAF evaluated the alternative approach. After conducting interviews with BLM staff, the TAF team found that "when BLM Washington, D.C. management staff and/or higher authority within the BLM or the DOI are involved in land transactions or exchanges, the most serious controversies and applications of the alternative approach are likely to be found" (TAF 2002:44). TAF found that in each controversial case, the Washington Office had been involved. Controversial cases occurred only in those state offices where State Directors were political appointees. The report concluded that there was a relationship between the Washington Headquarters' approval of the "alternative approach" and the selection of political appointees as state directors. The stronger the chance of sponsorship by the Washington office management, the stronger was political influence in the selection of the agency state director.

Finally, the report discussed the conduct of the BLM's Senior Specialist-Appraisal. According to the report, some of his appraisal reviews were in violation of professional and federal standards. In addition, TAF found that "his actions in connection with the alternative approach went beyond the limits permitted to protect his independence from the outcome of appraisals in which he was involved" (TAF 2002:46). TAF stopped short of publicly accusing the Senior Specialist but hinted at the fact that likely only "the absence of BLM records that would have been used in such evaluation"

(2002:46) had stopped the team from doing so. The team concluded, in accordance with its interviews of BLM personnel, that "the Senior Specialist-Appraisal exhibited bias with regard to application of appraisal standards and the operation of the BLM's appraisal function in his Washington County, Utah conduct. . . . These actions have resulted in a circumvention or misapplication of [appraisal] standards" (2002:47).

Conclusions

Several recurring issues are evident when the reports issued by the GAO, TAF, and the OIGs are examined together. Appraisers are blamed for a failure to account for different values, whether economic, cultural, historical, or environmental, and this failure always ends up negatively affecting the government by causing an increase in the valuation of the offered lands. In other instances, unskilled or incompetent personnel reject or approve land appraisals (USDA 2000; TAF 2002). In some cases, they even fail to oversee the work of their subordinates (DOI 1991). Simultaneously, the agencies fail to obtain equal value (GAO 1987; GAO 2000). Unclear departmental policies are blamed for lack of consistency throughout the different agencies' offices in the U.S. (GAO 1987). However, the consistency in the data demonstrates that valuations of federal lands are frequently lowered (DOI 1991). In addition, the agencies' personnel fail to consistently disclose information vital for an equal value determination (DOI 1998). These personnel even disregard legal opinions issued by the OGC (DOI 1998). Finally, some employees receive gifts from proponents, fail to disclose their financial information or conflict of interest, or give preferential treatment to the proposals of a facilitator (DOI 1998). These omissions are too systematic to be simple mistakes (DOI 1998).

The agencies, especially the BLM, clearly demonstrated their greater interest in pacifying local, county, and state politicians and streamlining the process for an expeditious transfer of federal land ownership into private hands rather than protecting the public interest by obtaining equal value (DOI 1996). In these cases, the "code words" used by the agency refer to the "essential tool" of land exchanges as "a management measure" to assist local and state governments in the reconfiguration of their land assets (TAF 2002). Agency officials are always under pressure from proponents, whose actions create conflicts of interest among agency personnel (DOI 1996). These practices create issues of lack of accountability of agency staff (DOI 1998). This is especially true in those instances where appraisers are reassigned when they fail to obey and instead "kick over every stone." Appraisers are deemed "obstructionist" when they submit valuations not identical with the appraisals of proponents (DOI 1998). A lack of accountability allows regional and local management to publicly challenge and criticize the appraisals of staff appraisers whenever a private party becomes dissatisfied with their work (DOI 1998). Ultimately, these actions question the authority of the appraisers and undermine their independence from external pressure (DOI 1998; TAF 2000).

It is evident that the BLM believes its organizational structure, especially with regard to the alternative approach, is partly to blame for swaps that fail to serve the public interest. However, the alternative approach is not used by the USFS. This demonstrates that in the USFS, loss of value in land swaps may be due to individual malfeasance (DOI 1998; TAF 2000). Private parties pressure managers and employees in the lands and realty offices of both agencies who, by profession, training, and attitude, already embrace a utilitarian view of natural resources (DOI 1998). This leads them to accommodate the concerns of private landowners (DOI 1998). These line officers are evaluated solely in terms of successfully completing swaps (DOI 1996).

These circumstances, combined with serious budget limitations which started in the Reagan administration, may ultimately lead a superior to reject an appraisal deemed too low by the private party and then rubber-stamp a new valuation. This seriously undermines the chances of receiving equal value (DOI 1996). In such cases, subsequent improper reviews are conducted that consistently fail to correct the undervaluation of federal lands or the overvaluation of private lands (DOI 1996). Such reviews complete the last phase of the land swap without properly demonstrating the public interest in the transaction (DOI 1996).

TAF found that undue influence is part of the danger of an appraiser's career (TAF 2000). Its findings show how important it is to protect staff and fee appraisers from the influence of the land and realty management (TAF 2000). In addition to protecting appraisers, Congress should provide a more serious set of consequences, including criminal prosecution, in those cases where evidence of malice or negligence is found by investigators. These more serious consequences are necessary because it has been regular practice for the last several decades to punish cases of malfeasance with only mild disciplinary measures such as transfer to a new position. These measures have been quite ineffective in preventing malfeasance. No criminal action has been initiated over a land exchange since 1905. It is time to reconsider restoring that option.

Table of Cases

Donna & Larry Charpied, 150 IBLA 314 (1999)
Desert Citizens Against Pollution v. Bisson, 231 F.3d 1172 (9th Cir. 2000)
National Parks & Conservation Ass'n (NPCA) v. BLM, 586 F.3d 735 (9th Cir. 2009)

References

The Appraisal Foundation. (2000). *Evaluation of the Appraisal Organization of the USDA Forest Service.* Washington, DC: The Appraisal Foundation.

The Appraisal Foundation. (2002). *Evaluation of the Appraisal Organizations of the Department of Interior Bureau of Land Management: Including a Special Evaluation of an Alternative Approach Used in St. George, Utah.* Washington, DC: The Appraisal Foundation.

U.S. Department of Agriculture. (1998a). *Land Adjustment Program: Fiscal Years 1990 to 1997* (USDA Report No. 08003–02-SF). Sparks, NV: Author.

U.S. Department of Agriculture. (1998b). *Title to Physical Improvements on the Zephyr Cove Land Exchange* (USDA Report No. 08003–4-SF). South Lake Tahoe, CA: Lake Tahoe Basin Management Unit.

U.S. Department of Agriculture. (1999). *Thunderbird Lodge Land Exchange* (USDA Report No. 08801–5-SF). South Lake Tahoe, CA: Lake Tahoe Basin Management Unit.

U.S. Department of Agriculture. (2000). *Audit Report: Zephyr Cove Land Exchange* (USDA Report No. 08003–6-SF). South Lake Tahoe, CA: Lake Tahoe Basin Management Unit.

U.S. Department of the Interior. (1991). *Audit Report: Land Exchange Activities* (USDI Report No. 91-I-968). Washington, DC: U.S. Government Printing Office.

U.S. Department of the Interior. (1996). *Audit Report: Nevada Land Exchange Activities* (USDI Report No. 96-I-1025). Washington, DC: U.S. Government Printing Office.

U.S. Department of the Interior. (1998). *Audit Report: Followup of Nevada Land Exchange activities* (USDI Report No. 98-I-689). Washington, DC: U.S. Government Printing Office.

U.S. Department of the Interior. (2001). *Land Exchanges and Acquisitions* (USDI Report No. 2001-I-413). Sacramento, CA: U.S. Department of the Interior.

U.S. General Accounting Office. (1987). *Federal Land Acquisition: Land Exchange Process Working But Can Be Improved.* Washington, DC: U.S. Government Printing Office.

U.S. General Accounting Office. (2000). *BLM and the Forest Service: Land Exchanges Need to Reflect Appropriate Value and Serve the Public Interest.* Washington, DC: U.S. Government Printing Office.

6 Improving the land exchange process

Elizabeth Kitchens, a business lawyer, has reviewed federal land exchanges from a legal perspective. Her study claims "to present a straightforward explanation of the exchange process, [by] viewing federal land exchanges as real estate transactions" (Kitchens 2000:22–23) between landowners. She finds the land exchange process, as implemented by the BLM and the USFS, to be "long and winding" (2000:22–51). However, she also acknowledges that federal land swaps have "helped numerous proponents to achieve their private development goals" (2000:22–50). She believes the best use of public lands is in terms of the potential resource value of the selected land.

Kitchens adopts a utilitarian-conservationist position and argues that public lands should be kept under government ownership until ripe for development. Thus, according to her, the most controversial swaps should be considered those initiated by the federal government to acquire large amounts of land, since their benefits to the public are debatable. Throughout her study she shows a tendency to see land as just a commodity, and she is more concerned with the "negative" effects of exchanges that dedicate large land areas to a dominant use (such as habitat protection) rather than with swaps directed at developing resources.

By turning her study into a legal guide to public lands acquisition, Kitchens gives instructions to her pro-development audience and stresses that a private party "must be proactive and have the staying power to maneuver through the lengthy bureaucratic process, maintaining the interest and support of the federal land management agency. When the agency and the proponent cooperate and coordinate their efforts, a land exchange represents a win-win situation for all parties" (Kitchens 2000:22–51).

Kitchens guides readers through the swap process and recommends that private parties always initiate the swap and create favorable conditions for a working relationship with agency staff. She suggests that private parties demonstrate their willingness to cooperate with agencies by taking advantage of the fact that the government always has staffing and funding shortages. Her message is that swap proponents should proactively assist agency staff as much as possible. Given the agencies' shortages of staff and funding, private developers should provide their own funds and personnel to facilitate and expedite the process. However, Kitchens does not take into consideration that this could create conflicts of interest for agency personnel. Clearly, she is not concerned that the government actually loses value in some exchanges.

Kitchens accepts faulty appraisals so long as the private developers are not held administratively, civilly, or criminally liable for them. Her recipe for success is a proponent's retaining "the power to maneuver through the lengthy bureaucratic process, [and] maintaining the interest and support of the federal land management agency" (Kitchens 2000:22–51). For Kitchens, it is an issue of cooperation and coordination, but she disregards whether the equal value and public interest requirements are actually met.

Introduction

Kitchens' article should be a reminder about what dangers lurk if developers get to control the appraisal process conducted by federal land agencies. Thus, this chapter examines a number of additional audits, distilling from them certain lessons for successful, corruption-free land swaps. It analyzes OIG, TAF, and GAO recommendations for improving the land-swap process and reviews how the BLM and USFS have received those recommendations. The final section of this chapter will discuss how these land-swap procedures might be further improved to avoid corruption and ensure fairness.

Summary of studies analyzing recommendations implemented by BLM and USFS

In May 2003, the Appraisal and Exchange Workgroup issued its final report on BLM land exchange appraisals. This report was aimed at providing urgent changes that would improve public confidence in BLM land exchanges. The Workgroup was spurred by the criticism faced by the BLM due to the previous reports published by the GAO, OIG, and TAF.

The Workgroup concluded that an organizational restructuring was necessary and recommended reorganizing the supervision and delegation of authority, applying established appraisal standards, and involving appraisers in early stages of any land swap. Furthermore, it recommended that an independent appraisal organization be established under the supervision of the DOI Chief Appraiser. This reorganization would end conflicts of interest among the Bureau's realty managers by creating an independent corps of appraisers. The Workgroup emphasized that realty managers should not be involved in land valuations and that discussions over value should be undertaken only after a proper appraisal had been completed.

Finally, the Workgroup studied the issue of public interest determinations. It addressed the reports by the GAO and OIG on the failure of the BLM to serve the public interest in land exchanges. It recommended changing the appraisal review policy to make sure that future decisions adequately document their public interest determinations.

In September 2006, the DOI OIG released a report on its study of the DOI appraisal services. Three years earlier, the DOI had consolidated the appraisal services of each of its agencies into the newly created Appraisal Services Directorate (ASD). Due to a shortage of staff, appraisers the ASD had been using contract appraisers. It was of the utmost importance to choose qualified contract appraisers to ensure that appraisals met federal standards.

However, the OIG found that the DOI's appraisal policies and procedures did not fully ensure compliance with standards. Even worse, the government had limited assurance that the valuations actually reflected market value. The OIG made recommendations to ensure the ASD would establish a periodic monitoring system for appraisals.

The ASD has not yet established a system for ensuring that appraisal reviews are performed consistently. ASD review appraisers still exercise significant discretion in how they perform appraisal reviews. In addition, the ASD lacks a management control program to ensure that appraisers conduct appraisals and reviews in accordance with applicable standards. Therefore, the OIG suggested measures that would assure ongoing monitoring of appraisal operations. However, that would solve only part of the issue. In fact, the OIG report uncovered another, even more serious problem: the Pacific Region's lack of proper appraisal document retention practices. At the time of the investigation, appraisers in ASD's Pacific Region could not locate nearly two-thirds of their appraisal reports.

The GAO issued its own report on the BLM and USFS land exchange processes in June 2009. As the GAO reported, officials of both agencies pointed out that the number of land swaps had declined since 2000 because of shortages of both qualified staff and funding. The GAO also discussed the issue of changing priorities at both agencies, which had shifted focus from land swaps to administrative land sales. The GAO then discussed the new nature of the land exchanges processed by the two agencies: swaps facilitated by third parties or conducted in multiple phases. As to facilitators, the GAO reported that the former often increased the pressure to complete land swaps and attempted to skew appraisals in their favor. As to multiphase exchanges, the GAO discussed the BLM's practice of tracking land value imbalances by using ledgers. However, since the BLM was not following its own bookkeeping rules, there is no certainty how much money was owed to the agency.

Afterwards, the GAO discussed a series of key problems raised in this and previous reports. Although the GAO pointed out that the most problems surround the legitimacy of appraisals, the report confirmed that no review of any appraisals had been conducted. The GAO was worried that neither BLM nor USFS could in all cases provide copies of key documents, including appraisal reviews. The GAO found that neither agency could provide any feasibility or decision review whatsoever.

Finally, though the GAO declined to evaluate appraisals, it did discuss the two agencies' restructuring of their appraisal functions. The restructuring of the appraisal function within the entire DOI led to a 2006 review of the new appraisal structure within the ASD. The GAO found that the DOI needed to take further steps to ensure that land transactions are based on appraisals adhering to recognized standards. On the other hand, the USFS created an independent organization within the agency by placing all appraisers under the direct supervision of a regional appraiser, who in turn was under the direct supervision of the regional director with land program responsibilities. The ultimate supervision of USFS appraisals by realty management was, and is, the opposite of the full independence of appraisers under the ASD.

In December 2009, the OIG issued its report on the ASD's appraisal function. The OIG found these appraisal operations to be impeded by several factors. The OIG found that the ASD was not a strong and independent organization. Interviews with staff in the different DOI agencies confirmed that each agency had repeatedly acted to regain control of appraisals, undermining the ASD. The failure of the DOI to intervene on behalf of the ASD had weakened it further. Furthermore, the absence of true leadership had rendered the ASD a dependent office. The original ASD Chief Appraiser quit his position in 2006; since then, the position has been filled on an interim basis only. Without a strong Chief Appraiser, the ASD could not become the organization envisioned at its inception.

Finally, on December 23, 2010, the GAO issued its most recent report on the BLM's land-swap practices. The GAO studied two particular assembled land exchanges completed by the BLM in California and Washington State. The GAO found that BLM had disguised impermissible land sales and purchases under the rubric of FLPMA swaps. In addition, BLM had failed to deposit into a specific fund of the U.S. Treasury the proceeds of these land sales, in violation of the Miscellaneous Receipts Statute. Once again, the GAO uncovered evidence that BLM, 10 years after the prior GAO study, was still bending the law to complete public land sales and use the proceeds to finance the purchase of private lands in violation of FLPMA.

DOI 2003 appraisal and Appraisal and Exchange Workgroup final report

In May 2003, the Appraisal and Exchange Workgroup (AEW) issued its final report on the BLM's appraisals and land exchanges. In February 2003, the BLM had commissioned this study in response to TAF's negative 2002 review of the agency's land swaps. The BLM formed the Workgroup with experts in land exchanges from the BLM, the DOI, the USFS, the Department of Justice, and state agencies in California, Colorado, and Idaho. Its purpose was "to provide definitive advice on how to make urgent and needed changes ... that ... will improve and restore public confidence in the BLM's Appraisal and Land Exchange programs" (AEW 2003:3).

The Workgroup found "serious and fundamental problems with the BLM appraisal program that require organizational restructuring" (AEW 2003:3). It recommended that the BLM reorganize the supervision and delegation of authority, apply established appraisal standards, and involve appraisers early in the process of a land swap. Given the inappropriate influence exerted on staff appraisers, the Workgroup recommended the creation of a separate and independent appraisal organization supervised by the DOI's Chief Appraiser (2003:4). According to the Workgroup, this reorganization "would prevent conflicts of interest with the realty function and enhance the independence of appraisers within the BLM" (2003:4). As for the application of established standards, the Workgroup pointed out that multiple reports had found the BLM's appraisals to be in violation of federally mandated standards (2003:4).

To correct such issues, the Workgroup recommended the early involvement of appraisers and the importance of effective supervision of appraisal staff to avoid inappropriate pressure from private parties. It recommended that experienced senior staff appraisers supervise line appraisers to counter that pressure (AEW 2003:4). Furthermore, the Workgroup acknowledged the flexibility that the use of private contractors provided. However, it suggested, "The BLM staff, rather than contractors, must manage . . . review appraisal products to assure the appropriate link to the needs of the BLM and to perform this inherently federal responsibility" (2003:5).

The Workgroup also discussed the resolution of disputes over the values of lands. The report stressed the importance of minimizing any procedural deviation from federally approved appraisal standards (AEW 2003:7). Among its recommendations, it emphasized training by which "managers recognize the potential for unreasonable expectations of value and either actively work to resolve those expectations, or make a decision not to proceed with the transaction" (2003:7). The report stressed the importance that appraisals should be completed even before any discussions over land values are conducted by management (2003:7–8).

Finally, the Workgroup addressed the BLM's public interest determinations. It reiterated the importance of stressing to BLM staff that the purpose of FLPMA's land swap regulatory authority remains the facilitating and expediting of land transactions to further the public interest (AEW 2003:47). Concerns addressed by the GAO and OIG about the failure of land swaps to serve the public interest "partially originated with the lack of quality documentation associated with land exchange public interest determination in land exchange decision documents" (2003:47). In response to these concerns, the Workgroup recommended that future appraisal-review documentation ensure that land swap decisions accurately and adequately address the public interest determination as the foundation for the exchange (2003:47).

Reorganize supervision and delegation of authority

By consulting with the GAO, OIG, and TAF, the Workgroup collected evidence of malfeasance by BLM personnel. It found that "responsible Bureau personnel did not effectively review land appraisals or properly prepare the required documentation on 71 of the 78 appraisals . . . reviewed" (AEW 2003:13). The BLM had "established land values based on appraisals that were not timely, independent, or adequately supported by market data" (2003:13). As for the organizational structure of the BLM, the Workgroup learned that TAF had found no real appraisal organization in place (2003:13). The Workgroup reached the conclusion "that the findings of the OIG, GAO and TAF reports . . . reveal symptoms of a deeper, core problem, that is, the organizational structure of the BLM's appraisal function is flawed, disjointed, and disconnected" (2003:13). According to the Workgroup, due to the commingling of the appraisal and realty functions, the BLM failed to provide an organizational structure guaranteeing independent appraisals free of undue pressure (2003:13).

The report suggested that the BLM create an independent appraisal organization. Ultimately, "the intent [is] to find an appropriate level of separation and independence between the appraisal and realty functions" (AEW 2003:13). The preferred recommendation of the Workgroup was to completely restructure the BLM's appraisal organization under the supervision of the DOI Chief Appraiser (2003:13). This reorganization would help prevent conflicts of interest among realty staff that affect appraiser impartiality, independence, and objectivity (2003:14). This would provide an organization change in which appraisers would "report to, and be supervised by, senior professional appraisers" (2003:14).

The rationale behind this recommendation was to create a structure that would curtail the "persistently evident instances of inappropriate pressure on appraisers to perform appraisals under duress and with a prescribed outcome" (AEW 2003:14). The Workgroup tried to provide a solution to the weaknesses in the BLM's appraisal organization found by the previous GAO, OIG, and TAF reports. According to those reports, these weaknesses flowed directly from ill-defined channels of supervision of and authority over appraisal staff (2003:14). The problem at that time was that the supervision of appraisers had been delegated to realty "managers who ha[d] no professional valuation experience or training and whose oversight of appraisal function conflict[ed] with their interest in the outcome of the realty transaction" (2003:14). The Workgroup report used the USFS's restructuring of its own appraisal program as a model because it had lessened the general perception of inappropriate pressure. Indeed, "Though USFS staff appraisers and contract appraisers still suffer some incidents of inappropriate pressure, the occurrences have been reduced dramatically over the past three years" (2003:15).

According to the Workgroup, this restructuring would:

- address the concerns of TAF and the OIG regarding the ability of the Bureau to provide unbiased valuation services that meet professional standards;
- create an organization that better insulates appraisers from management pressures;
- create an avenue of recourse for appraisers when confronted with inappropriate pressure to report artificial appraisal results;
- facilitate use of contract appraisers when appropriate and eliminate duplication of administrative overhead in appraisal contracting services; and
- restore public confidence in the department's valuation and realty staffs (2003:15).

Apply established appraisal standards

The Workgroup cited previous reports on BLM's misapplication of federal appraisal standards. For example, an "OIG audit . . . reported that the government's interest had not been properly protected and that the government had not received fair value for the land exchanged because the appraisal used by the BLM did not comply with federal appraisal standards" (AEW 2003:21). According to the Workgroup, in another instance, the BLM's office in Washington, DC, "did not fully conform to established standards . . . for appraisals and land valuations. As a result, if the Bureau had not obtained a second appraisal, the Government would have lost $9.1 million on the federal land selected for exchange" (2003:21). In addition, the report cited the GAO's 2000 findings that BLM and USFS had relinquished more than fair market value for the offered land and accepted less than fair market value for the selected land. In each instance, the appraisals used by the agencies violated federal standards (AEW 2003:21). The Workgroup cited another OIG report finding that appraisal reviews completed by a BLM staff appraiser in violation of federal standards were evidence that the independence and objectivity of the appraisal function had been compromised (2003:21). Finally, the Workgroup adopted the findings of the 2002 TAF report. Accordingly, the Workgroup reached the conclusion that realty management practices challenged the Bureau's ability and objectivity in the application of federal appraisal standards (2003:21).

The Workgroup stressed the importance of following what the law, in this case BLM regulations and procedure, prescribes. As the report stressed, the purpose of these policies is the protection of the integrity and independence of appraisers (AEW 2003:22). However, as the Workgroup pointed out, in "numerous cases cited over the past 12 years . . . practices of the BLM were in direct conflict with appraisal standard requirements. This has led to abuses of the appraisal process" (2003:22). On this issue, the Workgroup concluded, the status quo encouraged the neglect of proper appraisal standards (2003:22). Thus, the Workgroup recommended that the BLM perform all valuations in accordance with nationally recognized standards, and apply terms such as "appraisals" according to recognized standards rather than the layperson's interpretation (2003:22).

According to the Workgroup, BLM adoption of nationally recognized appraisal standards would:

- result in consistent work products throughout the agency;
- improve public trust and confidence in the BLM's appraisal and land exchange programs; and
- improve the quality of the work products because consistent criteria are more easily enforced and less subject to dispute (AEW 2003:22).

Involve appraisers early

According to the Workgroup's report, one cause of the problem was that appraisals take place at the late stages of a swap, leaving less time to complete a professional appraisal and its reviews (AEW 2003:23). The consequence is: "This environment creates the opportunity for inappropriate pressure on the appraiser to complete the appraisal or appraisal review without providing adequate time to do the work and meet all professional requirements" (2003:23). The result of this time pressure is an appraisal and review unsupported by sufficient evidence that become a means of facilitating the swap at all costs (2003:23).

In order to fix this problem, the Workgroup recommended that BLM "create an organizational structure that places responsibility for managing inappropriate pressure and the improper introduction of bias in the hands of experienced valuation staff" (AEW 2003:23). This could be accomplished by appropriate supervision of appraisers by senior appraisers, which would diminish undue pressure (2003:23). As the Workgroup tried to find a solution to this issue, the newly created supervision by senior appraisers would somewhat alleviate what is commonly perceived as internal pressure to deliver the appraisal on an unrealistic timeframe (2003:23). It is in precisely such circumstances that poor appraisals are made.

The implementation of this recommendation would:

- prevent "short cutting" of the process and produce[s] quality valuation products;
- provide clear direction and requirements to prepare and complete a valuation product;
- provide more supportable and defensible documents and decisions;
- provide supervision of the appraisal function by professionals with knowledge of the specific time, resource, and information requirements for completing quality valuations;

- eliminate unreasonable pressure or expectations that may introduce bias or abuse into the appraisal function; and
- result in fewer disruptions to the Bureau's realty transactions since senior qualified appraisal staff address problems (AEW 2003:23–24).

Continue current level of contracting

Another problem addressed by the Workgroup was the number of private appraisers used. According to the report, the BLM always acquiesced to a proponent's request to hire their appraiser, allowing it to submit appraisals completed without adequate BLM oversight (AEW 2003:24). "Such proponent appraisals typically do not meet accepted standards . . . These proponent-procured appraisals often exhibit considerable bias" (2003:24). The Workgroup found that the root causes of the sustained use of contract appraisers were an insufficient number of staff appraisers and the decentralized and scattered appraisal assignments due to the remoteness of the selected or offered lands (2003:24).

The Workgroup recommended that the BLM maintain the current number of staff appraisers and use an appropriate number of efficient and independent private appraisers (AEW 2003:24). The goal was "to develop and maintain a cadre of well-qualified contract appraisers to serve the BLM appraisal needs and provide service that is appropriate for the BLM mission and timing" (2003:24). Along with this cadre, the Workgroup envisioned the training of skilled staff appraisers to maintain quality control by overseeing contract appraisers (2003:24). However, if a swap included a proponent-funded appraisal, some safeguards needed to be in place to protect the public interest. These safeguards included the following:

- appraisers must be preapproved by the BLM;
- reports must contain a copy of the BLM-provided appraisal instructions including the requirement that the appraisal be prepared in conformance with UASFLA and USPAP; and
- qualified BLM Review Appraisers are responsible for the appraisal review process (AEW 2003:25).

The goal of these recommendations was to maintain public trust in the appraisal of properties in the expanding world of land transactions (AEW 2003:25). In order to do that, the Workgroup suggested, "The BLM must more closely control contract appraiser selection" (2003:25). The assumption made by the Workgroup was that the present ratio of staff to private appraisers was adequate (2003:25). As the report stated, "Given staff limitations, contracting provides important appraisal capability, flexibility, and expertise. However, review and oversight of appraisal products is an inherently federal function that must be maintained within the BLM" (2003:25). Although the Workgroup believed that both staff and contract appraisers should be used, the report stressed the necessity of reviewing private contractors' work.

DOI's policy response

On June 19, 2003, Secretary of the Interior Gale Norton announced the DOI's plans to consolidate all its agencies' appraisal functions into a single office. On November 12, 2003, Norton announced this would be the Appraisal Services Directorate (ASD) within the DOI's National Business Center. To confer more credibility on the new institution, she nominated Brian Holly, Chief Appraiser for the DOJ, to head this office as Acting Chief Appraiser.

Under the new policy, appraisers would report up the chain of command to other appraisers rather than to realty specialists. This was to ensure appraiser independence and that appraisals would be in accordance with professional standards to provide unbiased appraisals consistent with the public interest. The DOI had decided that this change would put to rest any allegations of political manipulation of appraisals at the BLM, the Bureau of Reclamation, the Fish and Wildlife Service, and the National Park Service.

DOI OIG 2005 report: managing land acquisitions involving non-federal partnerships

On September 29, 2005, the OIG issued its final report on the DOI's use of non-federal partners in land acquisitions. The OIG remained worried about using private parties' appraisers for land valuations (DOI 2005:1). These concerns centered on "the independence of DOI review-appraisers, who often faced the difficult decision of either approving a substandard appraisal that valued the land at a price acceptable to the landowner or rejecting the appraisal and derailing an important land acquisition" (DOI 2005:1).

The OIG was very concerned about a policy adopted in December 2004 by the Secretary of the Interior. According to this newly enacted policy, the ASD would conduct reviews of non-federal parties' appraisals as long as:

- The non-federal party consults with ASD before initiating the appraisal on the scope of work and the selection of the appraiser.
- ASD determines that the appraisal was prepared by a certified appraiser and meets applicable appraisal standards.
- The request to review the appraisal is made by a senior departmental manager who has determined that the land transaction proposal supported by the appraisal comports with applicable agency missions, priorities, and plans (DOI 2005:2).

The OIG believed this would make it more difficult for ASD review-appraisers to reject faulty private contractors' appraisals (DOI 2005:2). The OIG saw two problems. The first concern was that the creation of this regulated partnership would engender exactly an expectation that private parties' appraisals would be automatically approved (2005:2). In addition, the OIG was concerned about this policy since it required an ASD review of any appraisal provided by private parties. The OIG feared that "review-appraisers faced with a deficient appraisal may be put in the precarious position of having to disapprove the appraisal, thus impeding an acquisition that has high-level DOI buy-in" (2005:2).

The OIG felt that the solution enacted by the Secretary of the Interior was not actually solving the problems surrounding the DOI's land exchange practices. According to the OIG, to solve these problems, the DOI should change its newly released policy to:

- Clearly communicate in preliminary consultations with bureau managers and non-federal parties that consideration and review of a non-federal appraisal does not create an expectation that such appraisal will be approved. This would clearly signal to all involved that professional deference will be granted to an ASD review-appraiser tasked with reviewing the non-federal appraisal.
- Ensure that when ASD reviews an appraisal provided by non-federal parties and finds the appraisal deficient, decision-making authority reverts to the senior DOI manager to terminate the acquisition or to proceed, using a new appraisal obtained by ASD or alternative methods of valuation (DOI 2005:2–3).

2006 GAO report on Interior's land appraisal services

In September 2006, the GAO released a report of its study of the DOI's appraisal services. Three years earlier, the DOI had consolidated the appraisal services of each of its agencies into the newly created office of the Appraisal Services Directorate. However, due to a shortage of staff appraisers, the ASD has consistently used the services of contract appraisers. In fact, since the creation of the ASD, its staff has completed around 500 appraisals per year versus 1,200 appraisals per year performed by private appraisers (GAO 2006:3). The ASD assigns about 70% of its caseload to private appraisers (2006:30). Therefore, the GAO believed that it was of the utmost importance that only qualified contract appraisers be selected in order to make sure that only appraisals meeting federal standards would be submitted to the ASD (GAO 2006:3).

The GAO conducted its study by retaining four TAF appraisal experts to investigate 324 of the 2,905 land swap appraisals performed by the ASD from 2003 until 2006 (GAO 2006:4). The GAO selected those 324 appraisals because they exhibited the same characteristics as prior appraisals found faulty by past audits (2006:13). According to the GAO, these 324 appraisals represented nearly 50% (about $3.2 billion) of the total value of land appraisals completed by the ASD since its creation (2006:4).

The GAO found that the ASD's appraisal process still did not provide full compliance with federally recognized standards (GAO 2006:5). Of the 324 audited appraisals, the TAF experts found that 192 (about 60%) seemed to be compliant with federal standards (2006:5). However, 132 appraisals (about 40%) were completed and approved even though they were not in compliance (2006:5). To make matters worse, in 90 of the remaining 132 cases the ASD review appraisers had performed only simple, cursory reviews (2006:5). The result was that review appraisers repeatedly approved valuations that failed to take into consideration key property features that substantially increased the values of federal property.

The GAO successively confirmed that the ASD's appraisal process did not fully guarantee that the appraisals its staff completed or reviewed were in compliance with applicable standards (GAO 2006:13). This noncompliance meant that the land appraisals performed by the ASD for land swaps did not reflect market value (2006:14). The GAO cited two examples. In the first, the "ASD appraised a BLM parcel of land, as well as a parcel of private land, for potential exchange. . . . Because the [federal] land contained substantial amounts of timber, its value should have been considered by the appraiser in performing or reviewing the appraisal" (2006:15). However, the ASD appraiser did not use the appropriate timber valuation. "Therefore, ASD's conclusion that the properties being exchanged totaled about $2.3 million [wa]s not supported by the appraiser's analysis and [wa]s potentially incorrect" (2006:15). In the second example, the ASD staff appraised two parcels of offered lands totaling 154 acres (2006:15). The appraisal was based on the assumption that water rights were attached to each of the two parcels, which would significantly augment their valuations (2006:15–16). However, there was no proof in the appraisal or in its review that water rights were attached to the properties. Thus, the ASD's final appraisal of nearly $1 million was not supported by the evidence (2006:16). Fortunately for the BLM, the private party rejected the land swaps, stating his belief that the ASD's valuation of his offered lands was too low (2006:16).

Furthermore, the GAO "appraisal experts found that for 90 of the 132 appraisals that did not meet standards – totaling about $930 million in appraised value – the review appraisers approved appraisals without using adequate analyses to support the conclusion of value" (GAO 2006:16–17). More specifically, the ASD review appraisers had conducted only cursory reviews of these land valuations and had approved these appraisals, failing to acknowledge the existence of key characteristics of the federal lands that would have substantially increased their market values (2006:17). The GAO cited the example of a BLM land transaction in Douglas County, Nevada. The GAO found evidence that the private appraiser's own analysis of the market conditions was in violation of applicable standards, and yet the ASD reviewer still accepted the land valuation (2006:17). Despite

information in the appraisal report showed that lands with similar characteristics (comparables) had increased in value about 5 percent per month, over the previous year . . . the appraiser did not account for appreciation between the date of appraisal and the dates that the comparables sold – a period of about 1 year.

(GAO 2006:17)

The ASD staff reviewer approved the valuation without requiring the appraiser to reconcile it with the information available (GAO 2006:17). While the appraiser valued the federal parcel at $10 million, the new private owner resold it a few months later for $16.1 million.

According to the GAO study, the overall problem was that the ASD had failed to enact a management control process to guarantee that both appraisers and reviewers conduct their appraisals and reviews in conformity with nationally recognized standards (GAO 2006:20). The GAO recommended that the DOI take a page from the Forest Service's manual and apply a similar form of management control. Since 2002, the USFS had created a team of four senior review appraisers who would visit forest districts every three years and review certain categories of risky appraisals. The USFS had its own compliance inspection procedure which could identify those appraisals in violation of national standards, rescind them, and take measures that would ensure those issues would not reoccur (GAO 2006:20).

Furthermore, the GAO report addressed another issue. It discovered serious problems concerning the ASD's Pacific Region's failure to retain appraisal and review documentation (GAO 2006:21). Despite federal guidelines require appraisers to retain their appraisals for between five and seven years, "appraisers in ASD's Pacific Region could not locate nearly two-thirds, or 96 of the 150 appraisal reports" (2006:21). Each of the missing appraisals was supposed to be kept in conformity with the file retention time-frame guidelines set both by the ASD and the Uniform Standards of Professional Appraisal Practice (2006:21). However, when interviewed by the GAO team, the Regional Appraiser admitted that 96 of the appraisal reports completed for the regional office had indeed been lost (2006:21). The GAO was thus unable to audit these 96 appraisals (2006:21). Since the GAO found that many appraisals had not met federal standards, it was unclear whether any of them were indeed correct. As the GAO found, given the fact a number appraisals were not meeting federals standards, case studies selected in the report confirmed that the outcome of the land swap could have easily changed (2006:43).

2009 GAO report on federal land management

In June, 2009 the GAO issued its latest report on the land exchange processes of the BLM and the USFS. Congress asked the GAO to determine which actions BLM and USFS had implemented "to address previously identified key problems" (GAO 2009:69). In particular, the GAO evaluated the nature of land exchanges processed by the two agencies. According to data published in the GAO report, a number of these swaps were completed through third-party facilitators or in multiple phases (2009:19).

Regarding facilitators, the GAO collected some interesting data. Agency respondents confirmed that facilitators tended to increase the pressure on staff to complete a swap (GAO 2009:20). In addition, the GAO reported "that facilitators might try to skew appraisals in order to offset the costs they have incurred" (2009:20).

As for the multi-phase exchanges, the GAO discussed the practice of the BLM of tracking land value imbalances through the use of ledgers. According to the data in those ledgers, private parties involved in federal land trades owed the BLM over $2.6 million (GAO 2009:20). However, the GAO found that the BLM was not adhering to its own Handbook rules for maintaining land swap ledgers. Accordingly, there was no certainty the BLM did actually maintain proof of the balances owed by the private parties and no assurance that the total balance would ever be paid or even that the amount was accurate (2009:36). In addition, the BLM did not hold any form of collateral to secure the balances (2009:38).

This was in contrast to USFS practices. The USFS only conducts multi-phase land swaps "when each phase can be completed with the federal and nonfederal values in balance" (GAO 2009:22). Most importantly, it chooses not to use ledgers. As the agency explained, it "would not want to use ledgers because of the risk that the exchange would not be completed, and the Forest Service would be owed funds for lands already conveyed" (2009:22).

Afterwards, the GAO discussed a series of key problems raised by the data in this and previous reports. Unfortunately, as the report suggested, even though appraisals accounted for the highest number of problems reported by both agencies, the GAO chose to limit its study and did not conduct its own audit of each sample valuation (GAO 2009:71). Actually, the only example cited by the GAO was a BLM exchange terminated by the private landowner. According to the GAO's report, "the agency's Mesa Mood exchange in Colorado was terminated because of an appeal to the [IBLA] by the adjacent landowner, primarily about the appraised value of the federal land. Because of these actions, another appraisal had to be conducted" (2009:10). At this juncture, the landowner sold the Mesa Mood Ranch property to a third party. Evidently, the system in place worked, but only because the neighbor to the private party started an administrative proceeding to challenge the BLM's appraisal of the selected lands.

The GAO then examined data related to other specific swaps. It started with the BLM's Central Washington Assembled Land Exchange II (CWALE). In this swap, the GAO had questioned "the use of bulk discount value adjustments – an appraisal practice of grouping parcels at a discounted value – for the federal lands but not for the nonfederal lands" (GAO 2009:32). According to data available to the BLM, the use of bulk discounting could have led to a 28% decrease in the valuation of the selected lands, resulting in a loss of at least $576,620 (2009:32). Next, the GAO discussed a USFS exchange. In this swap, the USFS had reviewed the file and discovered that its own ranger district staff had failed to adequately support the public interest determination (2009:32).

Furthermore, the GAO was worried by the fact that "both agencies (1) could not in all cases provide copies of key documents, including the reviews, as well as the documents subject to those reviews, and (2) did not always document how problems were resolved" (GAO 2009:32). The GAO discovered that both agencies were unable to provide any of the decision reviews made by their local offices (2009:32). In addition, the GAO found that while in some instances the two agencies had proffered documentation of the resolution of issues identified in their appraisal reviews, neither could submit any papers documenting each single resolution (2009:34).

The GAO then discussed examples of the agencies' practices with third-party facilitators. The GAO examined the Blue Mountain Exchange, processed by the Forest Service. This was a failed exchange of about 18,000 acres of federal lands in northeastern Oregon appraised at $15.7 million (GAO 2009:43). The GAO analyzed the Forest Service's review of the Blue Mountain Exchange. The review noted that:

> the facilitator (1) tried to work on passing federal legislation without the Forest Service's knowledge, (2) was very secretive about its agreements with landowners, and (3) wanted to control the outcome of the exchange instead of working as a partner with the Forest Service to ensure an outcome that was in the public interest.
>
> (GAO 2009:45)

Failure to supervise the facilitator cost an estimated $1.4 million in processing expenses.

The GAO found that no specific disclosure policy existed for swaps involving facilitators. Agency officials stated that the disclosure policy became applicable only when a facilitator signed both the ATI and the swap agreement (GAO 2009:46). However, officials admitted that facilitators would never sign either document (2009:46). A facilitator interviewed by the GAO admitted that the disclosure policies never affected his operations because his company would not sign the documents under any circumstances (2009:46). He emphatically stated "that his company's relationships are 'open and clear' and that the agencies should have no questions about whom they are dealing with" (2009:46). In the previous four years, the agencies used the services of this facilitator for one-third of their swaps.

The GAO collected data from the agencies that showed the use of this facilitator in 13 of their processed exchanges. It interviewed officials who had worked on seven of these swaps. The agency officials "reported that the facilitator in four exchanges did not comply with the disclosure guidelines and two did comply, and in one case, the respondent was not sure whether the facilitator complied" (GAO 2009:47). However, for the two exchanges in which the facilitator was presumed to be compliant, the same officials were unable to provide complete documentation of the facilitator's compliance with the disclosure guideline.

Finally, even though the GAO declined to evaluate agencies' appraisals in their processed land exchanges, it did discuss the restructuring of BLM' appraisal functions and a pivotal 2003 controversial land swap, the San Rafael Land Exchange. This was the moment in which the DOI decided to change its appraisal process structure; BLM staff had negotiated the transfer of federal land resources after undervaluing them (GAO 2009:59). The DOI estimated that the BLM was about to lose somewhere between $97 million and $117 million because of faulty appraisals (2009:59). The consequent restructuring led to a 2006 GAO review of the new appraisal structure under the ASD. However, the GAO concluded that the DOI "needed to take several other steps to ensure that land transactions are based on appraised values that adhere to recognized appraisal standards" (2009:60).

2009 OIG evaluation report on the Department of the Interior's appraisal operations

Between May and July 2009, the OIG conducted a review of the efficiency and quality of the DOI appraisal procedures. It found that the appraisal function was actually obstructed by a series of factors over which the ASD had no control (DOI 2009:1). In addition, the ASD has not become the strong and independent appraisal agency originally envisioned by the Secretary of Interior (2009:1). According to the OIG, the cause of the ASD's problems was its dependency upon other offices to design its policies and their enforcement due to this agency losing its defining leadership over 3 years earlier when its first Chief Appraiser resigned (2009:1).

The OIG's evaluation demonstrated that the ASD had never received the support necessary to assert complete control over its own appraisals (DOI 2009:3). Interviews with the agencies confirmed that all "remain[ed] unconvinced of the need for a consolidated organization and have repeatedly acted to regain control of the appraisal function, thus undermining ASD as an organization" (2009:3). Moreover, the failure of the DOI to intervene on behalf of the ASD and protect its independence and operational integrity compounded the problem.

In 2003, when the Secretary of the Interior created the ASD, the original idea was to provide the newly created office "with a strong appraisal organization with unified lines of supervision meant to protect appraiser independence from undue influence, enhance the reliability of Department appraisals, and ensure unbiased valuation services" (DOI 2009:5–6). However, as the OIG found, the ASD became neither strong nor independent (2009:7). In fact, according to the OIG's report, internal struggles within the DOI prevented the ASD from being able to exercise complete control and therefore responsibility and accountability for the appraisal function (2009:7). In fact, the four different agencies whose appraisal functions were consolidated into the ASD "still refute the need for a consolidated organization and take actions to recover control of the appraisal function" (2009:7). Most importantly, these agencies have now regained control over directly contracting the services of private appraisers. As of June 2009, each had reacquired the power to assign appraisals to private contractors; thus, regaining much control over the appraisal process (2009:8).

Bureau of Land Management and General Services Administration: selected land transactions

In 2010, the GAO released its new review of BLM land transactions in the states of California and Washington. In particular, the review analyzed two assembled land swaps completed in several stages. The first was completed in stages between 2005 and 2008 in Washington. As the GAO pointed out in its report, its review showed that "none of the transactions was a permissible FLPMA 'exchange'" (GAO 2010:1). In this swap, the Bureau "sold public lands and, instead of depositing the proceeds in the appropriate account, used the funds to purchase nonfederal lands" (2010:1). The transactions fell in the category of land sales and purchases rather than swaps because, among other things, even the BLM referred to this terminology in its own documents (2010:1).

The second transaction took place in California between 1995 and 2003. While this transaction did include a couple of actual land exchanges, the GAO uncovered evidence that the majority were land sales followed by a land purchase (GAO 2010:2). In addition, the General Services Administration (GSA), an independent branch of the federal government, which operates under the mandate of supporting the basic functions of federal agencies, mishandled BLM's proceeds from its land sales. The problem was that the GSA was holding the proceeds of these land sales in a deposit account in the U.S. Treasury, in violation of the Miscellaneous Receipts Statute (31 U.S.C. § 3302). This law mandates that proceeds of federal lands "be deposited into the appropriate funds in the Treasury, 'without deduction for any charge or claim' 33 U.S.C. § 3302(b)" (2010:2). In reality, after amassing the proceeds of federal property sales, the "BLM and GSA used some of the proceeds to purchase lands" (2010:2). Afterwards, the "GSA improperly deposited the proceeds from land sales into a deposit fund account in the Treasury" (2010:2). However, it deposited the remaining proceeds into the wrong U.S. Treasury account fund (2010:2).

The GAO properly highlighted the concerns raised by these BLM practices. The BLM used its authority to exchange federal and private lands to complete federal land sales. The problem with this practice is: "By not using a competitive process in these sales, BLM may have lost opportunities to receive more proceeds for the land" (GAO 2010:2). Essentially, "instead of offering the land under competitive procedures as is generally required for selling land, BLM sold several of the parcels directly to parties who had been previously identified as potentially interested in buying the properties" (2010:2).

The GAO moved on to discuss the specifics of each assembled land swap. In the Central Washington Assembled Land Exchange II (CWALE II) the BLM was involved in seven different transactions. As the GAO reported, "No nonfederal party to the transaction both conveyed and received land; that is each nonfederal party either conveyed or received land in return for money" (GAO 2010:6). As for the California transactions, the BLM cooperated with the GSA. According to the GAO, "BLM and GSA tracked the total value of many of the lands transacted in a document they referred to as a 'ledger account.' . . . However, many of GSA's sales to third parties were not included in the ledger account" (2010:7). In 2009 the GAO noted that the "GSA provided . . . a document stating that about $8.39 million [wa]s remaining in the account. [However, a year later, the] GSA sent . . . a letter stating that about $7.9 million remained in the account" (2010:9). The GSA was unable to explain this discrepancy since no further transactions had been completed since November 2003.

The GAO was puzzled by the BLM's practices. As the GAO reported, "BLM must deposit the proceeds of such sale or exchanges into a separate account in the Treasury known as the 'Federal Land Disposition Account' 43 U.S.C. § 2305" (GAO 2010:12). Aside from the fact that the BLM deposited only part of the proceeds with the U.S. Treasury, and into the wrong account, federal law requires that these funds be disbursed on the BLM's behalf only to purchase specific in-holdings. The BLM did not use those funds to purchase any such parcels. However, BLM used land sales proceeds to purchase offered lands that were not in-holdings, thus ineligible for federal acquisition (2010:16–17). The "BLM's improper use of the sales proceeds depleted the Federal Land disposal Account of amounts it should have received to fund qualifying land purchases" (2010:17).[1]

Since the BLM financed its land acquisitions with funds obtained through the sale of public lands in violation of federal law, the GAO declared it in violation of "limitations . . . [that] prevent agencies from circumventing Congress's power of the purse" (GAO 2010:19). In other words, BLM's practices were directed at circumventing "the carefully crafted statutory framework governing the sale, purchase, and exchange of public land – a framework designed to protect the public interest" (2010:19). The GAO uncovered evidence that demonstrated BLM was in violation of safeguards that ensure both that a federal agency receive fair value from public land sales and these transaction benefit the public interest (2010:19).

Impacts of OIG, TAF, and GAO recommendations

As we have seen, since 2000 both agencies have decreased the number of land exchanges due to a lack of available qualified staff due to increasing

---

1 An account available in the U.S. Treasury is the Land and Water Conservation Fund, 16 U.S.C. § 460*l*-5(a).

retirements, decreased funding, and changing land management priorities (GAO 2009:17). For example, the BLM Nevada State Office only focuses on the land sales program. As for the USFS, the Forest Service Facility Realignment and Enhancement Act of 2005 codified the priority status of administrative site sales (2009:18).[2] Thus, two different Forest Service Regions (3 and 6) focus exclusively on administrative site sales because these land sales generate revenue (2009:18). Furthermore, some BLM and USFS staff interviewed by the GAO said that exchanges receive priority status only if "the nonfederal party pays over half of the processing costs" (2009:18). However, the GAO's report cautioned that "when nonfederal parties pay more of the exchange costs, pressure increases on realty staff to complete exchanges" (2009:19). This increased pressure is problematic because the overall goal of all the reforms is to create a corruption-free playing field.

Both agencies have refused to take action on GAO recommendations. The most egregious example is the failure to respond to the GAO's recommendation for the two agencies to list, or at least know, the cost of individual exchanges. So far, no action has been taken by the BLM because it did not agree with the recommendation. The USFS has never even expressed a final position on the recommendation (GAO 2009:26). The latest USFS dismissal of the GAO's recommendation concluded "that the cost of developing and implementing a tracking system would outweigh the benefit" (2009:67). However, a program leader admitted to the GAO the benefits of more cost information relative to land swaps (2009:53). The Service has yet to implement the recommended reforms. Similarly, the BLM has cited the additional expense of tracking the costs of individual land swaps as a disincentive to address this concern (2009:51). However, BLM field staff interviewed by the GAO acknowledged that though they "could track the cost of individual exchanges, they do not often do so because management has not asked about the costs of individual land exchanges and Congress has not asked specific questions" (2009:53). The attitude expressed by the agencies flies in the face of the GAO's belief that acquiring better data would lead to better outcomes (2009:65).

This cavalier attitude toward value tracking should be no surprise because since 1987 the OIG, GAO, and in part even TAF, have issued similar recommendations regarding the problems with the appraisal and land swap programs of the BLM and the USFS. These recommendations are detailed in previous chapters. Each agency reacted differently to these recommendations.

Following TAF and GAO reports in 2000 that had highlighted both the lack of independence of appraisers and the consequent pressure exercised by realty officials upon appraisal staff, the USFS somewhat reorganized its appraisal department. It resisted the full reorganization of the appraisal

2 Pub. L. No. 109–54, tit. II (2005), codified at U.S.C. § 580d Note.

department recommended by TAF, "stating that implementing this recommendation would require it to create an independent organization . . . that would be difficult to administer, to establish work priorities, and to hold accountable" (GAO 2009:62). Despite the partial restructuring, instances of inappropriate pressure were still reported years later. Following a 2000 Appraisal Foundation report, the USFS was forced to initiate its own compliance inspection program. The report confirmed that USFS appraisers had relied on inaccurate information (TAF 2000). The inspection program has been able to identify and rescind appraisals conducted in violation of federal standards (GAO 2006:20). However, in the State of Florida Exchange, the inspection program helped uncover evidence "that the field staff had not adequately explained why this exchange would benefit the public" (GAO 2009:32). In the Gray Wolf Exchange, the program "found that the public interest determination needed to be added to a key document" (GAO 2009:34). Such lapses have continued. As a matter of fact according to USFS sources, the inspection program was proven to be "behind schedule because of staff shortages, a lack of funds, and competing priorities" (GAO 2009:34).

At the BLM, the trajectory of recommendations and reforms took several steps. Due to the findings of previous reports starting in 1987, recommendations were made by the OIG in 1996 to ensure that the BLM processed land swaps in accordance with federal laws and regulations. The same findings in 1998 had prompted the OIG to request a moratorium on BLM land exchanges in Nevada. It was discovered that the BLM had just lost $18.2 million on three swaps there. The same OIG report stressed the importance of properly valuing lands and keeping those valuations in the exchange file. It also emphasized the importance of recommending that the appraisers' determinations of the highest and best uses of the offered and selected lands be adequately and fully supported by appraisals kept in the exchange file (DOI 1998). However, in 2006, the GAO issued another report in which similar problems resurfaced. The failure to retain documents was blamed on the ASD's Pacific Region and its lack of document retention practices; more specifically, 96 appraisal reports were deemed lost by the regional office (GAO 2006:21).

The presence of these valuation problems, at least at the BLM, was highlighted by a 2001 DOI OIG report that discussed the controversial "alternative appraisal approach" implemented by the Bureau in Washington County, Utah. Following the release of the 2002 TAF report that confirmed the failure of the BLM to protect appraiser independence, recommendations were made to change the BLM's appraisal process through organizational restructuring. Recommendations were issued to "provide proper supervision of appraisers by appraisers to reduce this pressure" (AEW 2003:23). By then, it was a known fact that the "Bureau appraisers' responsibility to determine market value frequently conflicted with, and was compromised by, realty managers' drive to expedite land transactions and 'make the deal'" (DOI 2009:5).

The reorganization of the appraisal structure as an independent function was long overdue as it originally had been proposed in March 1968 by the DOI's (later eliminated) Office of Survey and Review. By moving the BLM's appraisal function directly under the supervision of the DOI, the hope was that any conflicts of interest with the realty function of the Bureau would vanish. However, in 2003, the AEW's report found "that there are similar problems throughout the DOI's real estate valuation entities" (AEW 2003:14); thus, it recommended the creation of a new appraisal office within the DOI that would provide appraisal services to the BLM, the Bureau of Reclamation, the National Park Service, and the Fish and Wildlife Service.

However, as discussed above, three years after the creation of the ASD, a study by the GAO concluded that "[DOI]'s appraisal policies and procedures do not fully ensure ASD's compliance with recognized appraisal standards" (GAO 2006:5). As the same GAO study pointed out, "While trying to fix the systemic and egregious problems that threatened appraisal integrity in the past, the centralization of the appraisal functions has unintentionally caused inefficiencies in other processes" (GAO 2006:43). The GAO found the ASD to be a "dependent" agency (DOI 2009:1).

Another problem has been the use of appraisers retained by proponents. In particular, one report found that in many instances "the BLM succumbs to proponent demands to use appraisals prepared for the proponent with inadequate BLM oversight and coordination" (AEW 2003:24). These land valuations tended to exhibit a bias in favor of the proponent. At this time AEW recommended that qualified staff appraisers be put in charge of reviewing the appraisals completed by private contract appraisers.

This remained a concern in the new ASD since "ASD currently contracts out approximately 70 percent of its appraisal requests" (GAO 2006:30). Interestingly, unlike all the regional ASD branch offices that use a "best value to the government" methodology to assign appraisals to contract appraisers, the "Southwest Branch officials routinely award contracts using 'lowest bid' criteria" (2006:31). Thus, completely disregarding the criteria for evaluating "best value," such as the bidder's past performance and quality of previous appraisals, the Southwest Branch continued using its own "lowest bid" (2006:32). As the GAO discovered, the "ASD takes substantial risks when it has to use contract appraisers" (2006:34).

Another issue with the organizational restructuring was highlighted in the 2005 OIG report. The DOI OIG felt that the independence of DOI review-appraisers had been put at risk by the reorganization. It had become "more difficult for ASD review-appraisers to reject substandard and marginal appraisals" (DOI 2005:2). The fear was that it would be "likely [to] increase the expectation of bureau managers and non-federal parties that appraisals will be approved" (DOI 2005:2). That fear became reality when the GAO uncovered evidence that ASD review appraisers kept on approving appraisals that failed to reflect the existence of key property characteristics that would have substantially increased the value of public lands (GAO 2006:5).

The ASD has not yet developed a compliance inspection mechanism to ensure that appraisals under review meet recognized appraisal standards (GAO 2006:6). The "ASD [still] lacks an oversight mechanism to guarantee that the federal government is represented as fervently as the private parties that have a vested interest in transacting land at a more favorable price than that dictated by market value" (2006:43). When the DOI was confronted with this, it stated that "a 40 percent noncompliance rate is well within industry norms," adding that "noncompliance [only] . . . limits assurance that land the federal government appraised . . . reflected market value" (2006:14). The GAO was not satisfied with these figures either (2006:47).

Numerous reports have concluded that disagreements over the values of the offered and selected lands are to be expected. However, it is also noted that guidance should be issued to realty function managers to emphasize the importance of following the legal rules related to equal value. Therefore, the AEW has suggested to the BLM that training should be given to managers so that when they were faced with "unreasonable expectations of value . . . [they] either actively work to resolve those expectations, or make a decision not to proceed with the transaction" (AEW 2003:7). Recommendations were made for the realty office managers "to allow the appraisal process to be independently completed" (2003:58). However, once the appraisal reports were completed, realty office managers were allowed by the AEW to resolve any disputes over appraisals values as part of "management responsibility" (2003:58). Therefore, the "adjustments" were not eliminated but merely moved to a later stage.

Other studies have evaluated the agencies' (BLM and USFS) use of land exchange facilitators in the completion of land swaps. Strangely, these reports have overwhelmingly supported the increase in the use of third-party facilitators, due to their expertise in reducing both the costs and complexities of swaps. However, in 1998, the USDA OIG found that USFS staff in the Humboldt-Toiyabe National Forest had tended to provide an "accommodating relationship" with a specific third-party facilitator and that preferential treatment had cost the agency $5.9 million (DOI 1998). Nevertheless, a few years later, a recommendation was issued "that land exchange facilitators be recognized a valuable asset" of the land swap process (AEW 2003:8). Yet, evidence was also present of the existence of "a growing public perception that facilitators may have an inappropriate level of influence on the land exchange process" (AEW 2003:62).

Therefore, it was recommended that the "facilitators' role should be defined as serving a unique function to assist the BLM. The roles and procedures should be defined to ensure facilitators are perceived as assisting and not driving or influencing land exchange priorities or outcomes" (AEW 2003:62). While it was recommended that facilitators would also have input on the development of policy and guidance relative to their involvement in the land swap process, it was acknowledged, though, that facilitators would resist any formalization of their roles and relationship with the Bureau.

The GAO later discussed the negative impact facilitators have had. The GAO used the example of the failed Blue Mountain Exchange. An internal review of the accommodating treatment of the third-party facilitator revealed that "the facilitator . . . wanted to control the outcome of the exchange" (GAO 2009:45). Indeed, staff from the BLM and the USFS interviewed by the GAO "reported that facilitators often increased the pressure to complete the exchange" (2009:20). This is a clear example where a recommendation was adopted which in theory should have been an improvement but in practice was not.

Similarly, other recommendations that in theory should have corrected problems in fact quickly went awry, such as the new issue which surfaced with multi-phase exchanges. In 2000, the GAO reported that the "BLM was inappropriately depositing funds into interest-bearing escrow accounts outside of the U.S. Treasury and later using those funds to acquire nonfederal lands" (GAO 2009:36). Not surprisingly, its latest 2010 review confirmed the same findings. Thus, the GAO has asserted that this practice is in violation of FLPMA. However, these actions have been clouded by another questionable practice enacted, the use of land swap "ledgers to track land value imbalances in multiphase exchanges" (2009:36).

The GAO found that the BLM was not adhering to its own rule for the use of land swap ledgers (GAO 2009:36). For example, in the Birch Creek land swap in Idaho, the BLM could not even provide a ledger (2009:39). In consequence, the BLM did not have a way to know how much money it was still owed. Worse, there were other cases in which inadequate ledgers resulted in the probability it would be unable to collect the $2.6 million positive balance in three of its seven open ledgers (2009:38). Unfortunately, as a sad corollary, the DOI concurred with the GAO that the "BLM cannot now verify the cumulative imbalance" (2009:68). The ledgers were yet another example of a recommendation that should have worked in theory, but in practice failed.

Finally, numerous reports have noted that legislated land swaps have been underused. Since legislation is required to complete interstate land swaps, recommendations have been made by the AEW specifically to the BLM to seek out this form of land exchange. However, the GAO has cautioned federal agencies against the use of these tools since "facilitators . . . can create an unhealthy push to process legislated exchanges quickly, with insufficient public scrutiny" (GAO 2009:20). In the legislated swaps surveyed by the GAO in 2009, there were significant differences from the agencies' ordinary discretionary exchanges. For example, in three legislated exchanges the values of the offered and selected lands were declared by statute to be equal, "so the regular process of conducting an appraisal to determine land values was not required" (2009:25). In a total of six swaps the agencies did not conduct the NEPA analyses (2009:25). Thus, more recently the use of legislated exchanges has become somewhat another tool to circumvent FLPMA and NEPA.

Conclusions

If the answer to the historical problems detailed in this and previous chapters, and still not fully addressed even after the full implementation of the ASD operations, was to create an organizationally independent ASD, the "outside" contracting function should be transferred to the ASD rather than individual agencies. In addition, to maintain an independent organization, a strong and competent leadership in terms of the position of Chief Appraiser is necessary. Also, it is time that both agencies reinstate a system that ensures the public trust in terms of representing the federal taxpayer in land swaps. For example, an ASD review appraiser approved a private appraisal of federal lands in Douglas County, Nevada, at $10 million, and the same lands were resold by the new private owner few months later at the value of $16.1 million (see GAO 2006). This just followed in the footsteps of previous problematic land exchanges (see GAO 2000).

The basic mistake that has been made about this problem is the perception that outside pressure is solely responsible; therefore, solutions have been sought on the assumption that "the perception or reality of pressure . . . can be lessened" (AEW 2003:15). However, it is unavoidable that pressure will be exercised on staff or contract appraisers. All the reforms of the appraisal organization have been directed at fighting pressure when, in fact, as the USFS hinted when it resisted a restructuring of its appraisal organization, it is more essential to hold appraisers accountable to the agency.

It is of the utmost importance that the agencies be held accountable to the public at large. This could be accomplished by holding the agencies accountable for each land exchange, including holding them accountable if they fail to safeguard all the records of every step of the appraisal process in every transaction. On the one hand, an increased use of the U.S. Office of Special Counsel, as in the San Rafael Land Exchange, may provide a solution. This independent federal investigative and prosecutorial agency could allow the government to hold its employees accountable by actually referring, rather than merely threatening to refer, criminal cases to the DOJ. On the other hand, if faulty appraisals are approved, the agencies should not rely only on benevolent neighbors to challenge the values of the offered lands in administrative proceedings, as in the Mesa Mood Exchange. Thus it is of the utmost importance that accurate market value determinations be reached even at the cost of redoing appraisals, even after completion of an exchange. Only an *a posteriori* oversight mechanism, with officials accountable for their decisions, can "guarantee that the federal government is represented as fervently as the private parties that have a vested interest in transacting land at a more favorable price than that dictated by market value" (GAO 2006:43).

References

Appraisal and Exchange Workgroup. (2003). *Appraisal and Exchange Workgroup Final Report*. Bureau of Land Management (USDI Report). Washington, DC: U.S. Department of the Interior.

Kitchens, E. (2000). Federal Land Exchanges: Securing the Keys to the Castle. *Rocky Mountain Mineral Law Institute, 46*, 22–1–51.

The Appraisal Foundation. (2000). *Evaluation of the Appraisal Organization of the USDA Forest Service.* Washington, DC: Author.

U.S. Department of the Interior. (1998). *Audit Report: Followup of Nevada Land Exchange Activities* (USDI Report No. 98-I-689). Washington, DC: U.S. Government Printing Office.

U.S. Department of the Interior. (2005). *Managing Land Acquisitions Involving Non-federal Partnerships* (DOI Report No. W-IN-MOA-0085–2004). Washington, DC: U.S. Government Printing Office.

U.S. Department of the Interior. (2009). *Evaluation Report on the Department of the Interior's Appraisal Operations* (USDI Report No. WR-EV-OSS-0012–2009). Washington, DC: U.S. Government Printing Office.

U.S. General Accounting Office. (2000). *BLM and the Forest Service: Land Exchanges Need to Reflect Appropriate Value and Serve the Public Interest.* Washington, DC: U.S. Government Printing Office.

U.S. General Accounting Office. (2006). *Interior's Land Appraisal Services: Actions Needed to Improve Compliance with Appraisal Standards, Increase Efficiency, and Broaden Oversight* (GAO Report No. RCED-06–1050). Washington, DC: United States General Accounting Office.

U.S. General Accounting Office. (2009). *BLM and the Forest Service Have Improved Oversight of the Exchange Process, But Additional Actions Are Needed* (GAO Report No. RCED-09–611). Washington, DC: U.S. General Accounting Office.

U.S. General Accounting Office (2010). *Bureau of Land Management and General Services Administration – Selected Land Transactions.* Washington, DC: U.S. General Accounting Office.

7 Conclusions

Legal scholar Susan Jane Brown has examined in her study the manipulation of the land-swap process. She wishes to explain why USFS and BLM officials circumvent statute requirements and justify the completion of particular exchanges in violation of the public interest (Brown 2000:238–239). Brown is also effective in her analysis of the undervaluation of selected public lands. For example, by using governmental studies, she shows that the nation and its land assets have repeatedly been on the losing end in terms of failing to achieve equal value. According to her data, governmental officials do not look at the long-term potential for development of the land the agency trades, which results in the undervaluation of the selected public land. On the other hand, the offered private land is often overvalued when involving cases such as the presence of roads, which increase the value of the parcel because they provide a means of access. However, the agency official fails to look at the long-term management of the acquired land, which will require disbursing federal funds for the obliteration of the same road for which the agency originally had to pay a premium (Brown 2000).

In addition, Brown comes to an interesting conclusion regarding the agency acceptance of undervaluations. This is in accordance with the argument that she makes concerning shortages in agency salaries and budgets. According to Brown, the proponents of land exchanges often end up absorbing in their transaction expenses over half of the salary of the agency personnel involved in the swap. This happens whenever private developers offer to pay for required environmental studies, thus creating an incentive for the agency's official to complete the swap (Brown 2000). The proponents ultimately pay part of the salary of agency personnel when an agency is short of funds and cannot provide money for the studies needed to finalize a swap. This instance, a clearly unethical situation which gives the private proponent undue leverage over the agency, is rationalized by the fact that the payment of the costs of overtime for its officials is, financially, the only way the official will complete the swap (Brown 2000).

This study helps finalize our conclusions of the transactions that trade the public's lands to private ownership. Both her study and this book are based on the premise that a transformation of the present swap system is necessary to ensure that land exchanges are fair and corruption-free. This assessment follows a recap of the history of land swaps and the use of public choice in order to leave readers with a sense of whether any progress has been made. This book sadly confirms the results of investigative reports conducted on the practices of BLM and USFS officials. These reports systematically demonstrate that historical issues plaguing federal land exchanges are still present. Changes so far have affected only the exterior, the façade, of this instrument; we have changed the bottle, but the wine inside still tastes sour.

Unresolved problems in public/private land swaps

Although public policy has changed considerably since the "in lieu lands" selection clause of the nineteenth century, the problem of loss of federal assets due to faulty valuations in land swaps has continued up to the present. The GEA of 1922 did change the legal basis of land swaps from equal acreage to equal value. The federal courts, however, generally accept the USFS or BLM appraiser's valuations of federal lands, leaving to the discretion of the agencies the correctness of any appraisal. The wide scope of this discretion has been acknowledged by federal court decisions interpreting the FLPMA. This broad discretion is exploited by agencies' officials when they are protecting land developers' interests rather than achieving specific environmental goals.

If the agencies continue to follow the faulty practices known to result in undervaluation of federal lands, then the land exchange moratorium requested in 2000 by some members of Congress should hopefully become reality. However, Congress has enhanced its capacity to complete land swaps in the form of *quid pro quo* wilderness legislation (Blaeloch and Fite 2006).[1] Accordingly, "politicians . . . who wield disproportionate power over public land issues – are taking on the wilderness mantle with alacrity, while still holding the line for the ranching, wise-use, mining, and development interests they represent" (Blaeloch and Fite 2006:1). The problem is, "In the case of the land exchanges and giveaways that facilitate new wilderness, laws that would normally apply to the relinquishment of federal lands are simply waived" (Blaeloch and Fite 2006:7). Appraisals are cut short and land values disregarded, reinforcing the belief "that undeveloped federal land is essentially worthless" (Blaeloch and Fite 2006:8).

The BLM and the USFS justify these policies by declaring that land exchanges are necessary to facilitate relations between the federal government and state and local officials; however, when they conduct land exchanges, most of the time their counterparts are private parties (GAO

---

1 For example, see The Clark County Conservation of Public Land and Natural Resources Act of 2002 (Pub. L. No. 107-282).

2000). The agencies have had an easy time defending their practices before deferential judicial and administrative courts.

In both arenas, the agencies have been granted a high level of discretion. As illustrated in Chapter 4, IBLA, in its administrative decision-making, is very receptive to the BLM's discretion. The federal courts have adopted this practice as a form of legal argument. The IBLA is especially consistent in its unwillingness to overturn judgments reached by the BLM either in terms of the public interest in the transaction or the values adopted for the selected and offered lands.

As to the agencies' public interest determinations under FLPMA, the courts have been very consistent in upholding them. However, in 1984, a district court in Alaska rejected the interpretation of the public interest test adopted by the Secretary of the Interior in the St. Matthew's Exchange because it was in violation of the Alaska National Interest Lands Conservation Act (ANILCA).[2] This decision is considered unusual since such decisions are generally left by the courts to the discretion of the agency.

Frequently courts do not reach the merits of a case because the challenge is dismissed for lack of standing. When a court does reach the merits, it usually defers to the agency as long as the latter has weighed the statutory or regulatory factors, even if it fails to demonstrate which factor should prevail. Administrative judges are even more deferential because they defer to the agency's official even when challengers introduce evidence contrary to the agency's valuations. The only challenges accepted by IBLA are those regarding the appearance of partiality, such as in *Jolley* (see Chapter 4).

Federal courts have been reluctant to overturn land exchanges concluded between the agencies and private parties even when the land swap was found to be in violation of federal law. However, in two cases in 1999 and 2000, the Ninth Circuit enjoined the completion of land swaps (*Muckleshoot* 1999; *Desert Citizens* 2000). In the *Desert Citizens* case, the challengers proved that the BLM had wrongly relied on an outdated appraisal. The appellate court also found an improper determination of the highest and best use of the federal property. The Ninth Circuit scolded both the appraiser and the BLM for knowingly adopting a low valuation of the selected lands and for using an appraisal with an expired shelf life.

Since 1993, when BLM regulations were passed implementing FLEFA,[3] both agencies' officials have been assiduous for about a decade in their attempts to encourage and expedite land swaps. Agency officials used the bargaining provisions contained in FLEFA and implemented in their regulations to subvert the requirement of equal value. Investigative teams have successfully highlighted and criticized these practices of the agencies' officials (AEW 2003; TAF 2000, 2002).

---

2 *National Audubon Soc'y v. Hodel*, 606 F. Supp. 825 (D. Alaska 1984).
3 Similar regulations were introduced a year later by the USFS.

The response of both BLM and USFS officials is that the agencies are actually trying to meet the complaints of landowners. As ample data show, officials for both the BLM and the USFS allow negotiations where the appraisal is considered just the starting point. The valuation of the offered land is usually increased in accordance with the requests of the landowners.

Current policy has created an atmosphere where the agencies' officials know that challenges are mostly unsuccessful. Whenever a public interest determination or one or more appraisals in a swap are dubious, the only efficient remedy to challenge them is by using whistleblowers. Current or former BLM or USFS employees (as in the St. Rafael Swell Exchange; see Chapter 6) may decide to alert the OGC of any sort of malpractice or statutory/regulatory violations by federal officials.

Giving meaning to reports and their data

The reports issued by the AEW (2003), TAF (2002), and GAO (2000) all guessed that the serious problems with BLM appraisals were due to organizational structure. Until 2003, when reforms were carried out, the organizational structure of the BLM supposedly had failed to ensure the independence of appraisers. The BLM organizational structure subjected the appraisal function to the realty function, making conflicts of interest possible. However, the newly created office (the ASD) within the DOI immediately became subject to pressure from each of the four land management agencies within the Department (DOI 2009). Thus, the BLM and each of the other DOI agencies reacquired the ability to hire private appraisers (DOI 2009). Today, over 70% of appraisals are contracted out. More than 10 years after the organization reform, concerns over land valuations remain (GAO 2009; DOI 2009).

Another finding common to the DOI (2001), TAF (2002), and GAO (2000, 2009) reports is the role of BLM lands managers, who typically support the completion of land swaps. The data show these managers working actively in bargaining sessions to resolve unreasonable expectations of value held by landowners rather than withdrawing from the proposal, as they are specifically recommended to do (AEW 2003). Thus, in violation of the law, accurate land valuations become a point of negotiation rather than a requirement. The bargaining techniques used by BLM land managers to resolve disputes over valuation sidestep the authority of the appraisers and confer power to individual realty staff to meet the expectations of landowners (AEW 2003).

According to the reports, the practices of the BLM have consistently constituted misconduct. In 1991, the OIG reported that BLM staff had failed to review 71 out of 78 appraisals. Both in 1992 and 1996, OIG reports found the BLM had made land valuations on the basis of appraisals, which were outdated, biased, or lacking evidence in support of their conclusions. In 1998, the OIG again reported that the BLM had undervalued selected lands and overvalued offered lands. In addition, it found that the decision-making related to land valuations was not fully justified or documented. Finally, the report concluded that the BLM's Washington office had violated federal standards and the agency's own procedures in its review of appraisals.

Two years later, the GAO confirmed the inability of the BLM and the USFS to properly value offered and selected lands. Data showed both agencies had exchanged valuable federal lands in return for less valuable private lands. In 2001, the OIG issued another report finding that a BLM staff appraiser had approved valuations not in conformity with federal standards. Internal and external pressure exerted on the BLM appraiser had compromised the independence and objectivity of the appraisal process. One year later, TAF, concluding its analysis of BLM practices, found that the agency's realty management practices had in effect eliminated the appraisal function. These practices, coupled with inconsistent directives in the BLM's Handbook[4] and Manual, resulted in inappropriate valuations.

Following these findings, the Appraisal and Exchange Workgroup Final Report[5] of May 2003 stated that the BLM's appraisal function was a flawed, disjointed, and disconnected appendix within the organizational structure. The same year an investigation of the BLM's St. Rafael Swell Exchange prompted investigators to consider referring the matter of employee misconduct to the DOJ. In 2003, the general consensus was the organizational structure of the BLM was the culprit because it allowed private developers to profit from faulty valuations. Several instances of inappropriate pressure exerted on appraisers by BLM officials, private parties, and third-party facilitators had been documented by OIG, GAO, and TAF.

In response to equally perplexing claims, the USFS reorganized its appraisal function to correct problems similar to those in the BLM (TAF 2000). The reorganization worked insofar as inappropriate pressure exerted over appraisal staff has lessened. However, instances of "public choice" decision-making by appraisers who benefit from private landowners' unethical offers, although dwindling, remain a problem (TAF 2000). These data indicate individual official's complacency regarding unethical gifts and pressure in exchange for questionable practices.

In this scenario, public choice theory explains why federal land exchanges remain problematic. This theory emphasizes two sets of considerations: motivational and structural. The motivational aspect concerns the self-interested behavior of people involved on both sides of land swaps. The revolving-door system permits administrators or officials to rotate in and out of government service and regulated interests, possibly making them

---

4 Prior to 1956, no agency under the DOI had even prepared an appraisal handbook.
5 This Workgroup was formed in February 2003 by the BLM to advise the agency on the appropriate action to take to restore public confidence in its appraisal function and land exchange program.

receptive to unethical appeals from the private sector. Regulatory capture has for decades allowed control to run from interest group to agencies. Therefore, the possible corruption of federal land managers or officials is not surprising. Perhaps the ultimate culprit of this centennial controversy is traceable to that lubricant that motivates humankind – greed. Let us not forget that corruption has always been present and involves acts by government officers, lawyers, appraisers, reviewers, third-party facilitators, and even politicians (Blaeloch 2001).

Given the status quo, it is essential to evaluate the independence of appraisers and reviewers. The issue of appraiser independence was at stake before the reform within the Forest Service in 2000 and the corresponding creation in 2003 of the ASD (GAO 2009). Prior to both reforms, appraisers in the BLM and the Forest Service reported directly to their realty land management superiors. Thus, threats to the independence of the appraiser were inherent in the land-swap valuation process. Because of the study conducted by the DOI Office of Survey and Review in 1968, it was common knowledge in governmental offices that the independence of appraisers was compromised.

In 2000, TAF recommended that the USFS restructure its appraisal function due to improper influence that realty staffers (line officers) were placing on appraisers (TAF 2000). Though the Forest Service resisted the creation of an independent appraisal organization, claiming fear of lack of accountability, it did agree to a minor reform. Thus, in implementing this reform, the USFS later placed all appraisers under the supervision of regional appraisers who report to their realty regional directors (GAO 2009), which for all practical purposes simply replicated the previous system.

In 2003, the creation of the ASD was aimed at eliminating conflicts of interest and assuring the independence of appraisers (DOI 2009). The BLM Workgroup in 2003 found this restructuring necessary to fix the problems inherent in the Bureau's appraisal function. The idea was to create a completely separate office, with its own lines of internal supervision, to guarantee appraiser independence (GAO 2009). However, the ASD has been quite different from what was originally envisioned by the Secretary of the Interior (DOI 2009). The DOI failed to take into account the resistance of each of the Interior agencies that use the appraisal services provided by the ASD.

Since 2009, each agency has been able to regain the contracting function, which accounts for 80% of the appraisals completed on behalf of the DOI. Now, each agency is trying to regain control even of the appraisal function. There have even been cases where the agencies hired contract appraisers deemed by ASD to be "not recommended" or "not acceptable." In these cases, the DOI failed to intervene to regain control of the contracting function and thus failed to maintain the credibility of the appraisal process (DOI 2009). If the goal is to create an organizationally independent ASD, the outside contracting function should also be transferred to the ASD.

The basic mistake made in addressing the issue of faulty valuation has been the thought that improper pressure on appraisers can be eliminated; therefore, solutions have been sought based on the premise that "the perception or reality of pressure . . . can be lessened" (AEW 2003:15). However, it is inevitable that pressure will be exercised on staff and contract appraisers because appraisers must be answerable to their superiors. All reforms of the appraisal organization have been directed at fighting this pressure when, in fact, as the Forest Service hinted when it originally resisted a restructuring of its appraisal organization, it is essential to hold appraisers accountable to the agency and the nation. The Forest Service, however, did not move in that direction (GAO 2009).

Suggested changes for the future

The basic touchstone of all federal land swaps is the principle of exchange for equal value. This principle lacks meaning unless the federal government becomes serious about faulty appraisals. The principle of equal value was introduced in 1922 by the GEA in order to address the problems with the "in lieu" land exchanges of 1897, where the basis was equal acreage. Both the BLM and the USFS should accept that when the private party's offered lands are less valuable than the selected lands, the proposal should be summarily rejected and the agency should move on to other offers. Otherwise, the agency's appraiser might become the object of inappropriate pressure, co-optation, or other forms of corruption (TAF 2000; DOI 2000; AEW 2003; GAO 2009).

Knowing that both agencies will not terminate negotiations even when the offered and selected lands are not of equal value, this chapter proposes political fixes. With the caveat that normative reforms might not be feasible in the current political economy of rent-seeking and collective action problems, this chapter will rank several possible solutions. With the proviso that the necessity of a legislative fix is absolutely present, the reality is that if a bill is introduced in Congress then the same interests that skew land swaps could skew the bill. Thus, if appropriate legislative reform is not enacted, the issue becomes whether administrative reforms are likely to be sufficient. If we address this reform as a matter of changing agency practices, solutions might be found at the administrative level; however, any administrative solution could be overturned as soon as the swearing-in of a new president with a new stance on land privatization.

These suggested changes will be ranked in order of importance. The ranking reflects the importance of a political measure in terms of its salutary effect vis-à-vis nullifying the unethical advantages that private developers and third-party facilitators draw from contracting with the federal government. Thus, *in primis*, legislation should be passed to allow the federal land management agencies to recoup losses incurred whenever selected lands are retransferred by their new private owners at a higher price than the appraisal accepted during the swap process. Indeed, as long as the land exchange file reflects at least one prior appraisal (even if disregarded) indicative of a higher value, the agency should be allowed to recoup the value lost through a swap. Only an *a posteriori* oversight mechanism can "guarantee that the federal government is represented as fervently as the private parties" (GAO 2006:43).

A second possible solution is a retooling of the agencies' relationships with land exchange facilitators. This reform would require formalizing, via contracts, the service relationship linking the facilitators and the federal agencies (AEW 2003). This option could eventually eliminate any corruptive interference from facilitators. A formalized process not only could provide a higher level of quality assurance in the services proffered by facilitators but also could formalize their business practices and standards in the form of rigorous contractual terms.

The third-ranked suggestion is the imposition of criminal liability for any improper conduct by public officials. This would ensure that the public interest in a land swap transaction is more than a chimera (Stengel 2001). It is of the utmost importance that agencies be accountable to the public. This should include holding them accountable if they fail to safeguard all records created at every step of the appraisal process. An increased use of the U.S. Office of Special Counsel, as in the BLM's controversial St. Rafael Land Exchange, may provide the solution. This independent federal investigative agency could allow the government to hold its employees accountable by referring criminal cases to the DOJ rather than merely threatening to do so, as it has in the past.

The fourth normative reform would be to extend to the BLM the same general powers conferred to the Forest Service to use the power of eminent domain each time private owners become recalcitrant during a land swap. The Damocles' sword of eminent domain could be used as an incentive in the completion of an equal value land swap.

The fifth-ranked suggestion is the extension of legal standing to individuals who advocate prioritizing the public interest over economic development.[6] When faulty appraisals are approved by the BLM or the USFS, citizens should be able to bring a challenge through administrative proceedings (see the Mesa Mood Exchange in Chapter 6). Presently, however,

---

6 Presently, the precedent regarding standing of environmental organizations is *Friends of the Earth, Inc. v. Laidlaw Envtl. Servs. (TOC), Inc.*, 528 U.S. 167 (2000), now confirmed in *Summers v. Earth Island Inst.*, 555 U.S. 1142 (2009). According to the Supreme Court, in order to prove legal standing, "a plaintiff must show that he is under threat of suffering "injury in fact" that is concrete and particularized; the threat must be actual and imminent, not conjectural or hypothetical; it must be fairly traceable to the challenged action of the defendant; and it must be likely that a favorable judicial decision will prevent or redress the injury" (*Summers* 2009:1148).

the courts reject actions by private parties who base their challenge only on their status as regular taxpayers (*Northern Plains Resource Council* case).[7] According to the Ninth Circuit, it would be different if the plaintiffs were acting to ensure federal guardianship of the federal lands (*Desert Citizens* 2000).

In 1970, the PLLRC suggested that judicial action be one of the means used by government agencies to find proper valuations. Devolving to the court system the appraisal of lands could be the solution. Judicial action over land appraisal controversies is either the first or last option (depending on its feasibility) against the depredation of federal assets (PLLRC 1970). This policy would, admittedly, contradict the American tradition of strongly protecting private property. However, the court system is well-equipped to deal with private owners' resistance to condemnation proceedings. In the United States, where the court system is the last bastion against violation of the law, the courts should be protecting the public's interest against private parties' depredations. Thus, we could demonstrate to our progeny that our nation finally learned from the historical mistakes tracing back to the Oregon land frauds.

Table of Cases

Desert Citizens Against Pollution v. Bisson, 231 F.3d 1172 (9th Cir. 2000)
Friends of the Earth, Inc. v. Laidlaw Envtl. Servs. (TOC), Inc., 528 U.S. 167 (2000)
John R. Jolley, 145 IBLA 34 (1998)
Muckleshoot Indian Tribe v. U.S. Forest Serv., 177 F.3d 800 (9th Cir. 1999)
National Audubon Soc'y v. Hodel, 606 F. Supp. 825 (D. Alaska 1984)
Northern Plains Res. Council v. Lujan, 874 F.2d 661 (9th Cir. 1989)
Summers v. Earth Island Inst., 555 U.S. 1142 (2009)

References

Appraisal and Exchange Workgroup. (2003). *Appraisal and Exchange Workgroup Final Report.* Bureau of Land Management (USDI Report). Washington, DC: U.S. Department of the Interior.

Blaeloch J. (2001). *The Citizens' Guide to Federal Land Exchanges: A Manual for Public Lands Advocates.* Seattle, WA: Western Land Exchange Project.

Blaeloch J. & Fite, K. (2006). *Quid Pro Quo Wilderness. A New Threat to Public Lands.* Seattle, WA: Western Lands Project.

Brown, S.J.M. (2000). David and Goliath: Reformulating the Definition of "the Public Interest" and the Future of Land Swaps After the Interstate 90 Land Exchange. *Journal of Environmental Law and Litigation, 15*, 235–293.

---

7 *Northern Plains Res. Council v. Lujan*, 874 F.2d 661 (9th Cir. 1989).

Public Land Law Review Commission. (1970). *Final Report of Study of Appraisal Techniques and Procedures Utilized in Connection with Action Related to Federal Public Lands.* Sacramento, CA: Kronick, Moskovitz, Tiedmann and Girard.

Stengel, A. (2001). Insider's Game or Valuable Land Management Tool? *Tulane Environmental Law Journal, 14,* 567–596.

The Appraisal Foundation. (2000). *Evaluation of the Appraisal Organization of the USDA Forest Service.* Washington, DC: Author.

The Appraisal Foundation. (2002). *Evaluation of the Appraisal Organizations of the Department of Interior Bureau of Land Management: Including a Special Evaluation of an Alternative Approach Used in St. George, Utah.* Washington, DC: Author.

U.S. Department of the Interior. (2001). *Land Exchanges and Acquisitions* (USDI Report No. 2001-I-413). Sacramento, CA: U.S. Department of the Interior.

U.S. Department of the Interior. (2009). *Evaluation Report on the Department of the Interior's Appraisal Operations* (USDI Report No. WR-EV-OSS-0012–2009). Washington, DC: U.S. Government Printing Office.

U.S. General Accounting Office. (2000). *BLM and the Forest Service: Land Exchanges Need to Reflect Appropriate Value and Serve the Public Interest.* Washington, DC: U.S. Government Printing Office.

U.S. General Accounting Office. (2006). *Interior's Land Appraisal Services: Actions Needed to Improve Compliance with Appraisal Standards, Increase Efficiency, and Broaden Oversight* (GAO Report No. RCED-06–1050). Washington, DC: U.S. General Accounting Office.

U.S. General Accounting Office. (2009). *BLM and the Forest Service Have Improved Oversight of the Exchange Process, But Additional Actions Are Needed* (GAO Report No. RCED-09–611). Washington, DC: U.S. General Accounting Office.

Index

For Product Safety Concerns and Information please contact the
EU representative GPSR@taylorandfrancis.com Taylor & Francis
Verlag GmbH, Kaufingerstraße 24, 80331 München, Germany